The
Amadeus
Variations

The *Amadeus* *Variations*

A TALE OF TWO CONTINENTS, MUSIC, AND THE LOVE OF GOD

Kathy Webster

XULON PRESS

Xulon Press
2301 Lucien Way #415
Maitland, FL 32751
407.339.4217
www.xulonpress.com

The Amadeus Variations
© 2019, 2021 by Kathy Webster

This is a work of fiction. Any resemblance to persons living or dead is coincidental, with the exception of the role played by Mozart in the narrative. The fictional character of Mozart does follow generally known facts of the real Mozart's life and works.

Paperback ISBN-13: 978-1-6628-4048-7
Ebook ISBN-13: 978-1-6628-4049-4

Amadeus

Amadeus is a theophoric given name derived from the Latin words *ama*– the imperative of the word *amare* (to love) – and *deus* (god)... The name can be either taken to mean 'love of God', in other words, that the person is 'loved by God' or 'one who loves God'.

"Amadeus (name)" *Wikipedia*, last modified September 5, 2021, https://en.wikipedia.org/wiki/Amadeus_(name)

For George and Beth,
my own irrefutable proof of the love of God

Table of Contents

George Webster
2021

CHAPTER 1
North Carolina
October 2019

Irritation threatened to overshadow her grief at losing Aunt Alzbeta, Anna decided. Life in the middle of the semester never permitted any breaks or down time, but here she was, being forced into a long weekend away from Chapel Hill. The dreary gloom of the day mirrored her mood. She usually enjoyed the 90-minute drive to Winston-Salem, but today even occasional bursts of autumn reds and ambers among the pines couldn't lift the drab gray blanket wrapped around her soul.

The funeral at Home Moravian Church a month ago had only required a day away from her doctoral program in musicology. The old traditions had touched her more deeply than she thought they would. Her aunt mentioned her in her *Lebenslauf*–the ninety-year-old woman's life story and testimony–telling how proud she was that Anna had carried on the family tradition of musicianship. The band, gathered for the funeral procession, made up in volume for what it lacked in skill, evidenced especially by the enthusiastic trombones. Her aunt's favorite hymns, some like "Jesus Makes My Heart Rejoice" used by the church since the 1700s, rang out over God's Acre. Many of her family talked about Alzbeta, how she had entered "the immediate presence of her Savior." Anna believed it and gratefully took some of that peace back to school with her.

But now. Now she was expected to shoulder the responsibility of going through the old house to get it ready to rent or sell. Her parents were afraid of trusting anyone outside the family with the task. Aunt Alzbeta had no children of her own. Anna was her great niece, her brother's granddaughter. The yellow, three-story house had been in the family for centuries, literally. Over two hundred years. Who knew what treasures or horrors lurked in the basement, the attic? Probably spiders, she thought with disgust. Succumbing to pressure from her mother, as usual, along with the promise of some sorely needed financial reward, she reluctantly agreed to spend the next few weekends rescuing family heirlooms. Her parents lived too far away to help, and the realtor was salivating at the prospect of one of the original Old Salem dwellings hitting the market. No one could wait for the semester break.

Turning her radio to 88.5, she caught the strains of Mozart's "Gran Partita." Probably the Mackerras recording, Anna thought, automatically analyzing the sounds of the woodwinds. That meant she was within thirty minutes of her aunt's house, just at the point she could catch the classical station. The music triggered her familiar anxiety about a dissertation topic.

Her coursework was almost over. Just a seminar—Music in 15th-Century Florence—then preparation to defend her choice of research area. That is, if she could finally decide on one. The woodwind ensemble music of the classical period seemed promising. She could see herself wandering Vienna, losing herself in old libraries, unearthing some long-lost gem of a serenade by Stamitz or Triebensee. It would cost something, but there were grants, even big grants, like the Fulbright.

But a whole year away from Stephen would be hard. Her relationship with the high school band director who had shown up at UNC's Dept. of Music this year promised more every day. Even though they were enrolled in the same graduate school, seeing him was quite a challenge. Between his full-time job, her teaching position, and their programs of study, they were lucky to grab a couple of dinners together in a week. How would it be if they lived in different countries? She could almost hear Aunt Alzbeta chiding her, "Kümmere Dich nicht um ungelegte Eier." Don't worry about eggs that haven't been laid yet. And here she was, exit 193B.

It always felt like coming home. She had spent as long as a month at a time during humid summers in her aunt's yellow house near the town square in Old Salem, even though her parents lived only a few miles away in Clemmons. Just as she graduated from high school, her father landed his holy grail of a job in New York City, and they moved. The timing was terrible, because she simultaneously gained entrance to her heart's desire of a college, the University of North Carolina School of the Arts, less than two miles from Aunt Alzebeta's yellow house. As an undergraduate flute student at UNCSA she spared herself student loans by living with her through the school year.

She drove slowly, letting the peace of hundreds of years pull her in. She loved the imperfection of the old handmade brick buildings, leaning this way or that with the weight of centuries. Small squares of mostly dormant gardens broke the grass-covered, hilly back yards. Late maturing beet, broccoli and cabbage plants shone in the afternoon rain. Root cellars and hand water pumps sat behind antique homes. An old carriage sat forlornly beside a small side building, usurped by the car inside. Her little Prius shuddered over the uneven spots, cobblestones peeking through worn asphalt.

Aunt Alzebeta's house stared forlornly into the rain, not yet accustomed to being alone. It had no front yard, but its eight worn, irregular stone front steps began directly at the sidewalk of crisscrossed bricks. A low white picket fence outlined the lot, part of it built upon a layered stone wall. The wooden frame was a faded ancient yellow, set off by the darkest green door and shutters. Trees twice as tall as the structure embraced the south side. One large branch spilled over the front, a shy covering over half the house's face. Three-story brick chimneys flanked both north and south sides. The windows were smaller than those of a modern house and not all the same size. Less mechanical perfection in those days of building by hand in the newly settled "wilderness."

Before stepping out into the rain, Anna found the oddly shaped key in her purse. She grabbed her overnight bag and navigated her way across the wet bricks to stone steps, swayback with years of traffic. The solid weathered green door, placed off center in the front of the house, groaned as she opened it. Above the door, three small panes of ancient glass let just enough light through their ripples and dimples to allow her to find the switch. She dropped her things by the door and took time to inhale the woody, lived-in smell of the place.

Antique furniture greeted her like long-lost friends as she moved slowly through the bottom story, switching on lights in each room. Straight ahead lay the kitchen. The refrigerator always seemed uncomfortable on the uneven wide floorboards of heart pine, beside the thick wooden counter. Appliances were modern intruders, set among handmade pine and wicker chairs and a hutch full of pewter. A small microwave, knowing it did not belong, tried to hide itself on a centuries-old kneading board. The whole back half of the house was open, the kitchen flowing into the dining room. An old white ceramic stove dominated the north wall, looming over a table with a blue and white cloth. A fireplace of handmade brick, which she had been told was from the south meadow, took up the wall behind it. A Dutch door sat between two windows on the eastern wall. Opening the top half of the door allowed Anna a view of the still-green grass bordered by last summer's daylilies in the open backyard. No flowers now.

She turned left, back toward the front of the house, and entered the pale green sitting room. She liked the furniture, smaller and lighter than the big blocky things popular nowadays. A fireplace was painted the same green, just a slightly darker version. Two candles in pewter holders stood guard at either end of the mantle. Tears flowed a little as she remembered her aunt reading in the tiny dusty-rose armchair. They fell in earnest when she saw the music room and laid her hand on the ancient Bösendorfer piano. Those had been the best times of all. She sat on a worn burgundy settee and let the ache in her heart have its way.

Strange how giving in to the emotions she had clamped so tightly in place back at school felt like such a relief. Drained but peaceful, she rose from the settee, retrieved her bag, and climbed the stairs to the bedroom facing the street— "her" room. She even felt a little hungry.

A narrow four-poster bed with a lilac and green patterned quilt sat beneath simple white curtains pulled back with a green tie. She raised the modern pulldown shade a little for light, then tucked her bag beside a worn cherry dresser with sixteen drawers of varying sizes.

"I'll go to the tavern," she told the old stuffed rabbit leaning tipsily on the dresser, regarding her with one eye, the other lost years ago. The Salem Tavern, eternally proclaiming on every menu, napkin, social media site, and poster that "George Washington stayed here two nights in 1791," priced its meals to rob tourists blind. But it had some decent pumpkin soup. After all, she needed something comforting today, she decided as she grabbed her purse and an umbrella from an old ceramic stand on the way out.

The next morning dawned crisp and clear, a sky the shade of blue that caused natives of the state to declare that God must be a Tarheel, otherwise why would the sky be Carolina blue? She stepped out the back door in her robe, just to revel in it. The unique smell of bread baking in a wood-burning stove told her that Winkler's Bakery, which had been around since 1800, was getting ready for the day. Her spirits rose as the old town pulled her in once more.

Anna, innately organized, let her inner cataloger take over as she gathered a notebook and pen and began to go through the rooms. She inventoried, making notes as she remembered comments her aunt had made, like "this chair was built by my great grandfather" or "these dishes came all the way from Boston, before 1820." She marked things that she knew her mother would want to keep along with some she herself wanted. The rabbit made the list, along with the porcelain perfume and powder jars from her aunt's bedroom, the quilts that had been made by various relatives, family portraits scattered on the walls, and a heavy mahogany silver chest, so full its lid could never be totally closed.

By late afternoon, most of the main house was inventoried. Anna decided to survey the attic. It and the basement would be the hardest parts of her task. She had better get an idea of just how bad it was going to be. There were a few windows up on that third floor, so she should have enough light to briefly size up tomorrow's job. Skeptically eyeing the attic door, she shook her head. The way up didn't deserve to be called stairs, more of a ladder really. Climbing up carefully, she pushed the door open and closed her eyes as dust rained down on her light brown hair, mute testimony to the years it must have remained undisturbed.

It wasn't long before Anna realized that there were windows on only one side of the attic. By the dim light, she could make out boxes, piles of books and what looked like music, old lamps, clothes on some hooks on the wall, an ancient dress form, and some suitcases that had to be from the Roaring Twenties, if not before. She was going to head to Winn Dixie anyway, so she would see if they had battery lamps or extension cords so she could haul some light into the place. It looked like a full day's job for tomorrow. Closing the attic hatch, she carefully made it down the narrow stairs to her room where she left her list and grabbed a light jacket. Making sure to turn out all the lights on her way, she exited to her waiting car.

Anna started driving south on Main Street and slammed on the brakes about a block from the house. Checking quickly, she verified there was no one behind her. She got out of the car to stare at the sight that caused her startled reaction. The wind had come up and the tall trees on the south side moved dramatically, uncovering a fuller view. There, toward the top, were two windows on the south side of the third floor of her aunt's house. When she had entered the attic, she remembered distinctly that the only two windows letting in light were on the north side of the house. What the heck?

Curiosity taking hold, she went around the block quickly and parked in front again. This time, she took her cell phone with her as she scooted quickly up those ladder stairs and turned on the flashlight app. There were the two windows, definitely on the north wall. But there was a solid wall on the south side.

Trying to make sure, she stepped off the distance from the opening to the north wall. When she repeated the process toward the south, she proved to herself that side of the attic was about three or four feet shorter than the north side. And, she realized, though the house had two chimneys, north and south, visible from the outside, she saw only the bricks of the north chimney up here in the attic.

Pushing away some dusty boxes, she moved to stand before the mysterious wall and gently smoothed her hand over it.

"What's behind you?" she whispered. It appeared to be solid, with no doorway or opening of any kind. She rapped on it, as if knocking for entrance. She had no idea what she was hearing. It was as useless as thumping on a watermelon for her. She grew up seeing people rap their knuckles on the melons but had no idea why they were doing it.

Maybe she'd better stop at the hardware store, too. Maybe pick up a saw or an ax. There was probably nothing, but she dearly wanted to know what lay behind that wall.

CHAPTER 2
Dürnstein, Austria
December 1791

C arl lifted the small sheep's head into his lap, taking care to keep his large hands around her head to prevent any fearful pulling away. He didn't want her to knock over the small bottle of wolf's bane infusion by his side. Her eyes still looked pink, and she must be feeling bad, not to fight him any harder than this. Soothing her with his left hand, he picked up the bottle and carefully placed a drop in one eye. She blinked at him stupidly but remained still. The second eye received its drop, and he gently moved her head back to the thick mound of straw covering the stall's floor. His mother always said he had a way with the sick, especially sick animals. Maybe she was right, he thought as the animal dozed off instantly.

He rose to his full 6' 4" height, stretched, and looked down at her peacefully lying in the straw. She'd need some more in an hour or so. Smells of straw, sheep's droppings, and the wet sheep herself mingled with that of rain dripping outside. Scratching his hip, he debated whether he should bother to take the half-mile path back to his family's cottage or just try to nap a bit here in the ancient barn. It seemed to him that the drips came faster and louder. A nap

9

here it was, then. Just as he blew out the stub of a candle he had brought with him, the barn door creaked, and a gust of cold air announced someone's entrance. Carl stood still in surprise. It was past midnight. What the devil?

Another door noise and a frightened-sounding whisper, "Gustav?"

That sounded like a woman. Carl, used to being on the outside of whatever social happenings were going on around him, slipped quietly to his knees. Best to wait this one out, he thought. A thin half wall at the front of the stall afforded him a hiding place.

He could hear footsteps, then what sounded like something being pushed against the wall. Some low noises, perhaps a kiss? Carl sat without making a sound, growing uncomfortably warm with the effort. Then a dim light appeared by the barn's door.

Liese. He could just make out her beautiful face. How did he not recognize her voice? Since they were 10, he had followed her everywhere, memorized her every feature, worshipped her, longed to have the courage to speak easily with her, as the other young men of Dürnstein did. But he was slow. Big Carl, good with the animals, not so good with people. He knew he never had a chance with the prettiest, blondest, sweetest girl in the town. But at least she had not chosen another. Not yet anyway. But now?

"Gustav, I'm pregnant."

Carl's blood froze.

"Oh, no. Liese. How could you let that happen?" Another voice, this one male.

Anger began to rise in Carl.

"Me? I let it happen? I don't think I'm exactly the Blessed Virgin now, am I? You had something to do with this, Gustav. A lot to do with it!" Liese's voice grew shriller as she spoke.

"Ach, my father. He will kill me. He's had that Berte or Brette or somebody over in Melk on his mind. I think he talked to her father," Gustav took on a whining tone.

"Oh, I know," Liese sounded bitter.

Carl saw light appear between the two figures as Liese moved away, and he heard bitterness in her voice. "I'm not rich enough. Your father wants that fat cow whose parents own the big vineyard. I see now. I'm good enough for your filthy games, though."

"Liese..." Gustav closed the gap between them. Carl saw the two figures merge into one.

"Get away from me. I don't know what I'm going to do. Maybe I should run away..." Liese's voice broke and Carl heard small sobs.

"Liese, let me think. There's always something. Maybe..."

Liese began to cry in earnest, making Gustav seem extremely uncomfortable, from the worried tone of his voice. "Come on, now. There's always something. There's the nuns over in..."

He was interrupted by a deep, guttural roar of rage as something huge came barreling at him from the other side of the barn. Carl had heard enough. Gustav grabbed for the end of an old, rusted scythe without thinking, swinging it out on the rope holding it from the beam above. Carl, head down, ran straight into the broad side of the iron blade, braced by its handle against the wall. He fell like a large stone to the floor.

Liese and Gustav stared, mouths agape. Finally, Gustav began, "I think I have an idea."

Not long after, Carl opened his eyes as the loudest screaming he had ever heard pierced his consciousness.

"Rape, rape…help me, help me." This was coming from Liese, sitting propped up against the open barn door, her shirt torn and indecently open, her hair wild, filled with straw.

"What was she going on about?" Carl wondered. Then he remembered his failed, heroic attack and looked around for Gustav. The villain was nowhere to be seen. And still she kept up the screaming.

She looked at him as her shrieks filled the night air. He thought her face looked sad, even guilty. Why did she keep screaming? Then he realized he was being accused of something he would never, ever do.

Clambering to his feet, he headed to the open door. His head throbbed with pain, every step making it hurt worse. He cast a last painful look at Liese, who would not meet his eyes. Turning, he could see a couple of figures moving laboriously on the path, coming up the rise to the front of the barn. Better not go that way. He turned back, giving a last look at the love of his life, who was still screaming, and moved quickly to the back entrance.

When the old couple from the base of the hill got to Liese, they were too winded to speak for a minute or so. They listened as she told them how Carl, that big, strange young man, who never spoke, had dragged her here and done unspeakable things to her. The older woman crushed Liese to her ample bosom.

"Oh dear, oh dear," she began rocking the distraught girl as she held her. "Gunter, you must get the constable. Go, hurry. They have to arrest him."

Gunter, probably at least 80 years old, wasn't hurrying anywhere, but he did start down the path to the center of town.

Gustav was right, Liese thought, as her rescuer led her away from the barn. Carl frightened people, always lurking around the outside of things, staring at others. Staring at her. Anyone in Dürnstein would believe that Carl would do this. She looked down to find the path for her feet. Anyone except me, she thought with shame.

Carl's elderly parents knew they had little time. Their son exploded into their bedroom in the middle of the night, frantically trying to make them understand the danger he was in. His mother lit candles as his father drew a loose brick from the hearth and pulled out a small bag containing all the coins they had. She started packing bread and cheese and some clothes into a larger sack. This was not the first injustice they had suffered as poor farm tenants, but it was by far the worst.

"You have to go to Vienna," his father grasped his shoulder. "Look at me, Carl."

Carl's deep brown eyes looked down into his beloved father's face. How could he leave the only people in the world he loved?

"This may be a good thing. There are opportunities there. It is big. So many people. You will be safe. Only two days of walking. Find a job, maybe with animals. You have a gift," he was trying to give his son so many instructions. His son who was slow to understand things, shy to speak. God would protect him. He had to.

Before any of them were ready, they pushed Carl to the door. His long legs gave him an advantage, his great strength meant he could move quickly. And he had a knack for surviving. He could always find shelter and something to eat in the woods. Even hide there if he heard someone behind him. He would be fine, they kept saying. They say it too much, he thought.

He kissed them both quickly, tried not to notice the tears welling up in their eyes. Only two steps later he turned abruptly, his hand in his pocket.

"I forgot," he said, and he pulled out a small vial. "That sheep, with the black foot. She will need more of these," he told his father, as he handed him the ointment for the sheep's eyes.

His mother began to weep as Carl turned back onto the stone path leading away from home.

CHAPTER 3
North Carolina
October 2019

"Look, I can be there before 9 a.m.," Steve argued with her. Anna knew this would be a sacrifice for him and how precious a day off was, especially during football season. Another home game in five days, which meant another half-time show and several 13-hour days before that. He was probably counting on this three-day weekend to do laundry, groceries, or just chill in front of the TV.

"Steve, this is really nice of you to offer..."

He cut her off mid-sentence. "I've never seen Old Salem. We can take that wall down and maybe you can show me around a little?" And then he grimaced as he heard the pleading tone in his voice. He didn't want to sound that pathetic, not after only knowing Anna for a couple of months. But his hunger to see her drove him on.

"I'll leave by 7, ok? Just tell me how to get to the house."

She laughed softly and relief flooded his soul. "Ok, you win." She gave him the address, described the house, and wished him a safe trip.

A few minutes later, heading to bed, she went over the conversation in her head. Had she tried to manipulate him into helping her? She certainly hadn't any thought of that when she called him just to check in. She was excited about uncovering the secret behind the wall and couldn't hide it. Now the idea of Steve being with her in tomorrow's adventure made it all just that much more perfect. Maybe he wanted to save her from damaging more than the wall with the axe she had purchased that afternoon. Well, she could use a protector, that's for sure. She grinned as she climbed into the very high four-poster bed. One time her great aunt told her that colonial beds were so high because heat rose and a single fire in a room couldn't perform the miracle that central heating could. She pulled the faded lilac-and-green compass quilt up to her chin and couldn't get to sleep for thinking about Steve and how they had met.

At the end of last August, Anna had finished a busy week both attending and teaching music classes. Arriving at her apartment after 6 p.m., she was overcome with a deep loneliness as the quiet four walls surrounded her. Not thinking details, she grabbed her bag and headed back out. There was usually something happening on campus on a Friday night. She just couldn't stay in there by herself any longer.

Checking on her phone, she saw that there was a jazz concert by some of the UNC ensembles in an hour. Back in Hill Hall, the home of all her classes, in the Moeser auditorium. She liked jazz. And there was a wine and cheese reception for grad students right before it. Sounded like dinner to her.

Anna could tell the full-time students from those who already had jobs and attended school part-time. The fulltimers grabbed the large plates, heaping as much free food onto them as possible. She joined in. As she grabbed one end of a slice of ham, she was startled to feel it pulled from her tongs. She looked up in surprise into the blue eyes of a very tall, very red-faced young man opposite the table from her.

"I am so sorry," he said quietly, holding the ham slice in question dangling from his own set of tongs. He held it out toward her, a peace offering.

Anna burst into giggles. "That's ok. Guess we are both making dinner out of this, huh?" She nodded to his plate stacked high with cheese, bread, crackers, and grapes. It was far more heavily laden than her own.

"Guess so," he smiled, appreciating both her forgiveness and her beauty, which he was suddenly fully aware of. She was not tall, but had a self-assured presence that attracted him, along with large blue eyes and a stunning smile.

Putting down tongs and ham, he moved around to the same side of the table where she stood.

"Hi, I'm Steve," he switched his plate to his left hand and held out his right, almost sending the whole pile slipping onto the floor.

Anna carefully edged hers onto the table between serving plates.

"Anna Stohr," she said, gripping the offered hand firmly.

"Are you a student here, too?" he asked.

"Yes, musicology, doctoral candidate," she told him as she retrieved her goodies. This intriguing stranger would just have to understand that she was starving.

"Let's go over there," he nodded to a small corner table with a couple of folding chairs by it.

Before the concert started, she learned that he was new this semester, a band director working on his master's. He was a little self-conscious that she was already at the doctoral level, but they figured out that they were the same age. He had spent a few years teaching at a high school in nearby Carrboro while Anna had plowed straight through to grad school.

They sat together at the concert, then went for coffee after. Despite busy schedules and the death of her great aunt, they had managed to see each other two or three times a week ever since. Both were head over heels in love, but neither had the courage to admit it to themselves or imagine that the other felt the same way.

Bringing her mind back to the high bed and the soft quilt pulled up to her chin, Anna finally drifted off to sleep. She was grateful that the loneliness of her past few years seemed to have disappeared.

Steve left Chapel Hill's suburb, Carrboro, closer to 6:30 than 7 a.m., which put him at the yellow house just minutes after 8 a.m. He sat in his dark red Grand Cherokee after turning off the engine, wondering if it was too strange to be this early. Before he decided, the green door opened, and Anna waved a greeting. She wore jeans, a black long-sleeved tee sporting the name "Mozart" over the number 13 in a bizarre parody of a football jersey, and had her light brown hair pulled back in a ponytail. She looked fantastic, he thought, and couldn't take his eyes from her as he strode to the door.

"Oh, wait, I forgot," he did a quick turn around and opened the back of the red Jeep. "We might need these," he explained, lifting out the largest toolbox Anna had ever seen.

"Wow. Probably," she smiled as she opened the door wider. "I've got coffee made." She wished their relationship was just a little further along because the idea of greeting him with a kiss just wouldn't leave. As it was, she made way for him to enter, sighed, and closed the door behind them.

Putting the toolkit down on the kitchen floor, Steve stared back into the living area. "This could be a museum," he said quietly, acknowledging the dignity of the period furnishings. The white walls with medium blue chair rails kept the atmosphere light and airy and allowed the darker secretary, pie crust table, and wooden side chairs to stand out.

"Well, my family has owned this place since about 1800," she poured two mugs of coffee, handing him one. "And no one ever got rid of anything that I can remember. My Aunt Alzbeta lived here her whole life."

He declined the offered milk and began to walk slowly through the sitting room into the music room on the dark, irregular wooden floor. "That's quite a piano. Wait, does it have too many keys?" He walked to the bass end of the extra-long keyboard, admiring the black wood, the carved legs so thick at the top, tapering elegantly to the floor.

"It does. I think my aunt's father got it around 1910 or so. Bösendorfer made them with 97 keys instead of 88. Busoni talked them into adding the extra low notes, if I am remembering correctly." She knew he would have heard of the Italian composer and great keyboard artist. Just another perk that came with dating a fellow musician—they spoke the same language.

Steve wandered to the bookshelves lining an entire wall. But rather than books, they contained shelf after shelf of music. "So, your family has all been musical?"

Anna laughed, "Well, not everyone made a living at it, but everyone had to play something. Sort of required of the Stohrs."

"Not mine," he shook his head and sipped the coffee. "My father had some real issues with me majoring in music. He and mom couldn't figure out where I got it, because not a single relative they knew could even carry a tune. I think he still can't believe I'm actually supporting myself."

"My father went into law," Anna told him, "But he still plays second violin in a quartet with some friends from college. He calls it his 'therapy.'" She headed back to put her mug on the sink. "I really want to thank you for coming up here. I know you don't have much time for yourself these days."

Steve just shrugged, handing her his mug. "I'd rather be here with you."

"Do you want to see the attic?" she offered, discreetly ignoring the crimson flush spreading across his face as he realized what he had said.

He gave a low whistle at the sight of the stairs. "I think I'll have to go up those sideways. My feet, I mean." He pointed at the size 13s below him. The steps or rungs were only about four inches wide.

Anna went up first, carrying her new ax tentatively over her shoulder. "Maybe I can help with the toolbox?" she asked when she made it to the top.

"I can get it, I think," Steve had to hold it wrapped against his body with his left arm while pulling himself up with his right. She grabbed the side handle of the box when she could and helped slide it onto the wooden floor. Steve made it to the top but had to watch his head as he straightened up. Too many low-lying support beams.

Anna turned on three battery-powered camping lamps already in place from the day before. They fully illuminated the thick dust everywhere. She had cleaned the inside of two windows on the north, which allowed quite a bit of the morning light in. Steve breathed in the smell of age and hoped the dust didn't trigger his allergies. The flotsam and jetsam of ten generations, blanketed securely in dust, filled the area before the windows. There were old iron pots, a hat rack, a small table, something that looked like it had once been a wreath, and box after box of Lord knows what on old shelves. Lines in the dust on the floor marked the path Anna had used to drag piles away from the mysterious south wall. They had full access to begin their dismantling project.

"I want to start," Anna held the ax almost menacingly in both hands.

"Go for it." Steve stepped well away from the small woman brandishing the weapon.

Swinging the ax awkwardly back to prepare, Anna hit the middle of the wall as hard and fast as she could. She cracked a board loudly as the ax head sank deeply in and got stuck. It refused to budge in the face of her best efforts to extricate it. She growled in frustration.

"Let me try?" He exerted quite a bit of self-control in not showing the slightest trace of a smile at her efforts.

Anna stepped back, brushing back some loose light brown hair from her face, leaving the ax hanging from the wall for him. Steve pulled it out with one hand, positioned himself for a blow, and broke the board that Anna had cracked. Pushing the ax head into the wall, he used it as a claw to break the bottom half of the board and pull it toward them.

"Let's look!" Anna couldn't wait for a larger opening. He stepped back as she peered into the small opening. "Oh, it's too dark. The windows must be covered or something. I can't see a thing."

"I'll see if I can fix that."

She returned to the other side of the room to give him space to work. Within minutes, Steve had broken out two slats, leaving a foot and a half opening. He looked back at her, smiling. "Maybe bring one of those lanterns and see what you can see."

This time Anna stuck the lamp into the hole first, following it with her head and one shoulder. "It's just some old trunks, I think. Three of them." She tried not to feel disappointed quite yet.

"Well, let's get more of this wall down and see what's in there."

They began to work together, Steve breaking slats with the ax and Anna removing pieces of board wearing some too-big work gloves retrieved from his toolbox. After making enough room, he pulled out a small saw and carved off some jagged, splintery ends. Soon they had an opening large enough to fit through.

"Let me get some boards down, so we have room to move." Grabbing a hammer, he entered and began pulling nails from the inside of the wall.

"These look pretty old," he said, holding one out for her to examine. The head was a rectangle, but not perfect. The shank had irregular waves in its shape. Anna realized that none of them were exactly alike as she collected a handful.

"I think they're hand-made," she told him. "I guess that means this wall is about the same age as the house. There are others like this in some shelves by the kitchen. I wasn't sure when this was put up in here. Let me get us some more light."

Resisting the impulse to tear open one of the trunks, Anna grabbed some of her cleaning cloths from the day before. Thick, rough fabric had been tacked over the two windows, but it came down easily with a quick tug, the old threads disintegrating in the process and clouds of dust filling the air. Both sneezed several times before the particles

22

settled. She started wiping the blurry, distorted window glass until there was enough light to see the trunks clearly.

They were similar, but not exactly alike. About three feet long, three feet high, and a couple of feet wide. The one in the center looked like oak. Its edges were outlined in what she thought was decorative iron, though the dust made it hard to see. Three iron bands circled the girth of the chest with one wide latch in the center. She hoped it wasn't locked.

The sound of the saw stopped, and Steve came to her side. "Ready to open one?"

"They look really old," she almost whispered. "If they have been here as long as the house, that means more than 200 years."

"Wouldn't surprise me," he agreed, running a hand over the lid in appreciation.

"OK, here I go?" she looked up at him. His smile and nod reassured her. Anna was so grateful that he was here. She didn't know what these boxes held, but something told her it was going to be important.

The lid opened easily as she pulled the heavy metal latch up. There was dust everywhere, rising in clouds with the lid's movement. Steve stepped behind it to help her ease the lid all the way open, letting it down gently in back. The trunk appeared to be full of paper. He held the lantern, so it illuminated the contents more fully.

"It's music," Anna said in wonder. Stacks and stacks of it. Handwritten music. She picked up the closest page.

"Looks pretty old," Steve leaned over to stare into the trunk.

"This one is a piano sonata, I think." Anna examined it for clues but found no composer's name. "The paper does look old. There are tests you can do to find out." Her musicology training started to kick in.

Steve picked up the top sheet of another pile. "2. Violine" was written at the top. He turned it over. "I think there is a composer's name here." Squinting, trying to decipher the old-style handwriting, he barely made it out. "Pert-something? Could that be right?"

Anna laid down her paper gently and took the one he had found. "I think that's right. That's what it looks like. Never heard of him or anything close to that."

"Well, if you haven't, I sure haven't," he acknowledged her greater expertise in the history of their art.

The other trunks were filled with similar stacks of paper. In the top of the worst looking one, there was an old cloth sack. Inside lay several small porcelain containers, some round and some square. She stuck them into a corner against the wall to examine later. Anna handled the music carefully, trying to come up with a theory for what they were and why they were hidden away for so long. There were titles like "sonate," "quartette," and "hymne." And instruments were indicated, "klarinette," "flöte," and "klavier." But why no composers?

"There seems to be all kinds of things here—vocal, instrumental, anthems—this looks like a string quartet. A score and all the parts." She lifted the pages carefully to see what lay beneath, then hesitated, trying to find a logical explanation. "I think maybe they are copies someone did by hand. They're too perfect. When somebody writes music, there are usually all kinds of edits—lots of things scratched out, changed."

"Why would so much of it be in a house like this?" Steve wondered.

She realized that Steve didn't know about Moravian history and the vitally important role that music had played in it. She unleashed her inner music history teacher.

"The Moravians, or 'Unitas Fratrum'—Unity of Brethren— came here from a place called Herrnhut, near Dresden in Germany. They settled in Bethlehem, Pennsylvania, in the early 1740s, then a group came here to North Carolina in 1753. My family came with them. Music was incredibly important to them. It was central to their church, but they also loved it as one of life's great pleasures." Anna continued pulling one piece after another out of the trunk in front of her.

"They were very devoted to God, but not at all like the Puritans who settled in New England. They didn't see a big division between the sacred and the secular—they thought all of life should be offered to God in worship. When they settled here, they brought their instruments, to use in church and for entertainment. I remember hearing some story about how a Puritan criticized a Moravian for using the same violin in church that he used to entertain his family. The Moravian answered back, "I can't believe you use the same mouth to worship God that you use to eat sausage!"

Steve laughed at that one.

"In Bethlehem they had a pipe organ in 1746 and an orchestra a couple of years later. Then they received ship-ment of a complete choir of trombones–soprano, alto, tenor, and bass. The first trombones in this country," she lightly touched his arm as she mentioned the instrument Steve played. A sudden misgiving struck her.

"I'm sorry. I bet you didn't want a full-blown lecture on early American music."

"Go on," he nodded, folding his arms and leaning against the remaining part of the wall. "This is interesting."

"Moravians wrote the first chamber music composed in America and some of the first performances of famous works were right here, like Haydn's *Creation*. There was a lot of traffic back and forth to Europe and music was a valuable commodity."

"They also had several composers of their own, like Christian Gregor and John Bechler. They wrote mostly hymns, though," she sounded like she was thinking out loud as she looked again at the old music before them in wonder.

"But there were instrumental composers, too. David Moritz Michael lived right here in Salem for a while. He wrote some partitas for two clarinets, two horns, and two bassoons. I guess he was a Handel-wannabe. They played them on the Lehigh River up in Pennsylvania and called it 'Water Music.'"

Sitting back on her heels she continued. "Everything they did involved music. I guess they were as addicted to it as most of us are to TV or the Internet. I just wonder why all this was locked away up here, though." She moved again to the first trunk. "Help me look through it?"

Anna climbed downstairs and retrieved a clean sheet to spread over the dusty attic floor. Whatever the history of this music, she was very aware that it had to be handled gently and carefully. She wished she had gloves to protect it even more. After an hour, one trunk had been emptied, its contents sorted into piles by form.

"Maybe this isn't the best idea," Anna sat back on her knees, surveying the many stacks spread out on the floor. "I have to go back to school tonight. I don't want to leave this just laying out."

"It feels almost fragile," Steve agreed. "I hate to handle it too much."

"Well, I've got an idea now of what we're looking at. Small instrumental groups, lots of hymn settings, lots of solo keyboard things. I'll take a sample back with me to the department, see what they think."

Leaving the pages in their organizational units, they gently returned all save one page to the trunks. Anna climbed back downstairs and quickly returned with a gallon plastic bag. She carefully slid the paper inside and sealed it.

"Ok," she smiled up at him. "Hungry?" She was starving.

Back in the kitchen, they cracked up over their filthiness. Brown streaks adorned their faces and shirts. "Looks like we've been plowing a dry field," Steve laughed. Anna sent him to the tiny guest bath while she changed clothes upstairs. He had had the foresight to take off his outer shirt and work in a t-shirt, so he had something not quite so filthy to wear. She threw some things from the refrigerator into a cloth grocery bag. Presentable, they headed out the door.

The couple climbed a slight hill toward the town's center, passing Salem Tavern on the left and the long, brick and wooden-beam Single Brothers' House. Steve found the cars driving past the centuries-old buildings out of place. "Single Brothers' House?" he asked, reading a sign.

"The Moravians had a very structured society. Unmarried men lived together in the Single Brothers' House. The Single Sisters' House is over there by the Salem Academy & College campus. The whole community was organized into 'choirs,' as they called them, by their life status. Little Boys, Little Girls, Older Boys, Older Girls, Single Brothers, Single Sisters, Married Brothers, Married Sisters, Widowers, and Widows—all had their 'choir.' It made for a very tight-knit community. They even had specific church services for the individual groups." He glanced inside at a costumed employee explaining something to a group of children.

"Let's cross here and get some bread. We can do sandwiches," Anna led the way to the open door across the street under the sign "Winkler's Bakery."

The most heavenly smell accosted Steve's senses as they entered. A tall young man in knee-length brown breeches, a blousy beige shirt, white apron streaked with black, and oversized stereotypical baker's hat greeted them. Behind him, a second man, also dressed as if he had stepped out of the 1750's, slid a long-handled wooden paddle into the opening of a massive brick oven.

"Can I help you?" asked the man behind a table loaded with round loaves.

Anna picked out a whole wheat one and paid while Steve took in the sight of barrels of flour beside long kneading tables. He noticed other items for sale, round tubes labeled "Moravian sugar cookies" and boxes of something called sugar cake. His stomach rumbled.

Heading out once more, they turned right, still climbing slightly uphill. Anna led him to the right again, to a large stone house that reminded him of a small castle at the end of the street. A sign bore the name "Cedarhyrst (1895)." They turned left to "God's Acre," another metal sign proclaiming it as the Salem Moravian Graveyard, with its first interment June 7, 1771, and giving the name of its first resident, John Birkhead. Steve decided it was one of the strangest cemeteries he had ever seen.

Rows and rows of flat, white, square stones extended as far as he could see on top of rolling hills. "They are all alike?" he made the statement in a half-questioning tone, still looking out over the hills at all the white squares, identical in shape, size, and material.

"Moravians believe in equality, especially in death," Anna sat on a stone bench under a large, welcoming tree and pulled out a bread knife, ham, and butter, followed by a couple of apples and bottles of water. Thick trees and flowering bushes surrounded them, providing deep shade and privacy. Steve sampled the bread, amazed at the unique smokey, yeasty flavor.

Anna went on, "God's Acre kind of smacks of agriculture—we are sown a corruptible seed, our mortal bodies, and there will be a harvest of resurrected bodies. They used to bury people by 'choir.' Single men over there, single women there. No chance of any foolin' around in eternity!" She handed him a large sandwich on a paper towel and continued as he began to eat.

"You should see this place at Easter. I used to love coming to visit my great aunt every time. The day before, families and church groups scrub every gravestone and decorate them all with flowers. They also have a huge sunrise service. Starting at 2 a.m. on Easter, all the musicians gather. They play Easter hymns in little bands all over town—all night long. The idea is to get the faithful up for the sunrise service. Lots of renditions of *Wachet Auf*."

"How appropriate," he grinned. She appreciated a man who understood the reference to Bach's cantata, *Sleepers Wake*.

"I loved it. They bussed us around, then fed us a huge breakfast about 4 a.m. Scrambled eggs, country ham and biscuits and Moravian sugar cake along with Moravian coffee—really strong stuff. Then we would go out to God's Acre. Four different bands on four different hills around the cemetery. At the start of the service, we would all play antiphonally on the four hills, then march together. My aunt used to call it the 'Church Militant'—us—celebrating with the 'Church Triumphant'—them." She swept her arm in an arc to include the headstones spread before them. "A four-hundred-piece band. It's amazing and beautiful."

Steve thought he could apply those same words to the woman sitting before him. "So, they could hear your flute?" he teased.

"You underestimate the power of the piccolo!" she retorted. For a while, there were no more history lessons as they ate in companionable quiet.

They finished their lunch, gathered the paper towels, and Anna swept crumbs off onto the grass for the numerous birds twittering in the large trees sheltering the area. "Let's go back a different route." She led him past Salem Academy and College and the Single Sisters' House on the way home.

The lunch and tour had taken several hours. Anna thought she had better gather her things and close the house up so they could get on the road at a decent hour. She was pleasantly surprised that Steve suggested he could wait, and they could travel together on the way home. He picked up the plastic-encased sheet of music on the kitchen counter as she headed upstairs to pack up the few items in her room.

As she climbed the attic ladder for one last check on the trunks, she could hear Steve below, picking out a melody on her aunt's piano. Must be the mystery piece, she thought, while realizing that it was a pretty catchy tune. He repeated it with more confidence, just one line, no harmony. Actually, a very nice melody, she thought. All the trunks were closed, the old music resting once again. She hated to leave it, but decided that, since it may have been there for a couple of hundred years, a few more weeks wouldn't hurt. Making sure every lamp was off, she headed back down, calling out, "I'm ready!"

CHAPTER 4

Vienna
December 4, 1791

Carl reached Vienna in the late afternoon, exhausted after two days of fast walking punctuated by a miserably cold night on some damp pine needles. Staying in motion kept his fear at bay. He had followed the Danube, sometimes losing sight of it, but always keeping it to his left after crossing it at Mautern. The kreuzer he gave the ferryman was the only one he had spent on his entire journey. Now hunger made him think of spending another.

More and more carts and people crowded the road. He heard languages other than his own German. His father had told him about visiting the great city once and how it was full of Hungarians, Italians, Slavs, and people from the east. Taller than almost everyone, Carl scanned the crowd as he entered a stretch of road with buildings on both sides. Carts laden with farm produce all headed into the city. Perhaps there was a market nearby. He followed their lead.

A heavenly smell assaulted his nostrils. Sausage. Lightheaded with hunger, Carl stopped by a small booth where a man wearing an exotic round tower of a hat offered passersby sausages taken straight from a fire. He held one under Carl's nose, waving it on the end of a stick. Too hungry to wait, Carl grabbed it with one hand, dropping two small coins into the man's hand with the other. Eating quickly, juices running down his chin, he thought he had never had anything so good.

Energized by the food, Carl wandered deeper into the city, gaping at the majestic buildings around him. The streets were filled with elegant carriages, broken down wagons, dirty children, soldiers in uniform, and many who seemed to be common laborers. He passed cafes but refused to spend more of his precious coins. Running across a fountain, he quenched his thirst and sat for a while on its rim to take in the parade of life passing by. As he watched, he realized that he had no idea what to do.

He was amazed at the number of people, the number of shops, and the speed at which everyone moved around him. He wandered street after street with no goal in mind, simply taking in the sights and sounds. As the evening progressed, he saw fine gentlemen and ladies, wrapped in furs and traveling in carriages pulled by finer horses than any on the farms of Dürnstein. He imagined them on their way to plays or concerts or dinners hosted by the emperor himself. Carl felt very small and insignificant in the middle of the capital city. He had no idea where to go or what to do.

Carl had certain gifts, foremost among them a way with sick animals. His mother was known as a healer for miles around their little home. She had learned the medicinal properties of hundreds of plants from her mother and grandmother and passed on what she could to Carl. His happiest boyhood memories were of traipsing up and down hills and along the river, gathering plants as his mother told him their names, when to pick them, and what they could do. He also helped his father with planting and caring for their sheep, pigs, and chickens. He was totally out of place in this buzzing, frantic mess of people. The sounds overwhelmed him. His heart ached with missing his parents. What in the world could he do here?

Carl wandered aimlessly up and down Vienna's streets. Night fell. He continued to wander. People were drinking now. Loud voices and laughter, music and delicious smells spilled out onto the street from taverns and cafes. He spent another precious kreuzer on a small pastry filled with meat when his hunger overwhelmed him. A meal would cost 25 or 30. Best to stay hungry for a while.

Never one to take the lead or make decisions for himself, he continued to walk aimlessly. Perhaps he should find an inn. Indecision about spending any more paralyzed him. Finding himself on a street called Wipplingerstrasse, he noticed a line of poorly clad people before a doorway.

"What do they sell here?" he asked an elderly gentleman at the end.

"Ha," the man replied, "Soup! Soup for poor. Only one kreuzer. But it is terrible soup."

Carl joined the line, and soon proved the man's words correct. The thin, gray liquid warmed him up, but tasted terrible and left him unsatisfied.

The evening was growing very late. Decisions were always hard for Carl and now, with no father or farm manager giving him guidance, he could not find a direction or decide upon a course of action. He felt lonelier and more fearful every moment. If he had known how close several had been to robbing him, his fear would have been much greater. His size saved him, as predators left in search of easier targets.

He wandered into the Flour Market, noticing the few places with activity at night. An inn and a tavern or two. The warm lights of a tavern let him see a crowd still drinking and talking, but he was loath to spend any of the coins in his possession. The truth was that he simply did not know what to do and fear started to creep into his spirit. There were no open areas or forest to hide in, no spot under a bush or ledge to grab a few hours' sleep, as far as he could tell. People were everywhere, no matter how late the hour. The crowded conditions made him nervous. Coachmen drove by at speeds that made him dizzy. Panic started to squeeze his throat, made it impossible to think about what to do next. How would he ever find work? A place to sleep?

He kept wandering, despairing and helpless to decide where he should go. He doubted he could even find his way out of the maze of the city now. There was no way that he could retrace his steps. It was several hours past midnight when he found himself in a more residential area, with buildings no doubt holding apartments and their residents long asleep. No taverns, no traffic. At least these streets were quieter. Perhaps he could think, decide what to do next or even find a hidden spot to rest. Rauhensteingasse, a sign said. Carl kept walking.

CHAPTER 5
Vienna
December 5, 1791

Pain was real but not time. Time had lost all meaning. Miraculously, the spasms that had held the middle of his body captive for so long were gone. He felt nothing save the needles in his dry throat and a throbbing in his head that rivaled the loudest of timpani. He opened his eyes to darkness and forced a single, whispered name into it.

"Stanzi."

No response. He couldn't bring himself to push past the pain in his throat for a second cry.

Lying there, he held his head perfectly still while his eyes slowly made out shapes in the dim room. A dresser, a nightstand, the window opposite his bed. No fire. There was a gleam of light from down the hall, barely entering the open door and disappearing quickly again. On the nightstand a glass of some liquid, the stub of a dead candle. He had to have that liquid. His thirst was beyond all reason.

He pushed himself up against a pillow that smelled of sweat and reached for the glass. Weaker than a newborn, his arm failed him. Again, he waited. And again he reached out, this time dropping three fingers into the glass's opening and managing to pull it to the bed. Some of it spilled, but he lifted it with both hands to gulp mouthfuls despite his painful throat. It took a long while, but he drank all the stale water. Time wasn't real anymore, anyway.

How long had he been here, unconscious? He remembered months of illness, feeling off even since the Prague trip last August. A heavy cloud of depression accompanied his physical aches and pains. He had been convinced that he was being poisoned. Nothing else could account for the stabbing pains in his gut, the swelling and constant vomiting. It was several weeks ago, he remembered, that things became so bad that he stopped all work on the requiem. Awful thing to work on when you thought you, yourself, dying.

But then he had rallied and decided to continue. He remembered his student coming, scribbling and scribbling notes at his direction, hour after hour. The doctor kept interrupting. Didn't he know that this last child of his imagination was in danger of being stillborn? All the doctor did was bleed him, give him emetics which caused violent vomiting, and leave cool cloths on his head. After each visit, he felt worse than the one before. The fever laughed at their efforts. Then everything had stopped. For how long?

Was Stanzi even here? All those trips to Baden. Was she there even now? At some point, he angered her by asking her to act with more decorum, to remember that she was married, and to a well-known composer at that. She snorted in disbelief at his request for more reserved behavior. Though stories had made their way to him, stories that fueled a fire of jealousy in his heart. Had she left in a fit of rage?

His eyes were quite accustomed to the darkness. He held one hand up before them and marveled that the horrendous swelling had disappeared. His fingers had been over-boiled sausages. The headache, though still very much present, no longer threatened to split his head in two. How long had he been unconscious? It wasn't sleep; it was much closer to death. How long had he been dead? By God, he was thirsty, though.

There, a sound, just faintly from the hall. He tried once more to call out, "Stanzi!" His cursed throat had closed on him. Frustration fueled the helpless twitching of his hands on dirty bedding. He had to get up, get more water or die. The sound again. Was that a laugh? A giggle?

Anger giving him as much motivation as thirst, he swung his legs off the bed and pushed himself into a sitting position. His head swam and nausea threatened to undo him. There it was again, a gleam of light from the hallway. It must be the middle of the night; the city street lay noiseless. Trying to stand, he managed to get to his feet for a fraction of a second before sliding to the floor, dragging the sheets with him. The cold floor allowed no rest. Another low vocal sound tempted him from beyond the bedroom. He crawled with great effort toward the doorway, not even attempting to stand, and peered toward the light.

A hall stretched to the apartment's entrance. Where was she? Meager light came from the guest room door, left open just slightly. A wooden chair beside it held a pile of something large, looming menacingly in the dark. Stanzi must be in there. She must have become so exhausted watching over him that she had gone for a rest. That couldn't be blamed. It had been week after week of merciless sickness. He could get himself there. She must be asleep. She would be so joyful to see that he was not dead, that the swelling was gone.

He grasped a chair rail and managed to pull himself to his feet. Bent over, clinging to it, and bracing his shoulder against the wall, he inched his way down the hall before finally sliding once more to the cold floor. Too weak to move, he lay against the wall. Now he could see into the room through a finger's width of door opening.

There, by the meager light of one candle, he saw two forms on the bed. He knew his wife's low laughter by heart, but what was that other sound? That invasive, totally wrong, quiet whisper of betrayal? Incapable of sound anyway, he watched, unable to draw himself away from the sight no husband should ever have to see. He watched the two, entwined on the bed. Anger boiled in his heart, enervating his limbs, giving him superhuman strength. He wanted only to run, to leave this place, to leave her. He stood, grabbed the pile of heavy cloth on the chair, and forced his feet to take him to the front door.

The cold, damp Viennese air struck his face as he opened the door to the street. He gasped, unable to breathe, unable to think. Daggers of cold air assaulted his throat. He wrapped the heavy material loosely around himself and his soiled nightclothes. Determined to escape the voices behind him, he stepped out, but had no strength to slam the door closed in indignation. Instead, it shut with a muffled, impotent click.

He felt nauseatingly, insanely angry. Lost, he stood on the worn stone step just inches from the street, swaying like a flimsy reed despite bracing himself with a hand on the door. Another icy black hand encircled his heart as hatred possessed him. Never had he been so thoroughly betrayed. While he lay dying! Well, let her think that he had. He longed both to hurt her and to run as far from her as possible.

Numbness engulfed his soul as his body failed him and he fell forward off the stairs into the startled embrace of a huge stranger. It was as if God had placed the giant just there for that single purpose. But no, there was no God. No god would allow his creature to suffer this much.

"Take me away from here," he managed to force out. He didn't hear his savior's words as he lost consciousness.

"Ja, mein Herr."

The small man came out of the building right in front of him and fell toward him. Carl caught him without thinking. He heard him say to take him away from there, though it was hard to understand. He seemed hoarse, barely able to force a sound out. Well, that was a job to do, and Carl was very good at finishing any job he was given.

Whether drunk or ill, the man needed to be inside somewhere. Wrapping the oversized cloak around him, he lifted him from the damp paving stones as easily as if he were a small child. Stepping carefully in the darkness, Carl headed back toward the tavern he had seen in the Flour Market.

CHAPTER 6

Chapel Hill, North Carolina
October 2019

A nna found herself humming as she maneuvered her way around undergrads on the way to her advisor's office in Hill Hall. She still had that tune by her mystery composer in her head. Stopping abruptly in the middle of the hallway, she coughed softly. As if that would help dislodge it somehow. She shook her head at her own nonsense.

Anna's Tuesdays were full. First, MUSC 142, Great Musical Works, which had her introducing undergraduate non-music majors to the wonders of Western art music. Some days went better than others where that mission was concerned. Today's examples from the late Beethoven string quartets put most of them right to sleep. Then she had a graduate seminar, lunch, library research time, and a meeting with her advisor. Today's meeting with Dr. Fussell needed to be about nailing down a dissertation topic, but he was one of the world's leading experts on music of the Classical period. The surprise she was bringing with her looked to her like it came from the tail end of that era. She was going to have to shift the focus off herself and her lack of progress and onto her discovery. The single sheet of old paper, protected by its plastic sheath and the hard cover of the book it was stuck in, might just take up more of her appointment time than it should, she thought as she knocked on the already open door. At least she fervently hoped so.

"Anna!" the older bald gentleman with thick black glasses was genuinely pleased to see her. He always looked comfortably disheveled, with slightly wrinkled shirts, well-worn pants, and shoes in need of a shine. Today he had buttoned a navy sweater vest incorrectly, leaving the left side dangling four inches below the right. "Come in, come in," he said as he jumped up and closed the door behind his favorite graduate student.

Every surface of furniture and shelving in the rather large office supported piles of paper or books in varying heights, leaning at precarious angles. A few stray mugs, coffee long since evaporated, decorated some stacks. A MacBook Pro teetered dangerously on top of some slippery-looking folders. Used to the place, Anna moved a small stack of spiral notebooks off a wooden chair to the floor and took a seat.

"Hi, Dr. Fussell. Did you have a good day off?"

"Oh my, yes. Sarah and I raked leaves, cooked. It was wonderful."

She smiled as he rolled an uncluttered office chair around and took a seat facing her.

"So, what have you come up with?" His blue eyes sparkled as if musicological research was the most wildly exciting fun imaginable. Anna was incredibly thankful he had agreed to take her on as his advisee.

"Well," she carefully pulled a large flat book from her bag, "I got a little sidetracked this weekend. I had to start going through my great aunt's house up in Winston-Salem."

She opened the book to the middle and pulled out a gallon zippered bag encasing a single sheet of music.

Prepared to be disappointed by still no progress, Dr. Fussell stopped the admonishing words about to escape his lips and held out both hands. He wasn't very good at reprimands, anyway, so the diversion was just as well.

"I found some music in old trunks there. None of it seems to have any composer's name, but I brought a sample. I wondered if you could verify the age, maybe? It looks like a couple of hundred..."

"Well, well, well," his quiet words interrupted her. Standing, he turned toward the afternoon light streaming in from a ceiling-high window and held the page up before it.

"Yes, it is," he sounded certain. "Let me just verify..."

Putting the sheet of music carefully on top of a pile of books, he quickly sat and swiveled to face his computer. "There was a catalog published a while ago," he explained as he typed. "Of paper mills and watermarks in this country. Ah, here! You said Salem, right?"

Anna stood to look over his shoulder. A title appeared at the top of the screen: *American Paper Mills, 1690-1832: A Directory of the Paper Trade with Notes on Products, Watermarks, Distribution Methods, and Manufacturing Techniques.* Dr. Fussell typed in a password and photographs of the pages of a book sprang up. He clicked on "North Carolina" and read.

"A paper mill or paper factory was constructed in the original Moravian settlement in North Carolina —Salem— in 1790 by Gottleib Shober... by July 1791 it was producing paper with watermarks of S or NC." He stood up and moved back to the window. "Look at this!"

Anna stood closer and could barely make out the "S" watermark on the page. "So, it was milled in Salem?"

Dr. Fussell had returned and was studying the screen. "It looks like that mill produced paper until the 1870's," he read.

"Oh, so this might be from later in the 1800's?" She was a little disappointed it wasn't from earlier in the century.

"No, no, no," those blue eyes lit up again. "Look at the paper." He was in his element, leading a student to discovery.

Anna held it up to the light. The "S" was obvious, and the paper's color was near white. There was no discoloration or browning.

"What do you see? Or what don't you see?"

"Well, I see the 'S' but not much else. I don't see any yellowing or browning of the paper."

Dr. Fussell smiled. He loved a chance to teach.

"Very good. It's not discolored, because it's made from rags or linen. Paper mills didn't start making their products from wood pulp until the middle of the 19th century. So, it's ironic—the newer paper often looks older because lignin in the wood pulp oxidizes when exposed to the air. The color of this sheet means it was definitely produced before 1850."

He continued in full professor mode. "Another thing you don't see are lines, right? Long vertical ones or shorter horizontal ones?" He held the page out so she could clearly examine it in the light.

She agreed, "No lines. Just the watermark."

"And that means that it is what we call 'wove' paper instead of 'laid' paper. This technique came in during the late 1700's. Wove paper was made by stretching a very fine mesh over wooden ribs and it didn't leave the lines that you could see in older paper. So, conclusions?" He threw the ball back into her court, handing her the music.

"Ok," she put the page down. "The paper was produced between 1790 and 1850 right in Salem at the Shober Paper Mill." She hesitated while thinking, "But is there any way to date it more precisely? Figure out who the composer might be?"

For the first time Dr. Fussell looked at the music rather than the paper holding it. Like all trained musicians, he could hear the piece as he read the notes.

"This is quite nice," he seemed surprised. "Looks like late Classical period. Tell me about where you found it again?"

Anna described the trunks behind the strange attic wall and her inability to find much of anything attributing the music to specific composers.

"I really think they must be copies, maybe used in the church there or something. They all look like this—no corrections. They just don't look like someone worked on them as original compositions."

"Well, this is quite a catchy tune," he observed. *Tell me about it*, Anna nodded.

"Here's what you need to do. Show it to Frank Miller. He knows the most about keyboard works from this era. He also knows about inks, and I think he even has a connection with some handwriting analyst. Maybe you should bring some more of it back with you and let him see what he thinks."

Anna cringed at the thought of speaking with Dr. Miller. Her personal interactions with him had been upsetting and she believed his professional dealings were totally unethical. He was always weaseling his way into other people's projects and somehow stealing credit, often making money from them. However, she was also relieved that Dr. Fussell had not chastised her for her lack of dissertation topic. She would take what she could get.

But he had not forgotten. As she replaced the page into its book and slipped both into her bag, he commented, "Who knows? Maybe you could work on some of this...if it turns out they are not just copies. See Frank. Otherwise, I'll need a proposal in writing by next week." He smiled to let her know she was not off the hook as he held the door open for her.

That evening she invited Steve over for a Hello Fresh® meal, which in her mind qualified as home cooking. Anna loved the service for its delivery of exactly what she needed, no more, no less. She had no problem with cooking; it was the hunter-gatherer part of things that frustrated her. A Reicha woodwind quintet played loudly in the background in her small apartment as she chopped and drizzled olive oil into a pan. Her place was not large, but had lots of windows and adequate, if sparse, furniture. She barely heard the knock, preoccupied with thoughts about Dr. Miller. Her thrusts of the knife became more forceful the more she fretted about the man.

Anna wasn't just uncomfortable around Frank Miller. She hated him. Not just because he was loud and opinionated. He had been one of the faculty chaperones on a summer trip to Italy several years earlier. Anna had gone, along with several other graduate students, all of them male. That meant that she always had a room to herself, which suited her just fine.

One night in Florence, they had all overindulged in the fantastic wine and pizza at Il Pizzaiuolo. On the half mile walk back to their dorm, they locked arms to get through the crowded Piazza della Signoria. Anna looked down, concentrating on her feet, not wanting to stumble on the uneven stones. A large Italian man fell into the group, breaking their hold on each other, and she suddenly found herself staring up at the backside of the copy of Michelangelo's David that resided there. The off-color comment that escaped her lips was totally out of character for her. The others had howled with laughter, though, and teased her without ceasing all the way back to their dormitory. Of course, the elevator was not working again, so they had to clamber up two flights of stairs. Anna's room was a little removed from the others, at the end of a turn in the hall. Relieved to be on her own, she hummed a little to herself as she tried to find her key in the dark. "Ah ha!" she exclaimed as she found it and placed it in the keyhole.

Suddenly a man's hands grabbed her shoulders. She found herself pushed roughly to the floor of the doorway as the door flew open. A hand clamped over her mouth before she could scream. Then she struggled for her life, resisting being pushed farther into her room.

If only Dr. Fussell hadn't insisted on her taking the music to Frank Miller.

She let Steve in after his second round of knocking. Without asking, Steve moved to the computer and turned down the music. Then he faced her.

"You seem a little distracted." He kissed her lightly on the forehead.

"Come sit while I cook," she motioned to a bar stool in a corner of the kitchen.

"Dr. Fussell liked the music I brought him. He didn't recognize it." The oil popped and hissed as she dropped chicken breasts into the pan.

"So, what did he suggest you do with it?"

Anna stuck a pan of potatoes into the oven and turned to him.

"This is the bad part. He wants me to show it to Miller."

"And why is that bad?" Steve knew many of the graduate faculty, but primarily the instrumental specialists, not the history, theory, composition contingent.

She grimaced. "He is the worst. He's a pompous egomaniac, always managing to insinuate himself into everybody else's business. He takes credit for his students' work all the time. We think he's mafia or something, the way he dresses, the cars he drives."

Steve laughed, "A musicological mafioso?"

"Maybe not, but he is sleazy. And one time, on a trip, well..."

Her mind returned to Italy. Thank heavens another student, drunk but with perfect timing, had entered the hall and said loudly, "Dr. Miller! Are you ok?" Miller reluctantly backed away, giving Anna a chance to spring to her feet, slam the door, lock, and bolt it.

Steve asked warily, "What did he do?"

"He tried to get into my room one night in Italy. A group of us were doing some research at the Accademia. We all went out on the last night. He snuck up behind me when I was going into my room."

Steve stood up, hands clenched.

"Nothing happened!" She quickly let him know. "John Bagby, you know, the goofy guy I introduced you to at that reception last month? Anyway, he showed up right in time. Miller left, but it was such a close call. I've avoided him ever since." Anna returned to washing green beans.

"Did you file a complaint against him?" Steve barely kept his rage under control.

"No," she shook her head, turning to flip things in the pan. "There was no one there to complain to. And I guess it was just his word against mine. John really didn't see any details. It was too dark."

He didn't like it, not at all, but he let her continue.

"But Miller did write the article on the history of keyboard music for *Grove Music Online*. He's the leading expert in the world on the piano sonatas of Haydn and Mozart. He even discovered a short student piece by Haydn's brother and was able to prove Michael Haydn was the author."

She turned back to him, emotions rising, "I just can't stand him. He scares me. He hates women... he's creepy, he's evil..."

She was more upset than he had ever seen her. "And now Fussell expects you to talk to him?" Steve had an edge of angry disbelief in his voice. She loved the way he so thoroughly slipped into protector mode.

"Well, he doesn't know about it. No one does. As I said, I don't think John even realized what was going on. So, yeah, Dr. Fussell wants me to show him the music."

"I'm going with you."

"Steve, you'll probably have to take off work. You don't need to..."

"There is a conference day next Wednesday. I don't have any classes. Try to schedule it then?"

Adding the green beans to the baking sheet with the potatoes, Anna nodded. "Thank you. It really will help. Really. I do not want to be alone with him."

CHAPTER 7

Chapel Hill, North Carolina
October 2019

F rank Miller, PhD, DMA, had a knack for making money. If he caught wind of someone getting ready to publish, especially a grad student or novice faculty member, he was sneakily adept at offering to edit or verify facts for them, then making sure his name was added to the title page and that a cut of the royalties came to him. Not that there was a fortune to be made in publishing related to music history. He also dabbled in real estate, renting to students who less-than-affectionately referred to him as a "slumlord." And there were rumors of other, shadier business dealings. Something had to fund those summers in Europe and the BMWs he and his wife drove.

Two days later, Steve and Anna were coldly and formally welcomed into an office as different from the stereotypical professor's as could be imagined. Expensive mahogany office furniture gleamed in the late morning light. Rows of neatly placed books lined dust-free shelves and photos of Dr. Miller with celebrities of the music world sat in heavy, ornate frames by them.

Miller himself wore an expensive suit and tie, something none of the other teachers did during a regular class day. His dark hair and goatee were trimmed flawlessly. Anna thought he looked like the old actor David Niven and never liked that style of thin mustache anyway. The professor held up a pair of golden wire-framed glasses, his stiffly starched shirtsleeve sliding back to reveal what looked to be an incredibly expensive watch. Steve didn't see a single piece of paper or music anywhere. He was thankful for his height as he held Anna's hand and did his best to loom over the shorter professor. Dr. Miller would know that Anna was not alone and by no means at the man's mercy.

"What can I do for you, Miss Stohr? Mr....?" His voice was a perfect caricature of upper-class snobbery.

"Thorsen," Steve filled in. Everything about Dr. Miller's manner was off-putting. Even if Steve hadn't heard Anna's story, he didn't like the stoniness of the man's eyes or the down-turned corners of his mouth. No offer of a handshake. Not the slightest hint of even a fake smile. He resolved never to allow Anna around this jerk by herself.

"Dr. Fussell suggested I speak with you about this," she said as she withdrew the single page of music from a folder and handed it to him. "I found it in a library a couple of weeks ago. There is no composer on it, but he placed it from 1790-1840 or so."

Dr. Miller took the plastic-encased sheet, held it from a top corner and looked at it as if it smelled bad. He stared at it as Anna continued.

"I guess it's from a sonata or something. Dr. Fussell thinks that it sounds like it might be from the late Classical period." She could tell Miller was hearing it in his head as he sat without moving.

"You may be right. I don't think it's from anyone important, though. These kinds of things were a dime a dozen in the early 19th century," he spoke to Anna as if she knew absolutely nothing about the history of the period. "They didn't have television or iPhones or anything, after all." His false smile was all condescension. "They made their own entertainment."

"And how do *you* know Dr. Fussell?" Miller asked, abruptly turning to eye Steve up and down. He knew all the graduate students in the department. This was not one of them.

"Oh, he, uh, he is a friend of mine," Anna stammered. "He teaches band over in Carrboro, so it was pretty close for him to come here with me to campus."

Dr. Miller looked at him as if she had said Steve cleaned sewers with his bare hands. He turned again to study the paper, trying to hide his true reaction from this irritating young man. Excitement fired inside as he recognized the quality of the music he held. This might be quite a find, but he couldn't let these fools in on the secret.

"It's not very good, after all," he emphasized again. "I tell you what, let me keep it and I'll check some of my sources. I have a friend who specializes in obscure American composers of that era."

Steve wondered why Miller was being so negative about it. He kept repeating that it was not very good. But even he, lowly band director though he was, could recognize a good tune when he heard one. Both Dr. Fussell and Anna had been impressed by the piece.

Dr. Miller determined to find out where they had found this. There might be more. He could smell a money-making opportunity from a mile away and this had the right fragrance.

"So, where did you find it?" he stared directly at her coldly.

"The Forsyth Public Library," Anna blurted out. "It was by itself. They let me take it… because… you know… they knew I could bring it to school here. They don't know what it is either." She hoped the stuttering and stammering didn't give away the lie.

"Hmm. Really. Well, I think you had better leave it with me for now. I'll see what I can find out."

Steve and Anna got up to leave.

"And you are sure there are no more pages?" Miller's voice held a hint of accusation.

Anna decided to keep the game going. "Well, I'll check again. Their archives are not well cataloged." She repeated what they had planned beforehand to say.

"Anything with some writing on it would help. Even just dynamic markings. It doesn't have to be a signature." His eyes remained locked on her as she inched backwards to the door.

"I will look," she lied, leaving as quickly as she could, Steve holding the door for her before giving Miller an undisguised glare. He was totally on board with Anna's opinion of the guy as a first-class creep.

As soon as the door closed behind them, Dr. Miller pulled out his cell phone. Locating his contact, a friend who was most often a co-conspirator, he placed the call.

"Hey, Sam, Frank here. We're doing fine, thanks. I have some work for you, I think."

He waited as Sam described how overloaded his schedule was.

"You will want this one, though. It's a discovery of a new piece." His eyes scanned the music before him once more.

"It may be big. I don't have any written text yet, but I hope I will soon."

His friend asked for more details.

"A student found it in a library, she says. I'm not sure if she's telling the truth, but she gave me this sheet of music. It's definitely old. Piano sonata, looks like." He heard the melody in his head. "And it's good. Really good. Could almost have been written by Haydn or Mozart."

He shook his head, agreeing with the skepticism coming through the phone.

"You're right. I don't have any idea how it could have gotten to this country. Except there were a whole lot of Germans traveling to Salem back then. I've told her to find out if there is more, anything with text on it. And I thought I'd put you on alert in case she does."

Sam agreed to help, if he could, in identifying the handwriting. Miller ended the call with a promise to keep in touch and a greeting to Sam's wife.

Later that evening, over pizza at IP3 on Franklin Street, Steve and Anna rehashed the meeting. Without planning it, they had slipped into eating dinner together every free evening. The relationship felt good, comfortable, and absolutely necessary.

"You're right. There's just something so sleazy about him. I don't trust him," Steve took a drink of his iced tea.

"But we left the music with him." Anna swallowed a large bite of their favorite, caprese pizza.

"Hope he buys the lie the way we agreed, telling him it came from the public library archives," he sat back after taking a large bite.

Anna spoke thoughtfully, "You know, maybe we should do what he asked."

Steve's eyebrows lifted, his mouth too full to question her.

She continued, "Maybe I should get him a page with some writing on it. I probably ought to go back to the house this weekend, anyway. There were lots of sheets with things like instrumentation and tempo markings written on them."

"Why does he want that, do you suppose?"

"Maybe so his handwriting-expert friend can take a look," she speculated. "Sometimes you can tell the age of something written by the way they wrote it." Settling back against her chair, she folded her arms. "I just don't want him to know where the music is... or how much of it sits in those trunks."

Steve nodded in agreement and grabbed the last lonely slice of pizza.

CHAPTER 8

Vienna
December 5, 1791

No one paid any attention as Carl slipped into the back regions of the tavern's main room, maneuvering his way through benches and tables while carrying a large bundle. The late hour had allowed time for copious amounts of beer and wine all around. The establishment's usual working-class clientele argued and laughed too loudly to notice the large man carrying something over his shoulder in the shadows.

Finding a likely spot against the wall, he eased his still-unconscious burden onto a hard wooden bench in a dark corner and sat down beside him to prop him up. His arms were tired, though he had certainly carried larger sheep longer distances. Hunger gnawed at his insides. He couldn't remember his last warm meal. Carl had just decided that he had better part with a few of his precious coins for some dinner as a large, loud woman slapped his arm. Stains obscured the color of her tattered apron, and she wiped her hands on a gray rag as she took in the two.

"What'choo want, dearie?" Her breath was incredibly foul, and Carl couldn't stop his nose from wrinkling away from it. She wore a mob cap over uncombed, unwashed gray hair. Her bulbous nose and triple chin moved closer to him as he leaned back. Several large warts sprouted long white hairs.

"Beer," he answered quickly. "And food?"

She nodded to confirm that they had such things, then stared at the still form beside him. Carl tensed. Nothing but a tuft of dull blonde hair was visible, thanks to the large cloak. He wasn't sure why he was nervous, but the situation had him on edge.

"Your friend already had enough, aye?" Her grin displayed black holes between most of her teeth. She wrestled with the stained apron, wiping her hands some more, and continued to linger, staring at the unmoving figure on the bench. Carl nodded and slumped in relief as she finally pushed her ample bulk between empty chairs, clumping away to the kitchen area.

His meal came quickly, some unrecognizable meat, turnips, and bread along with a large beer in a not-too-clean pewter mug. Wolfing the food, he lost himself in eating his fill. Downing the last drops of beer, he wiped his mouth with his sleeve. The uncomfortable feeling of another decision to be made began to dawn on him. His companion had not stirred.

The tavern maid or owner's wife or whoever she was, came back. "Well, dearie, we need to be closing about now." He glanced over his shoulder to see that he and his charge were among only a few remaining customers.

Looking down at the lump on the bench, she offered, "We do have a room or two in the back. You know, for when fellows have a bit too much. Suppose you could hole up there for a bit."

Relief at a plan of action being offered outweighed Carl's vow of frugality. "That would be good," he stated, "seeing how he's not well, I mean." He nodded his head briefly toward the other man.

"Well, come on then. The sooner you get back there, the sooner me and mine can get to bed."

Carl gently picked up the man and followed her through a door at the end of the tavern's long bar. The kitchen area lay to the left of the door, where a tired-looking older man scowled at them as he rinsed mugs in a tin pail of gray water. The woman made an obscene gesture in his direction and looked back at Carl, explaining, "My husband." She picked up a lantern and entered a dark hall on the right.

Pushing open a creaking door, she went in first and placed the lantern on a small table. It was the only furnishing in the tiny room, other than a bed with a deep cavern sunk in its middle. Dingy bed linen peaked out from under worn gray and brown blankets. A small window was shuttered against the cold night air, though broken slats let in icy drafts from the wind blowing outside. His hostess turned, put her hands on her wide hips, and stood. When Carl laid his burden on the bed, she cleared her throat loudly.

Realizing what she was waiting for, he turned and dug a small cloth bag from his jacket. Pulling out a single gulden, he turned back and placed the coin in a now-outstretched hand. That should cover the meal and one night in the room.

Satisfied, she shuffled out, saying as she went, "Chamber pot's under the bed."

Carl turned to see exactly what he had gotten himself into. He crossed his arms and let out a long sighing breath. The small man was wrapped in a winter cloak that appeared to be several sizes too large for him. Carl decided to take it from him so that he could arrange the moth-eaten blankets over him. As he lifted it, finally slipping it out from under the man, a heavy object thudded onto the floor. Carl folded the cloak as neatly as he could, laid it on the floor against the wall, and found the thing that had fallen. It was a large leather bag and felt quite heavy. He put it on the table holding the flickering lantern.

The man in the bed was short, probably only a few inches over five feet, he estimated. His hair was brownish blonde, dirty, and matted. He did not look especially old, but his skin was dull, not at all a healthy color, and bore the marks of smallpox. He wore only a nightshirt, and a smelly, stained thing it was at that. Carl managed to get him onto one side of the bed and covered him with the ragged brown blanket.

Seeing no other option, he lay down himself on the other side of the bed, as far away as he could manage from the sickly little man. He covered himself with the other half of the sorry bedding. Quiet descended over him. The kitchen cleaning must be finished, though he doubted anything in the place was truly kept as it should be. This is certainly a strange turn of events, he thought to himself. He should probably put his mind to decide what he should do in the morning. Before he could even start, his first bed in days, after his only meal in an equally long stretch of time, put him into an immediate deep slumber.

CHAPTER 9
Vienna
December 5, 1791

Well after daybreak, the sick man stirred. Before he was fully awake, he felt trapped against some large object. Opening his eyes, he saw that he was. He lay on his back in a hole, with a large thing on his left and a pile of cloth on his right. He could make out a door in the dim light but had no idea where he was. His thirst would kill him. Moving a little, his arm struck the bulk on his left and it moved.

There was a lot of motion, tugging and grunting, and finally the largest man he had ever seen stood up, whirled around, and peered down at him in surprise. The stranger's mouth hung open in stunned silence.

"Water," he whispered. Blinking, the blonde giant nodded, turned, and left. In his absence, he studied the room, failing to recognize anything familiar. Some daylight made it past cracks and gaps in window shutters, enough to show him his dingy, empty surroundings. "Where am I?" he thought to himself. Then, just as the black memory of the previous evening started to engulf him, the giant entered with a pitcher and cup. He pushed those thoughts back down, unable to face them, and tried to sit up.

His unlikely nurse set the things down on a small table, then matter-of-factly placed two huge hands under his arms and set him up against the wall at the head of the bed. Then he poured water into the cup and held it out to him. Noticing the frailty of the arm trying to take it, the huge man gently held the cup to his lips. The blessed relief of the drink was overwhelming.

"Who are you?" He stared into the face of his benefactor.

"Carl, mein Herr. Carl Bauer." He nodded his head quickly as if in greeting. "And you, mein Herr?"

He almost said his name, but the black fist that had been his heart made him pause. No, that man was dead.

"Johann Pertl," he whispered, picking another of his names and combining it with his mother's family name. Yes, that other man was dead.

"Herr Pertl," Carl nodded. "You are sick, yes?"

Johann pursed his lips in what was almost a grin, "Yes, yes, I am."

A pounding at the door caused both men to jump, water splashing onto the bed. Without waiting for an invitation, a very wide woman stomped loudly into the room.

"Oh, so, the little one's slept it off, has he? I'll be needing payment now." She stuck her hand out toward Carl.

The familiar panic about finances and bill collectors rose in Johann, causing his still aching throat to constrict. But Carl simply turned to the wall, reached into his clothing, and placed a coin in the filthy woman's hand.

"Good, then," she nodded. "For that you get another day and food. But you have to come get it. I ain't your servant." Her backside barely fit through the door as she left.

"Thank you," Johann managed. "Who are you?"

Carl refilled the cup and held it to him once more. "Me? No one. A farmer. From Dürnstein."

"Then how did I get here? With you?" Johann had finished the second cup of water and his voice seemed to be working again.

Carl sat on the very edge of the bed. "Well, you fell out into the street." He scratched his head as he remembered. "I can't even say where, exactly. I couldn't leave you lying there."

The blackness threatened to choke him again, choke his very soul. Johann remembered the worst pain of his life, the betrayal. But by some miracle he had not been left to freeze to death on his own doorstep. He was not sure that was a good thing.

"Thank you, Carl." Now he was exhausted. Carl could see the little man withdraw into himself. The grayish-yellow hue of his skin worried him.

"How are you sick?"

"What?" Johann sank into a more prone position, closing his eyes as an aching fatigue took over.

"Where?" Carl moved his hand in a sweeping motion over his body.

"I had some terrible pains, here, in my stomach," he opened blue eyes as he spoke. "Then I started swelling up everywhere. My hands, my feet. My head almost burst with the pain. At the end, I could only sleep, for days and days."

"Have you had any food?"

Johann shook his head, "Not in weeks. It all tasted like metal. Couldn't even..."

But Carl left before he could finish.

Johann had time to doze off before his new friend returned, carrying a bowl and spoon.

"This is what you need," Carl spoke quietly but with much conviction. And, after the first spoonful, Johann had to agree. Nothing ever tasted better, and its warmth soothed his throat. He managed to down about a third of the broth before he had to stop.

"That was truly good. Thank you."

Johann noticed Carl had pulled something from his jacket and seemed to be moving things around in his hand, brow furrowed in concentration.

"Is something wrong?"

"No, no," Carl quickly stuck whatever it was back in its hiding place. "I was just figuring. Numbers do not like me."

"Figuring what? What numbers?" Johann was amazed at how much more clarity he had. He must have needed the soup.

"Well, the landlady. She said two kreuzers a day for this room and meals. I do not know..."

"Forgive me," Johann interrupted him. "I was thoughtless, and I have imposed on your good nature."

Carl stared at him wide-eyed, a member of the upper classes having never apologized to him for anything before. They never spoke to him, never even looked at him or farm workers like him.

Johann continued, "I was unaware that we were at an inn. Let me think about this."

He closed his eyes. This huge farmer who had without doubt saved his life, was also having to pay for their use of this room and whatever else they needed. It was wrong, but how was he to correct it? He had not sold anything in so long, he and—no, he couldn't think her name—he had relied on the mercy of friends and patrons over the past months. Then, once he was so ill... His situation was impossible. He didn't even have clothes, for heaven's sake.

"Um, excuse me, Herr Pertl?"

Carl stood in a corner of the room, holding what looked like a massive cloak in one hand and a good-sized leather pouch in the other. He was staring into the pouch with open-mouthed wonder.

"Yes, what is it?"

"Mein Herr, is this yours?" He tipped the pouch's opening toward the other man, dropping the cloak to open the bag's mouth wider. Slowly, he began to pour a stream of gold coins onto the bed.

"No... I mean, I don't know... Where did you find it?" Johann had never seen as much gold.

"It fell from your coat." Carl picked the garment up off the floor.

"That's not..." Johann stopped as he remembered grabbing the coat in his hallway and whose it must have been.

"There must be hundreds of these," Carl was in shock as he handed one to Johann.

"An eight-florin coin," Johann muttered, doing the math in his head. Sixty kreuzers to a florin, and several hundred eight-florin coins?

"Well, Carl, we could stay an eternity in this room and eat all the broth we would like," he handed the coin back. "Better put those away. We need to keep them hidden. Forgive me, I have to sleep now."

Whoever had stolen his wife had just become the victim of a theft himself.

CHAPTER 10

North Carolina
October 2019

A nna and Steve drove together through a Friday afternoon downpour to Winston-Salem. Somehow the
music in her great aunt's old house overrode their other
priorities and pulled them back to the attic and its mystery.

The windshield wipers' steady beat accompanied rain
and water sounds so loud that they opted not to compete
with them by turning on any music. For a while, they traveled comfortably in silence.

"Did you grow up going to church?" Anna asked finally.
She wanted to know everything about him, all the nooks
and crannies of his years before they met.

"Yes, my parents made me. First Baptist, Clemson, South
Carolina. I was in RAs, VBS, church camps. You name it,
they made me do it."

Anna laughed. "Sounds like you resented it a little."

He raised an eyebrow, glancing toward her, "You
think so?"

"So does that mean you stay away from churchy things
now that you are all grown up?"

"Not exactly, not now. It's a story," he responded.

"We've got over an hour," Anna folded her arms and leaned back in the passenger seat. "Tell me."

"OK, well, I pretty much played by the rules through high school. I tried a few things... beer, cigarettes, a few girls my mother didn't like."

It was Anna's turn to raise an eyebrow.

"Nothing serious. Just teenage stuff," he assured her.

"Teenage stuff can be pretty intense."

"Well, I was kind of skinny and had a lot of acne. Never quite got the intense opportunity." This caused her to laugh.

"Anyway, I went to school in Columbia, University of South Carolina. It was only a couple of hours from my parents, but far enough. At first, it was all right. I was in the band, so it was easy to make friends. There were parties, football games, a lot of work at things I mostly loved. But for some reason I started sinking."

"What do you mean?"

"Well, I was able to go to classes and get homework done, but my heart wasn't in it. I'd get together with friends. We'd do some crazy stuff in the freshmen boys' dorm. You can imagine. But I just felt kind of depressed. It should have been the best time of my life. I was doing exactly what I wanted all the time. But I started getting scared at how down I felt," he ran a hand through his blonde hair.

Anna's heart warmed as she sensed his trust in her.

"I wasn't sure what to do. I've never been especially close to my parents. They were just, well, busy. I never talked to them seriously about something like that. Besides, my dad wasn't happy with my major. I wasn't about to open a door for him to criticize, to try to talk me out of music.

"One morning I was drinking coffee before a rehearsal. A guy I knew a little, a tuba player, sat down and started talking to me. Out of nowhere, he starts saying that he had been walking by and God told him to talk to me. That what I was going through was because I didn't really know Jesus.

"That knocked the wind out of me. Of course, I knew Jesus. Wasn't I Mr. Baptist? I hadn't done anything about church since heading to the University, but I knew lots of stuff. I was raised in the middle of Bible classes and church choirs.

"This guy told me it didn't matter. The only thing was knowing him, knowing Jesus. Then he left.

"I forgot about it and went to class. But it kept nagging at me, staying in my brain. He managed to find me a few more times right after that. After a couple of weeks, I started to get convinced that something had to give. I was sinking deeper and deeper. He invited me to his church, a small one that met at some guy's house. And that's when it all changed."

Anna waited in silence, knowing this kind of transparency was sacred. She didn't want him to stop.

"So, I went with him. There were a couple of people singing with a guitar and the music was fantastic. I'd never experienced that before. I couldn't have described it at the time, but the Holy Spirit was there, and you could feel God. It blew me away. Then the guy who was the pastor preached about the love of God. You would have thought that I had heard that a million times, but this hit me right here." He laid a hand on the middle of his chest.

"So, what happened?" Her tone was quiet, reverent.

"I stayed after and prayed with the tuba player and his pastor. I told God I was sorry for running from him, for doing my own thing."

"And...?"

A huge grin spread over Steve's face. "Everything changed. I went through the same routines, but it was all different. Well, I quit the partying. But *I* was different. I kept going to that little church and started learning about God for real. Not that the Baptists were wrong... I just hadn't really listened, I guess. The depression left. I've been trying to hear God's voice and follow him ever since."

Silence enveloped them again. Steve turned to her, "Ok, so, and you?"

Anna wondered where to start. She had the pat religious answer that she grew up in the Moravian church. Then there was the mystical, other-worldly story of the experiences she began having when she was about six. She glanced at Steve, realizing he had spoken about God talking to people here and now. She figured he deserved the truth and took a deep breath.

"My parents made me go to church, too. But it was the Moravian church. I pretty much loved it, especially the music. Since they have all kinds of little instrumental groups, I was able to play a lot as soon as I got into junior high." She remembered playing anthems in a small orchestra, staring at a stained-glass window with the lamb in front of a colorful flag with a red cross. The Lamb of God, who had accomplished it all for her.

"I guess I wanted to be close to God forever. When I was six, I woke up in the middle of the night and I saw him standing there."

Steve's head jerked around so quickly Anna feared they might veer off the road. He recovered himself and faced forward again. "You... *saw*... him?"

She appreciated that he didn't seem to doubt her.

"I think so. Then I would hear him, every so often, while I was growing up. Like a voice or an impression, telling me to do a certain thing or talk to a certain person."

"Just like the tuba player." Steve sounded totally open to someone hearing the voice of God.

Then he asked, "So did you ever rebel? Ever try to run away from the church?"

"Well, I'm not perfect," she started. "Far from it. I've had my moments. But I didn't have as much loyalty to the church or rules as I did to this friend of mine, this Jesus who stayed with me and told me things."

"What kind of things?" Steve was genuinely interested, not at all skeptical.

"Sometimes I would know what a friend needed to hear, or where they had gotten off the path. Or I would just have this feeling that God was right there with me, that he loved me, and..."

Steve waited silently, expectantly.

"...and that he just enjoyed being with me. And that he liked it when I played music for him. Is that too weird?"

Thinking that he enjoyed just being with her as well, Steve didn't believe it was in any way too weird.

"No, not at all. So, you would say you are sort of a mystic?"

"Ha! I like that. Maybe so. I've never really labeled myself, just told people I go to the Moravian church."

"Can I tell you something?" Steve asked in a quiet voice as he glanced at her.

Anna nodded.

"That night that we met. You know when we ended up at the same reception?"

"Fighting over the ham?" she smiled.

"Yeah, that one. I heard him that night."

"Oh?"

"Before I came. I was supposed to meet a buddy of mine in Durham. We had it scheduled for a while. But when I was heading out the door after class, I saw the poster advertising the concert and reception on campus. Suddenly, I knew I was supposed to go there. It was so strong. There was no way I could do anything else. I called my friend and told him something had come up. Not exactly a lie, really. Then I headed over to the place when the time came, wondering why God wanted me to go to a party on my own."

"And the rest is history," Anna stated.

"It sure is," he smiled. They sat quietly again, each happy in the new knowledge of the other's faith, feeling knit together even more closely. Steve slid his right hand from the steering wheel to gently hold hers the rest of the trip.

CHAPTER 11
Austria
December 7, 1791–January 6, 1792

The pattern of their days fell into a monotonous regularity that brought healing to Johann's body, if not his heart. He slept through long wintery nights, slept ten or twelve hours. His waking times slipped by in staring numbly at the dirty walls surrounding him. His brain used to dart about like the collared flycatchers around Vienna, full of melodies, his own along with everything he had ever heard. No longer. Oh, he could focus and pull them up out of the dark waters, but they no longer joyfully swam unbidden to the surface.

Carl, who now slept on a pallet of thick woolen blankets on the floor, usually rose before him and wandered the city streets. The displaced farmer often headed out of the city to fields and trees. Th   was no aimless wandering, though, as he was always searching for the healing plants that his mother had shown him around their home. More often than not, he returned with a sack of green and brown things. Even in winter, there were treasures to be found.

The woods near Vienna, so beloved by its citizens, yielded dandelion root and horsetail. Carl thoroughly enjoyed the bracing cold air and sunshine as he scoured the forest floor for the medicines his mother had taught him to seek for urinary issues. Johann had mentioned the difficulties he was having with that, and it gave Carl direction in his foraging. An apothecary's shop near the market gave him dried goldenrod. The stuff made him sneeze every time he added it to his soup, but he knew its power to heal.

The inn's proprietress grew used to the giant man in her kitchen, stirring a pot's contents and mumbling to himself as he dropped bits and pieces of plant detritus into it. Carl in turn grew used to the glares and curses from her husband, who concocted foul meals from half rotten food for their customer-victims. Carl found decent merchants, who had fresh meats and produce at fair prices. Not for his patient, the greasy gray stews fed to others in this place.

He recreated the best of his mother's meals for invalids, guaranteed to restore health and strength. As he cared for the sick man, his sense of himself returned. At times memories of that night with Liese and Gustav rose within him and made his heart race. Anger drove him to chop things quickly and violently until the mistress of the kitchen would ask loudly, "And what's wrong with you now?" He never told her, but his mind calmed as it returned to his strange new situation and his patient.

The swelling of Johann's hands and feet went down with every bowl of Carl's soup. He could now walk easily around the room but was terrified at the thought of leaving it. His face was too well known in Vienna. This place was cheap, just the kind of establishment to attract musicians, who never had quite enough money. He would be recognized instantly, and he did not want that. He walked around the bed and back, over and over, in a nightshirt purchased with his enemy's funds. These stretches of exercise alternated with periods of deep depression as he lay on his back and stared at the ceiling, trying to breathe through the thick cloud pressing down upon him. The cloud contained not only his wife's betrayal, but also the frustration of constantly having to write music for payment which always fell short of their needs. Never in his life had he been so totally without hope. He wanted to end this suffocating pain by any means available to him.

Johann believed in God. A remote figure, poised to strike those who displeased him and reward those who performed according to his rules. He also believed that God had created him with extraordinary musical gifts. His earthly father had hammered that into him daily. In spite of prideful boasting about those gifts and relishing the acclaim that they had afforded him, Johann always felt a vague, uneasy sense of inadequacy. His father saw it as his parental duty to frequently point out where his son could improve, both in his music and also in areas in which he was being a less than dutiful son. The church's message was that he was a miserable sinner, hoping to attain grace through obedience to its teachings. He had rebelled against both parental and ecclesiastical authority at times. But the only thing keeping him from taking his own life was the deep fear they had taught him. God was no comfort to him now. He never had been. He was a remote, vaguely displeased figure. Escape from Vienna fixed itself in his mind as his only possible path forward.

But how to do it? He and Carl had fallen into a master-servant relationship easily. He needed help and Carl had nothing else to do, it seemed. They never spoke about it, and there was no discussion of pay or definition of roles. Johann had the sense that Carl was as needy as he himself was, but in an emotional rather than physical way. The giant man never mentioned his family and Johann presumed he had nowhere else to go. He hoped this meant that there would be no question of helping in an escape from Vienna.

"Carl," he spoke one afternoon, startling his nurse who was used to the staring and silence. "We need to think about going south, going to Italy."

Carl's mouth dropped open. Vienna was already the farthest he had ever been from Dürnstein. "Going to Italy" sounded to him as if Johann had said they were going to the moon. What in the world did the man have in mind now?

"Yes, I think we need to start planning for that. I need to leave this city." Johann's voice held no eager anticipation of travel or adventure. He sounded defeated.

"How?" Carl asked. He knew that Johann, though much stronger physically, could never walk even a mile at this point. Who knew how far Italy was, how much walking it might take?

"Well, my father and I used to go frequently. You hire a carriage, or there is public transportation. Yes, that would be better. People would pay less attention. I could be your invalid master, heading south for warmth. The sun is wonderful in Italy." Johann smiled at that memory.

The scheme enlivened the little man. He began to give orders to Carl, where to go to find out about public conveyances, where to go to purchase a trunk for the belongings they had accumulated over their month in seclusion. Thinking along those lines caused him to realize how little they had in the way of material possessions. Dragging the leather pouch from its hiding place under the head of the bed, he examined its contents. Still mostly there, as far as he could tell. Their stay at this miserable inn had cost almost nothing. But clothing! He could hardly travel in the night-shirts that were his only garments. And to think that he had once paid such careful attention to his wardrobe. Vanity surely is meaningless, as he had been told in church during his youth.

"Carl, I think I might have an idea. Do you know the place where you found me that night?" He no longer thought of it as his home.

The giant, sitting at the foot of the bed, nodded. He had made a habit of passing the place frequently. In fact, just a few days after their arrival at the inn he had watched a remarkable thing, a funeral procession.

It had stormed all night, rain and snow mixing in an assault on the city, but by midmorning a gentle wind warmed Vienna. Carl noticed several women in black at the apartment door when he passed by on his way to the market. A funeral bier with black horses, bridles adorned with black plumes, waited at the curb. He slipped into an alley where he could watch the scene unnoticed.

One woman pounded at the door, which finally opened. A man in a military uniform held it and watched as the women entered the apartment. He motioned to two men waiting by the bier. They, too, entered the apartment, carrying what looked like folds of cloth.

Quite a while later, the two men emerged, carrying a sagging object between them. Carl froze as he realized that it had to be a body, sewn into the cloth they had carried in, as was the custom. They placed it into the bier as the women came back out. One sounded to be arguing. Another woman appeared in the doorway, not dressed in black, and shaking her head angrily.

The three women turned away and walked into the position of mourners behind the funeral cart. It began to move slowly, in the direction of St. Stephen's Cathedral. Several other men appeared to accompany the group.

Just as Carl began his way down the street, a fancy coach drove up to the same apartment and men hopped out. Now the other lady, the one in traveling clothes instead of the black of mourning, emerged on the arm of the military man. They waited as the carriage men carried trunk after trunk out of the place, loading up more luggage than Carl had ever seen. The soldier helped the woman into the coach, and they left. In all these following weeks, the pair had not returned that he could tell. He continued to pass by almost daily. The apartment remained dark and abandoned.

Since he had asked about it, Carl decided he would tell Johann all he had seen.

"Yes, I have been by there many times over these past weeks."

Johann exclaimed in surprise, "Whatever for?"

"It is on my way to the best market. I was curious," Carl continued. "There has been no one there, not during the day or night, as far as I can tell. No lights, no changes in anything. Not since the procession."

"Procession?" Johann couldn't imagine.

"Ja, for a funeral." He explained in detail all he had seen on December 7.

Johann questioned him to the point of exhaustion, making him repeat and describe every person involved in the event. He was especially intense in asking about the woman who was not wearing black, who left with the military man in the fancy coach.

Johann sank into a stony silence. So, she had run off with the bastard. And all this... a funeral procession... a body?! Lord above, where had they gotten a body? Some poor soul to sew into sacks to toss into a pit with four or five others. Was she pretending that he had died? Well, he had, hadn't he? That man was no longer among the living.

"This may be to our advantage, Carl," he spoke quietly. "If they truly are not there, perhaps you could get in?"

"What? Break in? I have no key."

"No, but I know a window with a broken latch. It is just beside the front door. If you could go with no one around, I know you could easily open it and reach the door. Open it from the inside."

Carl felt fear rising within him. Thieves were not treated kindly in the city. He had no desire to spend time in jail. "But, mein Herr..." He stopped as Johann held up his hand.

"We will take our time, Carl, and you will just walk by for the next few nights. You can discover a time that no one is about and check at that same time, over and over, until you are comfortable."

Carl looked as if he would never be comfortable again.

"And you are not going to steal anything. I simply want my clothes." He went on to describe which room to go into, where the wardrobe stood.

"And the snuff boxes! I almost forgot. They are all in the second drawer of the table beside the bed. Bring them all. They belong to me." Johann nodded to himself, remembering the porcelain ones presented to him as a child and several golden ones, including a real treasure given to him by the King in Berlin in payment for some quartets and sonatas. He noticed Carl's nervous hand motions.

"They are mine, also. This is not stealing, Carl. You are merely collecting my own things, which I need for our trip." If they are still there, he thought uneasily.

Carl nodded, still unhappy at the prospect.

They launched the plan that very night. About two in the morning, Carl slipped from the room and quickly walked to the apartment where this new manservant life of his had begun. He slid into a shadow just across the street and waited for an hour, staring at the place for any signs of life. Nothing. And no one passed by. He saw a candle in an upstairs window at the far corner of the block, but no one nearby was awake. He stayed another half hour or so, then headed back to the inn. Johann was awake and interrogated him about his mission. Satisfied, both turned to sleep, though it eluded Carl for quite a long time.

Three nights went by, and he did the same thing at the same time during each one. Never a person nor carriage passed and there was never a sign of anyone inside. Carl also watched the place during the day as much as he could without drawing attention to himself. No one.

Finally, the night of the escapade was here. Johann insisted. Carl had purchased four large burlap sacks for almost nothing. They decided to wait until they saw how much he was able to retrieve before buying traveling trunks sufficient to hold it. Johann wondered bitterly if she had gotten rid of all trace of him and there would be nothing to retrieve. But he had to send Carl to try.

That afternoon and into the early evening, Carl watched for any signs of the apartment's residents' return. After dark, he brought dinner to their room, and they ate silently. He tried to sleep for a bit afterward but couldn't. Getting up at

2 a.m. had become a habit for him and he could sense the time was upon him.

Johann had not slept, either. He whispered a parting encouragement, "Thank you, my good Carl. I depend upon you. You will be safe." Carl did not look as if he believed that at all.

It was actually very easy to open the window just to the left of the front door, then to stretch his long arm to the bolt above the door handle and pull it back. He forced the handle on the outside down with all his strength and was rewarded with a breaking sound. The door opened easily. He checked both lengths of the street and was mightily relieved to see no one. Slipping inside, he pushed the door shut behind him.

Carl's eyes grew accustomed to the dark. They had both agreed it would be too dangerous to light a candle in the abandoned apartment. On the left was a sitting room with a harpsichord. No, Johann had called it a fortepiano. Who knew there was a difference? Anyway, his charge had gone over and over the layout of the place, making him repeat it back to him until there was no chance he would ever forget. He whispered the floor plan as he made his way down the hall.

And here was the bedroom. It looked as it had been described, or at least the furniture shapes seemed to fit. He fumbled a bit opening the wardrobe. There were clothes there and from the feel of them, he judged them to be men's clothing. Hurriedly he stuffed all of it into two of the large bags. The drawers below held what felt like stockings and shoes, so those went into another bag. In the large armoire, he grabbed three or four coats along with several waistcoats.

He almost forgot the nightstand by the bed. Opening the second drawer, he felt the smooth shapes of glass and metal boxes and put them one by one into the bag. There was something that felt like loose paper at the bottom of the drawer, so he grabbed that also. Johann hadn't mentioned it, but Carl was never, ever going to return to this place, so he had better get everything.

Shouldering the bags, he headed to the door but stopped quickly at the sight of a light from the street, shining into the window he had opened. Frozen in fear, he backed into the bedroom's doorway and watched the light move around, as if someone were trying to peer inside the place.

"So, this is where he lived?" A man's voice at full volume asked the question. He was not trying to hide his presence.

"Yes, until the end of last year. So sad. What a gift!" A second man answered.

"Well, then, a toast!"

They must be drinking, Carl thought. A toast to Johann?

"To Mozart!"

"To the greatest composer ever to live!"

"Come, now, Ludwig, do you really think so?"

A snort of laughter, "No, I think I'm going to earn that title!"

Raucous laughter followed and a third voice slurred the words, "Oh, let's get on, Beethoven. I'm freezing my parts off out here."

The light moved away, and Carl heard footsteps fading off down the street. He went quietly and carefully to the window and just caught sight of three men, holding onto each other, quite drunk and staggering as they made their way down the street. Still fearful after the interruption, he waited at least ten more minutes before pushing the door open and running in the opposite direction, back to their inn, bags in both hands.

Johann greeted him with much relief. Carl realized that the confidence the little man had shown before was an act. He had been in as much fear about the whole thing as Carl himself had been.

"So, it went well? No one saw you?"

Carl swung the four very full bags onto the bed.

"There was a problem, actually."

Johann's eyebrows shot up as he waited for details.

"Some drunken men. Very odd." Carl sat down heavily at the foot of the bed. "They were trying to look in a window. And talking about someone called Mozart."

Even in the dim light of one candle, Carl could see all color drain from Johann's face.

"That man is dead," Johann stated in anger. "I don't want to ever hear that name again."

Carl shrugged, "But they moved off and I hurried out of there. Strange that they should come around on this night."

Johann had already begun pulling things from the bag nearest him. "Yes, yes, these are mine. This is so good, Carl, so good. I can be a person again, dress in proper clothes, wear shoes."

Carl sank onto his pallet on the floor, suddenly exhausted as he realized his ordeal was over. Johann stayed up the rest of the night, examining each item of clothing, each shoe, each snuff box, and, just as the sun came up, staring at the music Carl had snatched up at the last minute.

CHAPTER 12
Vienna to Venice
February 1792

Traveling in 1792 was arduous. Long distance land travel was by public coach for those who did not have the means to purchase their own carriage. Many wagons and carriages, including those the Mozart family had used as they traversed Europe showing off their child prodigy, often became stuck in the mud. Highwaymen lurked in preparation for an ambush, especially in Italy. Many travelers' complaints centered around the primitive roads, which made journeys painful and strenuous.

Traveling the almost 400 miles from Vienna to Venice in winter wasn't going to be problem-free. Johann had spent easily a third of his life in carriages crossing Europe; from Salzburg to München when he was only 6, then as far as London, Berlin, Rome, and Prague over the next thirty years. He was well aware of the delays that mud, tired horses, and broken wheels might cause. It could take several weeks, but he had to get away from this city he had once loved. It meant only betrayal and death to him now.

Carl gathered the necessities for their journey as he was instructed. All their belongings fit into two trunks, procured inexpensively from the sale of a deceased flour merchant's estate. Johann had devised a traveling outfit that should allow him to screen his face from anyone who might possibly recognize him as the recently deceased composer. The collar of his coat turned up and the oversized brim of his hat pulled down, rendering him anonymous. The bulk of their golden coins were hidden in the lining of Johann's coat, though some travelled with Carl and some lay hidden in the false bottom of one of the trunks, discovered by happy accident. Johann told several stories of the burglars lurking in wait across Italy, convincing his companion of the expediency of hiding their wealth.

Carl's longest journey had been from Dürnstein to Vienna, 50 miles, which he had traveled on foot in two long days. Johann knew Venice to be over six times as far away. He tried to explain the impossibility of calculating the exact length of time for the trip. The carriage would go about 15 to 20 miles between each post station, where they would exchange horses. This could take up to two hours. So, each one of these pieces of the journey could take 6 hours, including the changeover in teams. If they spent the night at the rough, dirty stations along the way, and did not become stuck in the mud or break any wheels, they could possibly get there in 10 days. But a fortnight or longer on the road would be a strong possibility.

"It will be very important that no one knows who I am," Johann stressed many times to the farmer who had become his manservant and trusted companion.

"Who are you?" Carl asked blankly.

"A very...oh, never mind," Johann closed his eyes, shaking his head. "I just can't let that treacherous lady who used to be my wife know that I am here. I have to leave this place."

"Start over?" Carl asked, again without expression. He knew a bit about having to escape a situation. He dearly wished he could somehow get word to his parents about this adventure he had stumbled into, but he did not write well enough to send a letter. And he still feared discovery himself.

Johann shook his head without answering. Start over? He could do but one thing and now that one thing was lost to him. Perhaps he could teach music lessons in obscurity somewhere, but never could he compose or perform again. Not in Europe. His dear departed father had so successfully waged a campaign to spread the fame of his miraculous son across all the courts of the continent that he feared he could go nowhere without the danger of someone recognizing him. Perhaps the clouds of heaviness enfolding him were not totally due to his wife's betrayal. Perhaps they were also partly from the loss of the only identity he had ever known, that of musician and composer.

Carl had his own fears about leaving Austria. He spoke only German. Johann assured him that he himself was fluent in Italian, French, and English, but Carl wasn't so sure he could pick up those languages. He was the one who did all the day-to-day errands and shopping for the two. The loss of his family had put him adrift but having to care for Johann gave him focus once more. He had always had something to take care of, from the time his father had given him his first lamb to see to. Carl had a special gift, as his mother told him, in caring for the sick and weak. A gift from God, she had said. He missed her stories about God, which always comforted him. On his own, he rarely thought about the Almighty. One time he had felt particularly shunned by the young people in his village but caring for a calf rejected by its mother caused him to forget it. His mother told him that he had needed the sick calf just as much as that calf needed him. He didn't understand at the time, but perhaps now he did. If he worked his hardest at watching out for Johann, his fears went away. No need to worry about God for now.

Their landlady instructed one of the public conveyances to stop by the inn for several passengers, after they turned over a few more coins to her. She would be sorry to see them go, since they paid so regularly. Early on a frozen gray morning, Carl dragged their trunks to the rear of the coach. Johann, using a cane for support, followed behind. When he passed through the tavern's empty main room he slipped a small stack of music, the same that Carl had retrieved from his old apartment, into the fireplace. His old life was truly over, he thought as he climbed into the carriage and claimed the seat facing away from the driver.

Johann had not left the back room of the inn for almost three months and found himself on the verge of panic as a gentleman in a worn coat helped his plump wife into the cabin. They greeted him cordially, but Johann kept his face covered and looked away. Better they think him a boor than that he be recognized. Carl entered and Johann felt better hidden beside his massive form. The offense written on the faces of the couple so close to them lasted only briefly and the uncomfortable silence soon seemed normal.

Their first stop was Guntramsdorf. Johann felt exhausted and wondered what he had been thinking to imagine he could make such a journey. But Carl bought them both some strong coffee and cake, which they ate in the farthest, darkest corner of the hall, away from the other patrons of the station. Revived and less fearful, Johann returned to the waiting coach with its fresh horses.

Both men managed to doze during the second stage of their journey. Light snow fell, not enough to interfere with the condition of the road. The lady across from them appeared to feel ill, so her husband's focus was entirely on her as he tried to get her to take some liqueur. At least he ignored their unsocial traveling companions. Cold silence within the coach mirrored the gray day without. Snow fell more intensely as the dim daylight grew even dimmer. Their coachman decided to stop in Kottingbrunn for the night, even though that meant only 25 miles for the first day. Johann resigned himself to discomfort and boredom, probably for many hours ahead.

Their days blended into each other, mostly made up of long, bouncing rides in the carriage, during which Johann stubbornly refused to be civil to anyone around him and Carl served as a buffer between him and the world. The couple who began the journey from Vienna departed at Bruck an der Mur, a pleasant city at the juncture of two rivers. Other travelling companions came and left, never succeeding in eliciting even the most superficial of remarks from the rudely unresponsive small man.

Johann began to feel weak again. The months in the room at the back of the inn in Vienna, resting and taking Carl's herbal remedies and broths had caused a noticeable improvement in his health. He had felt penned up before their trip, ready to walk or sit outside. Now the poor food available at the post stations, the drafty, uncomfortable carriage, and loss of sleep were bringing back the old familiar malaise. He had to lean heavily on Carl's arm whenever they disembarked.

One morning, after a particularly noisy and smelly overnight stay in Udine, Johann had a nasty scare. They had left the Alps behind and the air at this lower elevation was not as frigid as before. The first blue sky of their journey, even though they were well over halfway, lightened his spirits. He stood in the station yard, waiting for the horses to be completely hitched to the carriage. Thinking himself alone, he lifted his face uncovered to the morning sun, relishing the delicate warmth as he leaned on his cane. His reverie was interrupted by a gasp and a crash.

Startled, he locked gazes with a middle-aged woman who stared open-mouthed at him. Carl appeared from nowhere and placed himself between the two. Another gentleman moved to the lady and grasped her arm. "Bettina? Are you all right?" He bent to retrieve an open violin case from the paving stones. It's drop must have caused the crash. Carl quickly helped Johann into the carriage, where they took up their usual positions, Johann burying his face into his high collar and pulling the hat as far down as possible.

Johann heard the couple outside, despite their efforts to keep their agitated voices quiet. "I tell you; it looks just like him. I sang under him, you know, in the Altes Burgtheater. He conducted *Die Entführung aus dem Serail*." Johann felt as if he would be ill. He could barely breathe.

"Dear, you know what we heard. He died months ago."

Bettina, still agitated, continued. "But it looks exactly like him. Oh, I am so foolish. Is your violin quite all right? I thought I was beholding a ghost."

Her husband reassured her that the instrument was fine.

That was the most uncomfortable day of the whole journey. Johann kept his face averted from the couple. Carl explained that his master felt ill. The couple whispered story after story dredged from years past about their favorite dead composer, who could hear every word quite plainly. At first his thoughts refused to line up in any kind of order, as fear made him stupid. But as the hours wore on, the carriage moving as if both horses were lame, Johann calmed enough to catch exaggerations and outright lies that irritated him more and more.

"I never threw anything at anyone," he screamed silently after hearing of his supposed reaction to a poor viola player butchering his Sinfonie Concertante. Carl watched his master twitch as a reddish flush spread up his neck to disappear behind the hat and collar shielding his face from view. Though he did not understand what those people were going on about, it made him nervous. The spreading redness reminded him of the many evening rants and ravings about Johann's despicable wife that he had endured. Johann could certainly work himself into a frenzy of anger. Those never ended well.

Just as Carl worried his master would explode and just as Johann devised a plan to throw off his coverings and tell them he had risen from the dead, the carriage stopped.

"Oh, there is Friedrich! He must have been waiting for hours." The man gathered up the violin case and eagerly opened the carriage door.

"My son, my son!" The woman trilled a greeting, waving a gloved hand at a cold and unamused-looking young man on the front steps of the post inn.

Johann and Carl hung back, waiting for the reunited family to head toward another carriage at the side of the inn, before exiting themselves. The driver told them it would be a short stop, so they should be quick about getting food or whatever they needed for themselves. Outside of the carriage, with no one near, both men let out loud sighs of relief. "Blessed, blessed quiet," Johann murmured and headed toward the inn's shabby door.

Finally, the driver announced that they would make Venice before nightfall on the next day. Johann felt physically incapable of deciding anything. The weeks of cold, bad sleep, and worse food tore at his health. Carl, on the other hand, never showed any signs of tiredness or weakness. Thank heaven for that, Johann thought. They would have to worry about lodgings when they arrived.

"We should stay out of the center of the city," Johann told him that evening. They were in a small room for the last night of their trip, furnished with several hard benches and ragged blankets. "There is little chance, but I could be recognized. The Italians are a marvelously musical people."

Carl nodded, still unbelieving that he could be in another country, Italy no less.

"Maybe, when we get there, I can stay at the post inn, and you can ask around." The words were out before he remembered that Carl spoke no Italian.

Realizing his error, he continued, "Well, that won't work. Let's just rest a bit when we get there. And hope I am up to Italian conversation soon." He pulled up a rough blanket as Carl removed a plate of food mostly untouched, grabbing it quickly before it could clatter to the floor.

He ate quietly as the small man's breathing slowed to the pace of sleeping. Johann was not doing well. It was going to be up to him to find a clean place to stay, decent food, and some hills or fields to search for restorative herbs. Tasks to do would keep his mind off the impossible distance between him and his family. He sank onto a thick comforter on the floor, spreading a dirty blanket over himself. Before sleep claimed him, he imagined himself back with the sheep and cattle on his father's farm, being welcomed home by the sweet smile of his mother.

CHAPTER 13

Venice
February 1792

C arl thought that Venice must be hell itself. He did not like being on water. Despite Dürnstein's proximity to the Danube, he had never learned to swim well enough to overcome his body's tendency to sink like a large stone. And Venice seemed to be nothing but water. The buildings floating on gray mist unnerved him. They arrived at sunset after a short ride in a barge-like conveyance. Johann told him they had arrived at the Place of St. Mark. "Piazza San Marco," he had called it.

Johann had no patience for his younger companion. He explained briefly that one really could walk everywhere here if one desired, but the boats called gondolas, lined up along the walls, were for hire. Carl stood by helplessly as Johann conversed with one of the gransieri, the porters who held the gondolas, in Italian. Nothing could be farther from German, he decided in dismay.

Carl stared in disbelief at crowds of people passing by, many of them wearing masks, most already drunk. Some wore fantastic costumes, dressed up as clowns, angels, and devils. A pair went by all in white, wearing long elaborate gowns with full-sized swans on their heads. The skin of their faces and hands was coated with white paint or grease, giving them a fearsome, ghostly appearance. Beside them walked two more revelers with every color imaginable throughout their coats and with skulls as masks. Many wore tricorn hats, sporting tremendous feather plumes. He noticed a golden-winged angel on the top of a belltower across from where they had landed. Was this a land of angels or devils?

"Come, Carl, this man knows of a place we can stay," Johann called to his friend who gaped open-mouthed at the crowds.

"Why... why is this place so strange?" Carl asked Johann in a hoarse stage-whisper, not wanting to offend any nearby Venetians.

"Carnevale," Johann replied and stepped down into the flat boat.

This meant nothing to Carl, but he nodded gravely and passed trunks down to its captain. As he made to climb into the long, narrow black boat, fireworks blasted across the square. He jumped as if dodging musket balls and reddened at the gondolier's laughter.

As they navigated the canals between buildings, Johann explained how Venice had been built on many islands. The gondolier used a pole to push them along. The ride was eerily silent after days in jangling carriages, and the gray palaces rising on either side of their small boat loomed menacingly. The front and back of the gondola rose high above them. This is the queen city of Italy, Johann explained, the center of music, and her citizens celebrated Carnevale before Lent more vigorously than any other people in Christendom. The Venetians had many festivals, both religious and historic. The strangeness of it all made Carl distinctly uneasy.

He was grateful when their gondolier finally stopped at the foot of some stairs. A square of white paper was fastened to window shutters above them.

Johann pointed to it, "That means they have rooms to let." Their gondolier was able to ring a bell by the door without leaving his craft.

After much more gibbering in their strange tongue with a servant who answered the bell, their trunks were unloaded, and Johann paid the boatman. The small man looked exhausted but seemed totally at ease with both the language and their situation. Carl was glad to finally enter a building which indeed had rooms for them. He followed his master down the stone floor of a narrow hallway. The colored marble was cold and polished. It led to a couple of dismal, dark bedchambers.

Everything about the rooms spoke of dreariness. No carpets, a few ugly square prints of buildings nailed to the walls. There was a dirty window in each with bars across the lower half and shutters that would not quite close. The furnishings in Carl's room consisted of a husk bed, flimsy washstand, and threadbare brown bench. He moved to Johann's room and found it no better.

Curious, Carl stepped to the window to examine their surroundings. There below was a square and people walking on solid ground. Relieved, Carl wondered if perhaps he could find a market. Would it even be possible to get to fields or forests for fresh air and herbs, he wondered? He turned back to ask his master, but Johann was already fast asleep after their long day's journey.

The next day Carl set out for the market which he learned was close to their lodgings, called a "palace" by their owner. These people were beyond belief, putting on such airs. He left Johann, worn out from their journey, and ventured out with the landlord's young son Antonio as guide and translator. The odd pair made their way down the narrowest, most crooked streets imaginable. The crowds around them moved at a slower pace than Carl was used to in Vienna. No one hurried anywhere. And the streets seemed quiet. He finally realized most likely the lack of wagons and carriages was the cause. Antonio spoke a smattering of German with a heavy Italian accent and was happy to earn a few coins leading the big oaf, as he called him, around. Rather than struggle with the languages, they spent their journey in silence.

Looking around, Carl identified a church at one end of the square and an apothecary. He stood and cataloged the other shops around it: mercer, draper, blacksmith, shoemaker, cafe or tavern, grocer, fruit stand, and what looked like a second-hand shop. In addition, people had various tables outside laden with wares. Some sat on mats and spread their goods on the ground beside them. Women gathered around a stone cistern, hauling up a bucket and pouring water from it into their own. Men wandered by, pushing small hand carts laden with piles of sticks, probably for fuel, Carl decided. A young man walked by with milk in two tightly woven baskets, swinging them by handles, losing drops of it as he passed. Children watched a puppet show beside an old woman selling chickens, plucked carcasses swinging above a pile of feathers that grew as her hands swiftly denuded still another skinny bird.

The market smelled strange. Carl noticed one man sitting on a dirty mat, roasting something in a cylinder over an open fire. He turned a handle that kept whatever was inside the metal container moving.

"Kaffee," Antonio threw out, noticing Carl's interest.

More smells wafted on the breeze, from someone roasting what looked like chestnuts and another booth full of hot pumpkins. A fishy odor surrounded a table on which long pieces of eel lay grilling. A few feet away, altogether different, delicious aromas arose from several booths. Antonio told him that the bits of dough he saw frying were called "frittelle." His mouth watered at the sight. The weather was quite cold, despite a bright sun, and he decided the Venetians must be used to battling twin enemies of cold and damp.

Looking around, Carl noticed some piles of vegetables across the square. He pointed to them and asked Antonio, "Gemüse?"

Antonio hesitated only briefly, "Si, Signor. Verdure." He led him to the farmer's stalls.

Carl recognized cabbages stacked into large pyramids, cucumbers, wreaths of garlic and garlands of onions. He was not familiar with the large varieties of squash available. He asked Antonio to find the price.

"That is too much for these old, wilted things!" Carl waved a mottled zucchini in his translator's face. Antonio, fourteen and obnoxiously sure of himself, sighed. He said something in Italian to the vegetable seller. Both dark-haired, dark-eyed men laughed as they glanced up at the blonde giant towering over them. The seller waved his hand dismissively and Carl was told to pay half of the original price. Let them laugh, he thought, gathering several other overripe vegetables. I won.

After a brief stop at the apothecary's shop, and just in time for the large meal enjoyed by every Italian at midday, Carl headed to the set of rooms they had rented. Not in the center of fashionable Venice, but not a slum either, Antonio had said, defending his family's trade. At any rate, they met the pair's needs well enough. Opening the door to his room, Carl placed his parcels on a table.

"Mein Herr?" he asked, approaching Johann's door.

"Kommst du herein."

The familiar German words were welcome after all the sing-song babble of the morning. Carl entered the room.

On a plain bed, propped up with several worn pillows, Johann nodded to him to enter. His face was a pale grayish color, his eyes tired and sad. A familiar anxiety gripped Carl. What was he to do? What if Johann refused to return to health? Carl planned to make the same healing broths, with familiar herbs he found to purchase and perhaps with new varieties that the local apothecary swore by. He had tried his best to find what he needed while shopping. But he feared there were no open lands here to walk and search for fresh plants. The long journey from Vienna was a mistake. The damp chill of this city entered their bones. Now what would happen if his master died, leaving him on his own among these incomprehensible foreigners?

"Did you have success?"

"Ja," Carl answered. "Many things to cook, to make you strong again. Do you want to dine with the others?" Carl motioned toward the door, beyond which lay a dining room where the landlady provided several strange foods that looked bewildering.

"I don't think I can today," Johann answered. "Could you make me some soup, perhaps? Later?"

Carl nodded. He had permission to use the kitchen, after explaining that he was caring for an invalid gentleman. At least that is what he hoped Antonio had translated.

Johann, fluent in Italian, said the boy was faithful to rep-resent the truth whenever he heard him. But Carl had wit-nessed the young man slip a stolen biscuit or two into his jacket when leading him on the shopping venture. It was enough to plant a seed of mistrust. Antonio also looked around the room whenever he came in it, as if sizing up arti-cles worth stealing. Carl usually kept him out and disliked having to rely on him so much.

As the days passed, he wished he could get Johann to leave the apartment, to get some air, some sunshine. The little man steadfastly refused, preferring to sit and stare at the walls in stony silence most of the day. The dampness of the city in winter was uncomfortable for Carl also. It could not be healthy. Who ever heard of building a city on water? Perhaps it was just as well that Johann could not be persuaded to leave the rooms.

"Do you suppose you might find some paper on one of your trips?" Johann asked one morning.

"I can ask. There is everything in a city this size."

"Good. I don't require it right away. Your next trip."

Carl left to see if there was a corner of the kitchen in which he could make soup and perhaps find himself some food. He was starting to like the noodles swimming in tomato sauce that were served everywhere. And the strong cheeses here in Italy were delicious.

Johann lay back in bed, lines of melody weaving around each other in his mind, refusing to stop, begging for exit. Copying out had always seemed to him a laborious chore. His music lived in his head, fully formed. But something to do with his hands had a strong appeal now that his physical strength grew daily.

He had never felt so depressed, so utterly lonely and abandoned in his life. At the same time, a black hand of hate locked around his heart. He supposed she was with her lover. Bitterness so strong he could taste it rose in his throat. His hands gripped the blanket under him, as if squeezing the life from it, from someone. With a groan of frustrated rage, he threw the cloth from him. And still the music welled up in his soul. How could he long for a keyboard at such a time? How could he even imagine returning to the profession that would uncover his secret and propel him back to that life—that person he used to be—whom he now despised with his whole being? Despite all the hatred for the two who had destroyed him, part of it was directed toward himself, along with a distinct sense of guilt. Who could understand? Nothing but rage and bitterness for all, including himself. Sinking back into the notes in his head, he made a feeble attempt to calm himself and eventually succeeded in escaping into sleep.

Antonio came in the next morning. He enjoyed talking to the small man in the bed. The big lug of a German was so hard to understand. But the other gentleman, the master, spoke excellent Italian. Today they discussed where he might find some paper, though Antonio could not imagine why he needed such a quantity as he requested. But, looking forward to his tip, he headed out with Carl to seek blank paper, ink, and quills.

They were gone longer than ever before, until Johann imagined they had simply left with the rather large amount of money he had given them. But, no, Carl was loyal. He mistrusted Italians and had often called the musicians of the country treacherous. But Carl was a good German and would return. And, within an hour he did, shaking off rain and dropping a package wrapped in brown paper onto the foot of the bed.

Sitting up, Johann unwrapped a pile of blank paper. Carl handed him a smaller bundle, holding ink and quills.

"I will need a flat board, about like this," Johann said as he held his hands about shoulder width apart. "And a small one, with a very straight edge." Carl stared blankly at him.

"I must draw lines!" Johann's voice betrayed a burgeoning frustration. He had an almost physical need to get notes on the page. "To draw music staves. Do you read music at all?"

Carl's eyes widened. He was too shocked to even shake his head in the negative. Music? He could not even read words. What a thought.

More patient now, Johann described what he needed to do to prepare the pages. He could work with any straight, light stick. So, Carl left on another exploratory mission.

Finding the needed items was much quicker than retrieving paper. A carpenter lived above his shop around the corner and sold scraps cheaply. Johann eagerly set himself to work, propping himself up in bed and shoring up his workspace with pillows. It wouldn't do to let the pewter inkpot slide off onto the bedding.

The simple act of drawing music staves, mindlessly pulling line after line across the page, soothed Johann. As he worked, he heard and even saw the notes that would eventually be placed there. For now, setting the stage by preparing the paper was enough.

What a dilemma, though. The one thing he could do, had to do, could spell disaster for him if anyone with any musical sense or training recognized his style, his voice. These months of illness and hiding had left him with a brain filled with notes ready to burst out faster than he could write. And then what? Just destroy the sonatas, the arias, even symphonies that he birthed? He couldn't think about the future. Best just to draw the lines for now.

Johann spent hours engaged in drawing lines, then writing. Carl ventured near and saw what he supposed to be music appearing on the papers. He also observed that his master was calm and as peaceful as he had ever known him. If all this required was paper and ink, he vowed to find as much as was needed from now on. He slipped out to take some air and look for the healing plants he sometimes found in booths and stalls in the market. He had discovered that he could manage transactions with a few words and hand signals well enough, which was helping him conquer his fear of the place.

Antonio wondered if his services would be required the next morning. It was probably time for the giant German to want to go out again. The late afternoon sun was slipping away as he knocked lightly on the door to their quarters. No answer. After a second knock, he pushed the door quietly open. Carl was not in sight. The smaller man, Herr Pertl, sat halfway up in bed, his head bowed as he slept over a board filled with papers, quills, and an inkpot leaning dangerously close to its edge. The boy crept silently to the bed and stared at the pages of manuscript spread before him. Music! Herr Pertl must be a musician. Antonio's eyes narrowed, thinking of the music-crazy Venetians all around them. He could sell music.

Pushing the inkpot more to the center of the board, he turned to go, vowing to snatch a few pages at another time to see what he could get for them. He left as quietly as he had entered but stopped as he was closing the door when Carl appeared before him.

"What have you been up to, you little thief?" Carl whispered angrily, intimidating the boy by leaning over to look down at him.

"Nothing, nothing," Antonio shook his head. "His ink almost spilled."

"Carl?" Johann asked from his bed.

"Ja," Carl responded, still glaring at Antonio, who slipped quickly away underneath his elbow.

"It's good you are back. I think I am actually hungry, though I can hardly believe it."

That was a good sign. This music obsession must be of some value after all.

CHAPTER 14
Venice
March 1792

C arl decided that everything was a sign of hope these days. The weather was warming slowly, and days were lengthening. More people crowded the narrow streets and squares, obviously enjoying the changing seasons. He himself was sick to death of the cold, made worse by constant dampness. Johann was able to sit for part of each day at a desk they had moved into the room. What's more, he wanted to. Carl discovered he could buy paper with those lines already drawn on it. Now they spent more on it than their food.

Antonio had talked to a boatman who knew of some lands only a short distance away. Carl learned that the fruits and vegetables he bought were all transported to the city from the mainland. He steeled himself to a brief water journey and the expense of having both the boatman and Antonio wait as he searched the land just waking up in early spring. It yielded a great variety of tender young greens that Carl served in salads or made into soups, having remembered his mother's teachings about their benefits in cleansing the blood and intestines. Whatever the cause, Johann's color was better, and his strength increased daily.

He still napped for several hours every afternoon. Carl took long walks during those times, escaping the damp, fetid odors of the city and soaking in the sun as he roamed through markets filled with more varieties of plants every day. He was thrilled to find bay laurel, fennel, and basil. An old woman in the market had recommended juniper when he described his master's symptoms to her through Antonio's translation, so he gathered juniper berries from an apothecary. Besides their healing powers, many of the herbs added rich flavors to the dishes he prepared. It brought him deep satisfaction when he could return an empty bowl to the kitchen after a much-praised meal.

One afternoon he returned to find Johann standing at his desk, quickly turning over pages, searching for something. Clothes and papers lay haphazardly on the bed and furniture, as if the search had been going on for a while.

"Mein Herr, is something amiss?" Carl put his knapsack full of plants on the floor and removed his cap.

"I cannot find it. I know I wrote down a violin sonata. The thing had been plaguing me like a mosquito for days. I released it onto the page and now it's gone." Johann turned quickly to accuse him, "You didn't throw anything away, did you? Remember I instructed you never to touch any of the music."

"No, no," Carl was mildly offended at this. "Never. I only gather clothing from time to time."

"I'm sorry, Carl," Johann realized the injustice of his words to this man who had most likely saved his life many times over. "It's just upsetting to lose something like this." He returned to sifting through the pages at hand.

A knock at the door startled them both. Carl opened it slightly only to have Antonio push it quickly out of the way in his rush to enter. He looked at both men, grinning as he caught his breath.

"Herr Bauer, Herr Pertl," he greeted each man with a quick nod. "I have good news. Great news!"

Johann sat on the bed, clenching the cover tensely. What had this boy done?

"I have found a buyer."

Carl and Johann looked worriedly at each other.

"A buyer of music!"

Johann's face turned as white as his shirt.

"I took just a few pages to a friend of that paper seller. He looked at it and played a bit and bought it!"

Johann stood as Carl moved in front of the door, blocking Antonio's exit.

"You stole from me?" Johann's glare punctured the balloon of Antonio's euphoria.

"No! Not really. I just borrowed..."

"But you sold it? You sold my music?"

Antonio usually wriggled out of tight spots and quickly thought of a way to do that now. "For quite a bit! You see..." He held out a small gold coin, smiling encouragingly.

"Get out." Johann couldn't look at the boy.

"But mein Herr, he wants more! He said he would come see you himself. Maybe this evening."

Johann looked at Carl, who picked the boy up and set him facing the door.

"Think how much..." Antonio started to plead, before he was propelled into the hallway and the door closed firmly behind him. Carl restrained himself from placing a large boot onto the boy's backside.

"We have to leave." Johann sat heavily on the bed. "I cannot be discovered. I am dead and wish to remain so."

Carl did not understand but nodded. He opened one of their trunks to begin packing. Obedience no matter what was deeply ingrained in him. The music would go in the bottom, and they should be able to make everything else fit in as before. He wondered where they would go and dearly hoped wherever it was, the people would speak German.

A short while later that hope left as Johann spoke one word, "London."

CHAPTER 15
Venice to London
April 1792

A ntonio was astonished that the two men had left so quickly. His eager music-buyer right at his heels, the boy pounded on the door three times before daring to open it. Nothing. No clothes, no piles of paper, no little mounds of leaves spread by the fire to dry. The innkeeper's wife knew nothing of where they had gone, having summoned a gondola whose driver she trusted for them. She was happy that they had paid well before leaving and the handsome tip assured her silence on even the time that they had departed.

Johann insisted that they head to Rome. That would put them in the vicinity of a large port where ships to England were bound to dock. It was early spring, and the roads were good. Since the coach was empty of other travelers during the first part of the journey, Johann let the hat and collar shielding his face drop and spoke eagerly about their destination. He told Carl that he had always loved England, since his visit to the island nation when he was a child. He began learning English then and continued lessons in the language as a young man in Vienna. He spoke about English writers whom he admired and the parks and gardens he was sure that Carl would appreciate. Carl remained unconvinced that London would be less of a trial than Italy had been.

The trip to Rome took only a little over a week. Carl felt as if they were traveling into summer the farther south they went. The weather warmed and the landscape looked greener every day. Johann, hidden again behind a high collar and hat pulled down, survived this journey in much better health than their ordeal from Vienna to Venice. They stopped in Rome for a brief overnight stay.

Childhood memories from his three Italian trips flooded Johann's mind. He had a great desire to see the Sistine Chapel once more, the site of his triumph as a boy of just 14. There he had heard Gregorio Allegri's famous *Miserere*, a complex nine-part choral work that had not been published. He astounded the adults around him by writing down every part perfectly from memory afterward. But here he was now, the past done, and the day was warm with several hours of daylight remaining. He instructed Carl to hire an open-air coach to give them a tour of the city.

Johann grew comfortable enough to stop hiding his face as they rode slowly past the wonders of Roman architecture. Carl sat in stunned silence. He had heard of the Pope and the great churches of his empire, but never had he imagined this. They saw cardinals walking by St. Peter's, red robes swaying. The city was filled with statues, fountains spouting gushing streams of water, and churches on every corner. Finally, hungry as the sun set, they returned to their inn for a Roman specialty, bucatini all'amatriciana. It was a thick spaghetti with a hole running through the center and a delicious sauce of tomatoes, pork, and cheese. Even Johann finished a small plate, while Carl polished off three platters of the stuff.

They stayed at an inn not far from the ruins of what was called the Forum and gathered information about traveling to London. Carl found more shopkeepers who spoke German and had picked up a few words of Italian himself by now. Johann spent several days in bed after their tour of the city, then proceeded to have Carl bring people in who could advise them on travel to England.

He discovered that the "Port of Rome," Civitavecchia, was actually 50 miles away. One could travel there and book passage on any number of ships which would eventually make their way out of the Mediterranean and north. The trip could take three weeks, depending upon stops, winds, and weather. Johann had never had any difficulty traveling by ship, though the trips he had taken were relatively short compared to this. Carl had never traveled on water, other than an occasional short ferry ride, and looked forward to it with some trepidation. Soon, they were on their way to the port city.

A few days of making inquiries and purchasing supplies, and the pair found themselves on the good ship Molly, bound for London in the beautiful month of May. She was not the largest ship at the port, but her three masts looked sturdy. Her hull had weathered quite a few storms, as had her captain. Her main attraction was that she carried primarily cargo but had a large cabin in steerage that could hold two passengers very comfortably. Johann's privacy was assured.

The sea air agreed with Johann, who spent much time on the deck, totally unconcerned that the few sailors going about their duties would recognize him. The captain was an American, which made Johann even more confident his anonymity was secure. The sun and sea air had him feeling better than he had in months.

Carl, however, had never been on anything other than a flat-bottomed river boat for brief trips to and from farmers' markets. Though they were blessed with a calm sea, he spent his days in bed, trying to throw up as little as possible. His mother had never seen the sea, much less given him any instructions about plants that might help with this particular malady. He closed his eyes and quietly waited for death.

The ship's crew grew used to the little man who stood most afternoons leaning against the rails, basking in the sun and salt air. The captain stopped to chat and found his passenger widely traveled and agreeable. After a day or two, Captain Handford invited the gentleman to join him on the quarterdeck.

"So, you are from Germany, Mr. Pertl?" The captain asked, as starved for conversation and fellowship as Johann was himself.

"No, Austria, but we all think of ourselves as German, sir." Johann welcomed the chance to practice his English. "And you, sir? What do you call your native land?"

"America," the captain said proudly. "Born in the state of Virginia, before the Revolution. I married an English girl and followed her back home." He lowered his eyes, "But she took sick and died a few years ago. I suppose I ought to head home, but I'm afraid I buried my heart with her here." He looked up. "And you? Are you married, sir?"

Johann quickly answered, "My wife is dead as well." His tone did not invite further inquiry.

"And your man? Is he quite well? My men told me he was a bit green around the gills."

"I think he is better, but I'm afraid this is his first time at sea. Poor fellow." Johann watched as some large fish jumped about the side of the boat. Sea travel fascinated him.

"Well, sir, if you would do me the honor, I would much appreciate your company at dinner tonight."

Johann inclined his head in a small bow. "Thank you most kindly. It would be a great pleasure."

Entering the captain's quarters that evening, he was struck by how much more spacious it was than the confined space he shared with moaning, retching Carl. Johann admired the heavy table, elegantly set for two. A pair of upholstered chairs sat by the wall as if inviting pleasant conversation. In the corner opposite sat a small clavichord with a black keyboard and yellowed ivory halftone keys. He wondered if the captain played.

The captain reigned as king over his tiny domain. His ship's cook served a masterful meal, including several fish dishes, English peas, and a pudding with some fine wines. As they were finishing, Johann ventured to ask about the instrument in the corner.

"No, I don't play, I'm afraid. That was my wife's." Johann heard the sadness in his tone. "She loved it so, I can't bring myself to part with it. What about you, sir? Do you play?"

Johann smiled, "A little."

"Well, why don't you play something, if you please? It's been a very long time since I have had the pleasure of music. Cecile and I used to go to all the concerts. I've dearly missed it."

What could it hurt? They were miles at sea, with no one from the great musical centers of Europe nearby. And he dearly wished to play again.

"It would be an honor."

Johann played a few soft chords and was pleasantly surprised to find the instrument in tune. Within seconds, he was lost in a sonata. As the music drifted into the night air, the crew gathered quietly as close to the cabin as possible. The captain had heard enough music in his lifetime to recognize an artist when he heard one.

"You are no amateur, sir," he said in wonder when the piece ended.

"I have taught music for years," Johann told a small part of the truth.

Content to be making music again, he continued to play pieces that had been born in his mind over the past six months, new to both his own and the captain's hearing. He improvised, losing all sense of himself in the cascade of notes coming from the small instrument. Finally reaching a logical ending place, he remembered his audience.

"I apologize, sir," he said as he stood. "I have taken far too much of your time."

"Not at all, sir. That was most welcome, most welcome indeed. I am sorry that I have no fortepiano. What you play is too large by far for this little instrument."

Johann smiled, "No, this is fine. I, too, have been unable to play for a long time, what with illness and travel. I... I have missed it." If only the captain could have understood the depth of that statement.

The rest of the trip's evenings passed so enjoyably in conversation and music for the two men that they truly regretted the journey's approaching end. They were blessed with calm weather throughout the journey, which left the captain free to entertain his passenger. He spun endless tales of his home country, captivating Johann with its freshness and promise of freedom. He told tales of savages and dense forests and newly birthed cities promising opportunity for all. Democracy and equality had found a home at last.

Johann had always admired the American ideals. His father had believed, along with most of Austrian society, that God placed kings and noblemen in their positions and bestowed upon them all the wisdom and knowledge that they needed to rule. It behooved the rest of humanity to obey and defer to them, much as children owed the same to their parents. That had not stopped Leopold from bowing and scraping to garner favor and scheming to advance himself and his family. Johann remembered many humiliating instances when he had been forced to agree and obey the wishes of some idiotic minor nobleman, always hoping for an appointment which would guarantee a steady stream of income. At heart, he rebelled against political inequality. He dearly loved to see aristocrats put down and looking foolish. Writing *The Marriage of Figaro*, with its servant far wiser than his lord, had made him suspect in some circles. If America had no ruling class, that might make it the ideal place for him to be. And where else could he be certain of anonymity?

"Tell me more about Virginia," Johann encouraged one night over an especially good claret.

"Ha, well, it is a beautiful place, miles and miles of green hills under bright blue skies, most of the time. The land was full of natives a hundred years ago, but those who stayed now live peacefully enough. Many moved away, farther west and north. There are all types of people there now. Wealthy landowners, workers such as you and me, and those who do the more common sorts of labor, both slave and free."

"Slaves?" Johann asked, surprised. He had always heard about freedom in America. This idea of slaves troubled him.

"Yes," the captain looked down. "I don't hold with such, but the large planters in the south insist they cannot work so much land without them. They are black-skinned, from Africa."

"Did they choose to come to such a place?"

The captain looked even more uncomfortable, "No, no, I am afraid not. There are those who steal them from their homes, ship them across the Atlantic, and sell them to masters there."

Johann was horrified. "And is the whole place full of these slaves?"

"No, not at all. In the North, there are many who don't like it. But the Southern planters insist. It's only the very wealthy who have such. Especially those who grow tobacco. At the same time, there are many who fight it, who wish for no slaves in Virginia at all." He wished they could move to another topic.

"I am surprised. I have only heard of freedom in relation to your country."

"And it is there, for most of us. Freedom of religion, freedom of thought, freedom to choose our own governors. It is a land most blessed by the Almighty, without doubt."

Johann, for his part, wrung more music from the tiny clavichord than any human would have thought possible. Whole symphonies condensed to miniature, but nonetheless magnificent for it, captivated the ship's company. If the crew noticed a certain sadness, a certain preponderance of minor keys, none mentioned it. They were awestruck at the beauty pouring itself into the evening skies.

By the time the Molly slipped into London harbor, the blackness threatening to engulf Johann had been pushed away again. Playing for Captain Handford evening after evening built up the strength of the undamaged part of his soul. Carl saw and understood that this man, his master and companion, needed music as much as he needed the vegetables and broths, sun and fresh air, that had healed his body. Nothing was as complicated as the human soul, he decided, and perhaps healing the body was only part of what Johann required.

CHAPTER 16

London
May 1792

Johann reluctantly bade his friend Captain Handford farewell, then picked his way along a plank bridge to the dock. He sincerely believed the man to be one of the best he had known and would miss both his company and the keyboard sorely. The captain vowed he had never heard such marvelous music as his passenger provided and knew he never would again. The two men bade each other a reluctant God's speed.

Looking up and down the Thames, Johann took in other ships tied up as far as he could see. Men carrying or pushing loads scurried everywhere, on the dock and on the many ships tied to it. Pungent, exotic smells and the cries of animals lay over the crowd. London was certainly as busy as he remembered it.

Carl, ecstatic to be on land once again, waited for him by their luggage. Fortunately, Johann thought, he felt well as they embarked on this new chapter in their journey, as he would have to handle the conversations necessary to secure lodgings. As if to underscore his thoughts, he watched Carl stand obliviously in the way of a dockhand asking him to move, not understanding a word the fellow shouted at him.

Johann intervened in the one-sided exchange and asked the worker if he knew where they could procure a carriage. For a tip, he sought one out for them. As the driver and Carl stowed trunks on the top of the vehicle, Johann asked the man if he knew where they might secure lodgings for a short while. He was a bow-legged fellow, not very clean, but that was probably because he spent all day driving about the dirty, crowded city.

"I know of an inn or two what might have rooms for a night. But longer?" He reached up under his faded tricorn hat to scratch vigorously at his scalp through the greasy gray hair covering it while wrinkling his nose and forehead in puzzlement.

Johann suddenly remembered a name. "Might you know where Edbury Street is? In Chelsea? My family stayed there several years ago. I wonder if that might be a possibility?"

"Aye, I know whereabouts it is. Hop in."

The coach took off just as Carl managed to close the door behind himself. Johann's mind wandered back to his childhood. He believed he was about eight years old when he was fortunate enough to have a series of lessons with the English Bach, Johann Christian, in composition. He remembered the youngest son of the famous Johann Sebastian helping him to arrange some of his sonatas as keyboard concertos. Bach was always encouraging and kind, a different experience for the young boy, who had known only the strict discipline of his father. Johann recalled those lessons as the best and most formative of his musical life. And he had lived on Edbury Street while they happened.

Another cold, damp pit of a place, Carl thought to himself, as they rode several miles through the densest traffic

he had ever seen. There were so many horse-drawn conveyances that they practically scraped each other in the narrow
streets. People were everywhere, selling everything imaginable. Carl wondered at the girls with trays of nosegays,
the men with apples and some type of small pastries, all
shouting at the top of their lungs. Fine carriages went by the
quickest, and pedestrians scattered out of the way. Everyone
seemed to be screaming at each other. Carl longed to hear
German and even more to understand the voices he heard
around him once again.

Their carriage driver found Edbury Street. Johann
had him wait as he went to inquire at a house he remembered. Carl accompanied him and heard his friend mutter
something about writing his first symphony there as they
knocked on the door. It did not, however, have anything for
them now. Discouraged, they turned to leave. The young
woman with a babe in arms and a toddler pulling at her
skirt called after them. She thought a smaller, red brick
dwelling down the way had just lost a tenant. Johann muttered a quick "thank you" as an ungodly shrieking began
from behind her skirts.

"This place will do," Johann proclaimed, returning to
the coach after a short time inside the red brick. The driver
clambered down to retrieve their now travel-scarred trunks.
A pleasant-looking young woman stood surrounded by several children, watching them from the door. Carl picked
up one trunk as Johann paid the coachman and wondered
if all the English reproduced like rabbits. Children were
everywhere.

"Kommen Sie herein," the young mother instructed him,
and Carl almost dropped the trunk in his joy. He could
understand her! She led him to a sitting room on the east

side of the house which had two bedrooms adjoining it. Lots of windows let the pale light in and a small garden lay outside. The light-yellow walls and clean white bed coverings gave the rooms a happier atmosphere than any place they had stayed before. Carl chose the room with a door leading to the yard, though it was probably presumptuous of him. In their travels, he had learned that Johann was easy about such things and rarely gave much notice to his surroundings.

"Well, what do you think?" Johann dropped his black tricorn hat onto a corner table in the sitting room after Carl had moved both trunks to their rooms.

"The garden is nice. And the landlady—she speaks Deutsch, ja?" Carl couldn't contain a wide grin.

"I tell you; you will pick up English. It's much more like your beloved German than Italian is. Though Italian sings much better, Lord knows. And you can use the kitchen. Though the lady has a few children you will have to wade through."

Johann wandered into the room in which Carl had placed his trunk. He was suddenly weak and sat down on the thick white cover on the bed. "I believe I will sleep now for a bit. Travel is exhausting."

Carl hoped Johann had not pushed himself back into a sick place. He decided to check out this kitchen and garden of theirs. Down the hall to the left lay the cooking area, his nose told him. The lady of the house balanced a baby on her hip while stirring a large pot with her other hand. A young girl sat peeling potatoes quite skillfully for her age, he thought. The young mother noticed him in the doorway and greeted him, again in German.

"Are you from Germany?" he asked, wondering at her skill with the language.

"My mother was," she turned back to check the pot once more.

"Oh," he was always short on words when speaking with women. "My mother is in Austria. I haven't seen her for more than half a year." He couldn't keep the sadness from his voice.

"My name is Berta," she offered with a smile, "and this is John and Mary." Mary had given up peeling vegetables and stared at the big man with her thumb in her mouth. Berta put down her spoon. "Is there anything that you gentlemen require?"

"No, no," Carl shook his head. "My master is resting. He has not been well for a long time. Might it be possible for me to cook some things for him from time to time? Soups and teas?"

"I'm sorry to hear that. He seems nice. And, yes, of course. Make yourself at home here."

Carl nodded. "We have had too much travel. Is there by chance an apothecary nearby?"

"You are in luck! My husband is such. His store is just down the street, toward the church at the bottom of the hill."

"That is good, very good." He never knew how to end a conversation gracefully. "I think I will go, now, while Herr Pertl is asleep."

Berta smiled and turned to pay attention to Mary as Carl left to find the shop. This street was quieter, not so intimidating as downtown London. He strolled in the direction he had been told, relishing the feel of solid land beneath his legs. The English in this neighborhood kept the street clean, their houses cheerful with small hedges

119

and flowers. He could feel the tension leave his shoulders in these pleasant surroundings. He recognized an apothecary shop by the bottles lining the street-front window and bunches of dried herbs hanging from the ceiling and walls.

"Sir?" a pleasant-looking young man looked up from chopping something behind a counter.

"Sprechen Sie Deutsch?" he asked. The man shook his head, replying "Nein."

So, he would have to use sign language. Carl recognized a number of medicinal herbs hanging in bunches from the ceiling. Not knowing the English name for them, he pointed to bilberries. He knew Herr Pertl needed it to restore his health. They managed to negotiate a price for that and some gorse he spotted in a jar behind the counter. His mother always told him that it would help those who had given up hope. Though he was not sure of everything that bothered his master, hope restored would surely be a good thing.

Carl returned to the house, unpacked a few items, and brewed some bilberry tea. Johann slept for several hours but was persuaded to drink some of it in the late afternoon.

"My one real friend here is dead now, you know." Johann stroked the handle of the teacup absentmindedly as he sat at a table watching a few birds outside. "He was a great musician, the son of the best of all, J.S. Bach."

Carl had no idea how to respond, so he replied, "Oh?"

"J.C. Bach taught me how to write symphonies. No, that's not really correct. He wrote them and I heard them. I was only eight." Johann sipped some more of the tea and the corners of his mouth pulled down. It was sour, but at least he was drinking it, Carl thought.

"I used to sit right beside him at the organ and listen as he played. For hours sometimes. Then I would go off and write the same things. Did you know I wrote my first symphony when I was eight?"

Carl nodded in the negative, not being entirely sure what a symphony was.

"Well, it wasn't very good, except Mr. Bach taught me the form to use. I'll be forever grateful for that. God knows, I miss him. He died a decade ago." Johann fell silent, watching the birds once more. He missed much about his former life in music. Though he could sometimes still write things as they came to him, there was no purpose in music never heard. No purpose. That was his life now.

The two slowly established the same kind of routine outside of London that had been their pattern in Venice. Carl kept up the supply of healthful herbs and plants, much easier to find here than in the Italian city. He bought paper, so Johann wrote music endlessly, but there was no keyboard instrument of any kind nearby. When not writing, the composer sat staring out the window into the garden for what seemed like hours. His mind refused to stop circling the old places of pain.

It was hard for Carl to tell if his master's health was improving. Melancholy was as detrimental to the body as the spirit and mimicked illness perfectly at times. He could not tell where sickness of the soul stopped, and sickness of the body began. Johann paced restlessly, spent long blocks of time writing out notes on lined paper, and often woke in the middle of the night unable to return to sleep. Something kept him agitated.

One day, Johann threw his quill into the inkpot, almost turning it over. "I cannot abide staying here longer!"

Carl, mending a pair of socks, looked warily at the little man now up and pacing around the room. Moods like this never produced anything good.

"I cannot feel in any way safe from discovery here. Who knows how many people saw me as a youngster and might recognize me now? We were here for over a year. These London audiences are well-educated. They know my music."

Carl thought he was too fearful and possibly prideful, as well. His companion had a sickness of spirit that drove him to unreasonable worry. To his mind, no one was looking for them. No one would see him, hiding away in this room as he did. No one was thinking about Herr Pertl as much as Herr Pertl seemed to be. Not many would connect a youngster with a man thirty years later, but he did not dare contradict Johann.

"No, what Captain Handford said was true. America is the only place. I could be free there. I could write, maybe play again. Our money will not last forever."

Oh, no, Carl thought. *I can't. How many weeks would that take? I would be sick the whole way.* He didn't exactly know where America was, but he did know there was a great deal of ocean between them and the place.

"We must look into it, see how much passage would cost. It's the only way."

And, since finding his way back to Dürnstein alone was impossible, Carl fell reluctantly in line with the plan. He obliged Johann by asking Berta where to begin to find this kind of information. She gave him directions to the Port of London, just downstream from London Bridge. She saw his dismay at the thought of trying to navigate such an errand with poor English.

"My husband has a helper, a young man who works in the mornings for him. Perhaps he could be persuaded to be your guide?"

Carl's face brightened. He asked her in German, "Could you tell him what we seek? Then he could ask for me. Ja, that would be way to do this."

Early the next afternoon a spindly young man of 15 or 16 knocked on their door. Berta introduced him to Carl, but Johann was spending the day in bed. After much exchange in English and German, Carl was satisfied that George, his helper, understood that he was to ask about passage to America—its cost, time, and what they might be expected to bring. The two set out for the heart of London.

It was a fair walk, but each man had long legs and they made quick work of it. Stopping at the bank of the Thames, Carl stared in wonder. So many ships! It was a marvel that they did not all collide and sink before his eyes. The water churned with its heavy traffic.

George led the way and began asking random ships' workers about any planning a trip to America. After an hour of fruitless seeking, they stopped beside a large vessel called the Isaac. George spoke longer this time to the sailor supervising the unloading of cargo. Carl saw barrels of salted fish, bags of rice, and bales of a strange plant unfamiliar to him.

George motioned him over to the man. "This ship sails to America and back regularly. They will head out again in a few weeks. They can take passengers."

The sailor nodded at the words. Carl understood none of them. Frustrated, George continued, "He doesn't know. Look, I'll have to take him back home and have my employer's wife to translate. How much did you say this all costs?"

"It's 5 pounds apiece for a stateroom between decks. That includes all the food you need for the seven weeks." The sailor turned to give an order to men carrying bales of some large leaves.

George shook his head in disbelief. Half a year's wage for someone like him.

"We'll be back." He motioned for Carl to follow him. The large farmer was fascinated with this new plant being carried by. He pointed to it and looked at the sailor, raising his eyebrows.

"That's tobacco," the man spat as he told him. "Biggest money-maker we carry most trips."

Carl repeated, "Tobacco."

George grabbed his arm, "Come on, you, let's get back to somewhere where they can talk to you." They had a long walk back to Chelsea. George was glad that the only burden they carried was information.

They returned home just at sunset. Carl had expected to go through a chain of translators to get the information to Johann, but he was up and eager to hear what they had learned. He heard the details straight from George, then paid the boy handsomely. The prospect of another journey invigorated the small man. Or perhaps it was the destination. So far, all their travels had been to places that Johann had already visited, even if only as a child. Here lay an undiscovered land, a new adventure before them. America.

CHAPTER 17

Atlantic Ocean to Philadelphia
July–August 1792

C arl would remember the ship's journey from London to Philadelphia as the longest, darkest time of his life. He and Herr Pertl could afford one of the five staterooms between decks on the *Isaac,* so their passage was infinitely easier than that of the poor souls in steerage below. They had mattresses and linens and a washbasin. Their door, with an ample number of slits for ventilation, opened into a cabin, where they took their meals with the other wealthier passengers and the captain. Still, the food was abysmal. Salt beef and dried prunes four days a week; salt pork and dried peas on two days; and salt fish on the seventh. All of that washed down with stale water and a little beer.

Thanks to the medicines prescribed by the Chelsea apothecary, Carl spent the 63 days not nauseated, but in a fog of malaise. He could easily nap three or four hours a day, in addition to getting a full night's sleep every night. Waking hours were spent with a sailor about his age who hailed from Boston. In return for Carl's help in moving heavy ropes and swabbing the deck, he gave the Austrian farmer lessons in American English. If not ready for polite company, Carl began to feel that he might be able to navigate day-to-day life in the New World more easily.

Johann, once he realized that the company on this voyage was nowhere as congenial as Captain Handford had been, spent most of his time in the cabin. He would take the air by venturing out onto deck in the early morning and late evening. No one was awake at dawn and his fellow travelers preferred drinking and cards late at night. Not that he didn't enjoy cards, but his heart was no longer in amusements. Weeks went by in quiet monotony. He often stared at night into the deep horizon with its myriad stars and rehearsed a litany of grievances against Constanze, wherever she might be. The black, cold waters mirrored the state of his heart and his physical body started to give way to weak sickness again. Everything he ate nauseated him, so he ate very little, giving most of his share to Carl.

They arrived in Philadelphia in September, thin, lice-ridden, and with legs that wobbled trying to walk on solid ground. A driver waiting for possible hire at the wharf took them to Oellers Hotel, an expensive establishment, but safe. Carl was sick to death of travel. He had given up all hope of ever seeing Austria again, much less his home or parents. All the cities they had stopped in seemed the same to him—dirty, noisy, and crowded. But Johann acted as a man driven to some irrational goal. He had in mind to settle on the frontier, as far away as possible from the more civilized parts of this New World. He instructed Carl to investigate coaches going west or south. Carl agreed at once, eager to try out his new American words as his master retreated to a thin bed in their room. First Carl would seek some of that powder derived from chrysanthemums to rid them of their pests. Then, after becoming more presentable, he would inquire about public conveyances.

Almost two months at sea with poor water and no fresh food had done neither of them any good, and Johann did not recover quickly. Carl scoured the city streets for herbs and vegetables to purchase, but many of the plants in this new world were unfamiliar to him. The one apothecary he located did not have much in stock and wasn't at all interested in trying to understand Carl's broken English. He grew desperate as Johann stayed in his bed once more, months of hard-won health undone in one cursed journey.

Wandering the streets late one afternoon, Carl heard some voices speaking in his native tongue. He couldn't resist staring in the open door to see who spoke. It was a tavern, small and cheap looking, but he spotted three young men speaking German over their beer. Their suspenders, worn trousers, and rolled up sleeves betrayed them as working men. One of them noticed him.

"Come in, come in," he smiled and waved to the curious large man staring at them. "Are you a fellow countryman? Aus Deutschland?"

Carl smiled at the German words, took off his hat, and entered the place. "My name is Carl Bauer," he said, nodding at each of the three. "I am from Austria, but I am very glad to hear German, very glad."

The man who had invited him in put a hand on his shoulder, "Well met, Carl. I am Hugo and this is Peter and Hans. All of us have come here from Mannheim, just weeks ago. Sit! Have a beer!" He motioned to the tavern keeper who turned to draw another as Carl found an empty spot on a bench.

Hugo was older than the others, his dark hair and eyes framed a lined face that betrayed a life of work in the outdoors. Hans looked about twenty, blonde and blue-eyed, much shorter than Hugo. He smiled frequently. Peter was the friendliest and most talkative, with light brown hair and blue eyes. He looked to be about Carl's age. He stood to make room for Carl, who noticed that he was at least his own height and had the solid frame that manual labor gave a man.

"So, what brings you from Austria to Philadelphia?" Hugo asked their new acquaintance, after a long drink from his tin mug.

"I am with my master, a man who travels overmuch, I think. We have just arrived this week from London."

Peter nodded knowingly. "That journey nearly killed us."

Hans added, "Well, at least we know we are here to stay. Nothing would get me on one of those God-forsaken boats again."

His friends lifted their drinks in agreement.

Hugo looked at Carl more seriously. "So, will you stay here? In this city?"

Carl nodded negatively, "I hope not. My master is not well. I don't think this place would be good for him."

"Are you from a large city yourself?"

"No," Carl couldn't disguise the longing in his voice, "from Dürnstein. A small farm. Beautiful mountains and river."

That sparked something in Peter. "That's just what I was telling these fools about before you came in. Beautiful farmland. There is so much of it here, just for the asking. This country is large and new."

"But dangerous!" Hans broke in. "The natives who scalp you!"

Carl had never heard of such. "What is that... 'scalp'?"

Hans slammed his mug down too hard. "They take you like this." He grabbed his thick blonde hair with one hand and pulled his own head back. "Then they cut your skin and hair off your head. All of it!" His other hand mimicked a slicing motion above his forehead.

Peter broke in, "But they have been driven west. They do not do such things now, not in the settlements."

"Who?" Carl asked, horrified at the thought. "Who does such things?"

Peter answered, "The natives. Savages. Shawnee. Susquehannock."

Carl marveled at the strange names, while Hans shook his head at the thought of such barbarians. The others went on to discuss the little history they had picked up about the place.

Peter sang the praises of North Carolina. "Green hills, many rivers, and full of people who have come here from Germany. Why, there are whole towns so full of them that you would think you were home. And the farmland. Like nowhere else. The winters are mild, much milder than we are used to. So, the growing season is very, very long. Some crops can be planted twice."

Carl was fascinated by the tales that followed, full of names he had never heard, like "Pennsylvania" and "Georgia" and "North Carolina." He allowed himself to dream of rolling farmland with his new friends before he realized it was already dark outside. "Oh, I must leave." He put a coin on the table for his beer.

"Well, come back. You know we are here after work most days. At least until I get enough money for that trip to North Carolina," Peter winked at him.

Johann was asleep when Carl returned. Days and nights did not seem to matter now. The small man was not well physically or mentally. *What if we could travel there?* Carl sat heavily to wait in case Johann awoke and needed anything. *What if we could go to this North Carolina?*

The idea stayed with him the next day. He began to mention it to Johann in their routine conversations. "It is farther south, so it is warmer. There are not so many people as here. And many come from Germany." Carl learned more and more as he met his new friends daily now at the Yellow Thistle Inn.

Johann had given up caring. His bowels hurt and he had no energy to even move from the bed. Every now and then he tried sitting, but there was no reason to move around, to get stronger. Even a drastic change in location had not helped. His black cloud had followed him from Europe.

He passed many hours amusing himself by rehearsing his hatred for his wife and her lover. In some way, the thought that his disappearance, his "death," might have hurt her pleased him. At least, she was not spending his hard-earned money anymore. He tried to add up what he must have spent supporting her adulterous trips to Baden over the years. The smoldering fire of his rage might seem to disappear at times, but it was too richly fueled by his imagination to die out. These periods of melancholy left him physically weak and lethargic. Not even Carl's remedies helped this time.

One day, Carl brought him a newspaper, thinking to distract him. *The Pennsylvania Gazette.* Perhaps it would take his mind off the things keeping him in such dark moods. Carl worked on cleaning some boots while Johann became absorbed in the paper.

He had not seen one in months and read with interest the stories of this new country, the United States, and the struggles it was having in finding its way. President George Washington had vetoed a bill about state representatives, and a new state, Kentucky, joined the union. He would have to learn about this government with no noblemen and how it worked. On the inside was news from the world, months out of date, but many stories from Europe. He began reading them with interest. Most told of France and the insurrection going on there. He read with horror that their queen, Marie Antoinette, had been imprisoned. Though he certainly sympathized with the revolutionaries' cause, he had warm memories of the French queen. He had met the young Archduchess Marie Antoinette at the Habsburg summer residence outside Vienna. She was just a few months older than him and had treated him with great kindness. He hoped she would not come to any harm in the middle of her country's turmoil.

A sharp intake of breath alerted Carl that something was wrong. Johann's face was white and his eyes angrier than Carl had ever seen them.

"She married!" he spat in disbelief and threw the paper onto the bed.

Carl could not read, so could only guess at what was so upsetting. Johann picked the paper up again, angrily reading the story through clenched teeth.

A brief article entitled "Mozart's Widow Remarries" told of Constanze Mozart nee Weber taking the hand of Georg Nikolaus von Nissen, a wealthy Danish diplomat who amused himself by writing histories of music. Several sentences waxed poetic about the sacred memory of the great composer and how the newlyweds would work to preserve his memory and music. Johann threw up violently on the paper and took to his bed for the rest of the day.

Over the next weeks, Carl found himself spending more time with Peter and his friends and less with Johann, who lay listlessly in bed every day. He refused all interaction with Carl or any of their landlord's staff. He hardly ate. Carl feared the small man would succeed in willing himself dead.

Peter introduced Carl to his sister, Greta, a tall, large-boned blonde girl who instantly captured his attention. She had a way of looking at him from under thick lashes that caused his heart to speed up. He discovered that they had escaped a tyrant of a stepfather after their mother died a year ago. Taking money that their mother had put away for the family, the brother and sister made their way out of Germany and finally all the way to a new life on the other side of the Atlantic. The three walked to a park one warm afternoon and found a grassy hill comfortable enough to linger on.

"Imagine owning a farm of your very own. It's possible in North Carolina. Never having to bow and scrape to anyone again. Plenty of food for those strong enough to work for it!" Peter's enthusiasm was contagious.

"Peter, you always go on. How can we get there? You work in the shipyards, and I cook and clean, but we never have this kind of money," Greta said. It was ground they had covered before.

"But, Greta, you don't know! I have been saving, I have been working extra hours. I have almost the price of the trip in hand."

"How could you have kept it from me?" She stared open-mouthed at her brother.

"Well, we are not often together. We work so much. But trust me, within a few weeks we will be able to go. I'm talking now about finding work there, just at first. There are some German farmers near a town called Bethabara in Wachovia, in North Carolina. They need workers. Hans found out about them. Both of us would be welcomed!"

Carl panicked. He liked Peter but that was not his issue. He realized that he could not entertain the terrifying thought of not seeing Greta again. He had to be with her.

She glanced shyly at him as she asked her brother, "And what about Carl? Could he find work, too?"

"Most certainly! They are hungry for people to settle there."

"But I could not go. My master is ill. He depends upon me and no one else," Carl responded in a voice full of worry.

"Didn't you tell me once that he is a musician?"

Carl nodded.

"Well, there is another town, just a few miles from this Bethabara, called Salem. It is a center for the Unity of Brethren, you know, those Moravians Count Zinzendorf brought over. A good German town, and they are crazy for music. What if your master would move there?"

The thought that he himself would decide upon their next destination, even suggest it, was an impossibility in Carl's mind. He was sick to death of travel, but he was also sick to death of cities. A German town in a warmer climate, perhaps some land to farm. This was too much to stay quiet about. And there was Greta.

"I'll talk to him," he resolved, clapping his hands on both knees. He who never made a decision would make this big one. Greta broke into a smile that he carried with him all the way home.

While Carl was away, Johann had a visitor, one of the other boarders at the house where they now lived. He was an old violinist, Robert Harold, born and raised in Philadelphia, who hoped to hear news about the musical life of Europe from this reclusive stranger. Carl had mentioned at table that his master was a musician. The old man was always looking for opportunities to speak with others in his profession.

Robert knocked and entered, startling Johann out of another black reverie. His visitor was short, bent over, and shuffled slowly into the room.

"May I speak with you for a while, sir?"

He sat before Johann could deny him and continued, "My name is Robert Harold. Sir, I have heard that you are a musician?"

"Yes, I was, but no longer."

Such sadness, such hopelessness of tone. What was this man's story? The older man's compassion was stirred, and he had to know more.

Mr. Harold continued, "It is hard to give it up. My aches and pains do not allow me to lift a bow any longer. But you, you are young! You have your life ahead of you. Once you get on your feet... why, you could be back at it in no time!" Blue eyes under bushy gray brows looked kindly at Johann.

Johann was drawn in by the concern of the older man, though his circumstances were too complex to explain.

"Thank you. I understand what you say, but I don't think that will happen."

"There is no need for such a tone of despair. Why, you could make a fine living here. And not just in Philadelphia!

The other day I was hearing stories of places all over this new land of ours, places where music is in high demand. There is a group of religious folk—the "Brethren" they call themselves—who have settled north of here in Pennsylvania and also farther south, in North Carolina. Music is the center of their lives! Just think of that... way off in the wilderness and probably listening to Mozart!"

Johann flinched at the name, then recovered himself enough to respond, "What a thought!"

"Salem. Salem is the name of the town, I believe. A beautiful place, with long summers and mild winters."

"Peace," Johann added quietly. "Salem means peace." He thought perhaps his sister had told him that once.

"Take heart, young man. The good Lord may yet have things ahead for you that you cannot even imagine now."

Johann could not believe it but thanked him as the older man shuffled away.

At the noonday meal the next day, Carl brought up the topic of moving out of the city. Johann knew that his dependable companion did not like city life, so he was not surprised that Carl had listened to his new friends who dreamt of fertile farmlands in the southern colonies. He listened, despite his black mood.

"There are several towns, they said, which are settled and even have churches and music and things."

Johann nodded, leaning over to take another spoonful of green soup.

"Salem," Carl said. Johann's head shot up. "Peter said it is a good German town and its people are hungry for music."

CHAPTER 18

The Road to North Carolina
October 1792

C arl packed the trunks for what he hoped was the final time. They had three of them now, one half full of Johann's music. The composer had come around in just a week to the idea of North Carolina. Something about the remoteness of it and the name "Salem" attracted him. Carl looked at the pale, drawn face of his companion, eyes sunken in dark circles, and hoped he would survive one last trip.

Peter and Greta had already gone a month earlier. Carl rose early to walk several miles to bid them good-bye. They promised to find him there, but Greta's eyes welled up as she stood before him at the last. Peter turned around, pretending to examine the front of their conveyance to give them a moment's privacy.

Unable to stop himself, Carl grabbed her hands in both of his. "I will find you there." He stood awkwardly, wanting to tell her about his love for her, but far too fearful to begin.

She nodded, but the tears spilled over. She did not want to leave this gentle man so recently met.

Their driver called to them, "Time to board! Time to go!"

Peter turned back and saw Carl releasing his sister's hands. He gently took Greta's arm and helped her into the carriage.

As they started to move, Carl walked with them and shouted into their window, "I promise." He stood until he could see their coach no longer. On his way back to Johann, he vowed to himself not to give in to the sadness, but to work all the harder at getting himself to North Carolina as soon as he could.

Weeks later, Carl and Johann boarded the same carriage to head south. The roads were the worst they had ever travelled and the inns the poorest they had seen. Some nights they had to make do with a pile of straw in a corner for a bed. None of the walls in this country were free of holes, Carl decided. Drafts were their constant nighttime companions, and he was thankful that the evening temperatures remained pleasant. Johann grimly refused to complain, but Carl hovered nervously about, trying to keep as many warm covers over the small man as he could find.

The farther south they traveled, the fewer settlements and farms they saw. The land was heavily forested, and Carl thought the air had a clean, pure vibrancy in it. He eagerly examined every farm they passed, noting the crops and how the barns had been built. An older man and his wife, who sported a white bonnet with a blue ribbon, joined them for a portion of the trip. They regaled the coach's occupants with stories of wars with the natives from forty years' prior, bloodcurdling tales of scalping, torture, and the abduction of women and children. Johann, who had given up keeping his face covered in this New World, asked question after question of the long-time settlers. Rather than being frightened by the tales, he was fascinated. He discovered that they were from the Moravian settlement of Bethlehem in Pennsylvania. There had been another, earlier group from their church that had tried to settle farther south, in an area call Georgia after the British King. But the land was a swamp and the colony failed. Now, however, many of their brothers flourished in both Pennsylvania and North Carolina. Upon telling them that he himself was headed for Salem, they proceeded to give him a complete history of their church in Moravia, Count Zinzendorf, the Unity of Brethren in Pennsylvania, and the towns of Bethania, Bethabara, and Salem to which they were headed.

Their church, the Herrnhuter Brüdergemeine or Unitas Fratrum, had been born out of persecution and the martyrdom of Jan Hus in 1415 in Bohemia. Earlier in this current century, some of the remaining Brethren had settled on the estate of Count Nicholas of Zinzendorf, who supported their beliefs and whose sponsorship allowed the group to grow and flourish. The couple spoke of the Count with utmost reverence, listing all he had done for their church.

Count Zinzendorf placed a great emphasis on the heart. He believed that faith is set not in the intellect of man, but in his heart. Jesus was the center of that faith, the sole means by which man can understand God. In this, the Unity of Brethren agreed with their Lutheran cousins. Salvation was surrender of the soul, body, and intellect into the hands of a loving Father who wishes all to come to him, as they explained it.

Over the long hours in the cramped coach, the couple, Hubert and Ida Mueller, shared the basic beliefs of their church. It was the first time that Johann had listened in depth to anything other than the teachings of his Catholic upbringing. They spoke of a Father God who loved fallen humanity, who sent his perfect Son to die sacrificially for their sinful rebellion, but who was now resurrected and seated at the right hand of the Father. Johann couldn't understand their description of salvation as the "joyful apprehension" of a sinner by a loving Father. They were concerned with being pleasing to this Father, with pure morals and upright conduct. None of this was unique to the Unity, but their emphasis was on Christian living and relationships with each other and with God. In their view, this Father God did not sit to judge and condemn mankind but waited patiently for his errant children to run to his loving arms. Johann asked question after question. His thoughts kept swirling in a thick fog, never coming together to satisfy him, but his heart was waking up, wanting more.

"So do you think it is necessary to attend mass for salvation?" He was starting to question the teachings of his childhood.

"No. Repentance, confession, and belief in the Lord Jesus Christ are necessary," Hubert clarified. "We celebrate the Lord's Supper because it is commanded in the Holy Word that we do so. The Bible is our sole standard of religious doctrine and practice. It is always good to take time to ask the Spirit to show us our sins. It makes the presence and forgiveness of our Lord real in our lives and especially precious during Holy Communion."

Johann was struck by all the talk of a relationship. He was used to approaching God through a priest, a mass, or music. Ida and Hubert made the Lord seem uncomfortably close. Christ himself was the head of their church, not a human leader like the Catholic Pope. They spoke over and over of their loving friend, Jesus. It seemed almost irreverent or lacking in respect, but something within him longed to know more.

"Jesus atoned for our sins, fully and completely. We do not have to walk in eternal penitence," Hubert admonished him.

Ida nodded, "And He brings joy." Her pure smile perfectly illustrated the truth of her statement.

Hubert described their faith as having five aspects: simplicity, in a focus on the essentials of the faith; happiness, because of the love of God; unintrusiveness, a true acceptance of other denominations; fellowship of equal brethren, there being no difference in artisan or aristocrat; and service, which meant happily putting others before oneself and believing that all have gifts or talents useful in the kingdom.

These words resonated deeply with Johann. "Equal brethren... no difference in artisan or aristocrat... all have talents useful...`` How he wished he could believe them. They gave meaning to ideas he had struggled with his entire life. He had been raised in the Catholic church and had spent many hours in the composition of music for various religious uses. But something about this couple before him, holding hands and smiling at each other after 50 years of marriage and hardship on the frontier, painted a truer picture of faith than any ornate cathedral's service.

After ten days, they reached Richmond, Virginia, a busy new city where the Muellers' children had settled. Upon climbing down from the coach steps, Hubert turned to Johann, "You will be among many who love God and serve him in Salem. They can answer any questions you have. Blessings be upon you in the rest of your journey!" He and his wife turned to their son and grandchildren who welcomed them with open arms.

The realization that such a life was out of possibility for him now hit Johann with an icy reality. He held too much hatred. No family or children waited in his future. He sank into deep depression upon their departure and let black thoughts peck up the grains of hope that had been sown in his mind and heart.

Their journey continued through thick forests scattered with a few small settlements. One day, some strangely dressed people on horseback passed them. The men wore shirts of pale leather with fringes and hats on their black hair that looked like a band around their head with a few feathers. They all carried bows across their backs and led a pack horse with a dead deer slung over its back. The carriage driver called a greeting to them and the man in the lead raised one arm to acknowledge it. Later, the driver confirmed that Carl and Johann had seen their first group of natives. They were pleasantly surprised that there seemed to be nothing savage or violent about them.

Finally, four weeks after leaving Philadelphia, they arrived late in the afternoon at what they were told was the Salem Tavern. The village buildings on Main Street looked well-kept and reminded Carl of the neat smaller towns in his beloved Austria. The inn was of brick with a long porch, swept clean, with bright white columns along its front. Many people were about, men in plainer clothing than they were used to seeing in larger cities, and women in simple brown or gray dresses, always with a white bonnet decorated with different colored ribbons. Everyone looked busy, intent on some errand or another.

Johann entered the clean and airy public room on the first floor of the Tavern and had to sit quickly as his strength left him. A kind-looking woman hurried to him, "Sir, are you quite well?" She wore a simple brown gown covered by a white apron. Her hair was concealed under a white bonnet with a blue ribbon tied neatly under her chin. He heard the heavy German accent in her English words.

"Yes, just... tired," he responded in German. "My man is there, seeing to our things. Might you have a room for a few days?"

"Jawohl, mein Herr," she nodded enthusiastically and continued in German. "We have several rooms upstairs for guests. Why, just months ago General Washington himself stayed with us!"

Johann nodded at the mention of their president. A military hero who had led them to win their freedom. All Americans adored him. What a country, where the people chose who would rule over them! His religious past had received a shaking through the words of the Brethren in the coach and his political past full of emperors and lords stood to be shaken as well.

Carl entered, carrying one of their trunks on his broad back.

"Carl, this kind lady says that they do have rooms for us," Johann told him. He let them take over the arrangements. Carl rejoiced to be able to converse in German again. The landlady, Frau Gierke, sent one of the boys from the kitchen to help carry the trunks upstairs. She brought tall mugs of cider to the travelers.

Carl returned from the second floor quickly and stood before Johann, who still rested on a wooden bench before the large fire in the public room. "May I show you to the room, sir?"

"Yes, I suppose you may," Johann stood, then eyed the stairs doubtfully. "I may need some assistance."

Carl nodded, both of them knowing that he was more than capable of carrying his master upstairs if need be. Johann began the climb with Carl close behind him. Though he had to stop several times on the way up, he made it and sank gratefully onto a soft down mattress covered by a clean quilt of bright red and blue design in fine repair. These Brethren were making a good impression on him.

After seeing his master settled, Carl descended to the inn's kitchen and to the heavenly smells coming from it. He was given a tray with chicken pie, a salad of dark green vegetables, and ale for them both. After carrying it carefully upstairs, he ate gratefully as Johann picked at the food before him.

He cleared away the remains of the meal, then saw Johann settled for the evening. There was no one on the porch of the tavern, so he sat heavily into a rocker in deep shadows on the end. A cool, clean breeze bore scents of pine with a faint undertone of animal odors. The village was quiet. Peace descended on his spirit. Not one to think much about God, Carl surprised himself by speaking aloud the words, "thank you." A few minutes later he rose to head upstairs.

He made himself ready for the night in his own small, simple room. Bright white walls contrasted with a dark blue-gray chair rail. Clean bedding, neat and tidy surroundings swept clean, everything in good repair. He wondered if they could have arrived in heaven and if Greta might possibly be nearby.

CHAPTER 19
Salem, North Carolina
November 1792

Peace. Johann lay in the good straw bed under several quilts, marveling at the early morning quiet of Salem Tavern. His room faced west, away from the main street of the town, which apparently had little traffic at this hour. Standing up on wobbly legs, he moved to the solitary window and pulled back the white curtain. A stable and a few small gardens lay close to the tavern, then a cleared field on low, green hills and thick forest in the distance. *I am at the frontier's edge*, he thought, *the farthest end of civilization.* A knock caused him to turn just as Carl opened the door with a tray.

"Guten morgen, mein Herr," he greeted Johann.

"Good morning, Carl, English, ja?"

"Yes, goot mornink." Well, he was trying.

The smells from the tray caused Johann's mouth to water. It had been a very long time since he had had any interest in food. A heavy white mug with a sweeping, large handle sat by a pewter plate full of some kind of buns.

"It is coffee," Carl explained, "of a special kind that they make only here."

Johann nodded appreciatively as he sampled the strong brew, mixed with large amounts of cream and sugar. The buns were equally good, yeasty, and spiced with something he did not recognize.

After finishing the coffee and two buns, to Carl's astonishment, Johann was ready to talk. "So, what do you think?"

Carl looked at him quizzically.

"Of this place? Of Salem?"

"Well, we have only seen a little of the town. It reminds me of my home in many ways. Good farmland, hard-working folk."

Johann nodded, "I think we must see more. I am very intrigued with this place."

After helping his master to dress, the two made it to the public room downstairs. A few tables of men drank coffee and talked, but there were not many customers this early in the day. A low fire in the room's only fireplace kept the fall morning's chill at bay.

A woman in a light brown gown and white bonnet with white ribbon approached, wiping flour from her hands on an apron. "May I help you, sirs?"

Feeling weak after only the exertion of leaving his room, Johann sat at the table closest to the fire. He asked, "May we have some more of that wonderful coffee?" She smiled widely as she nodded and turned back to the kitchen. Carl sat across from him.

"Don't worry, Carl. I can walk. I will just have to sit when these legs fail me."

They watched the people of Salem go about their business through the inn's window. Their landlady approached once more. Farm wagons pulled by large horses drove by and men dressed in more formal shirts, waistcoats, and breeches talked with each other on the sidewalk.

"May I help you, sirs? Are you here on business?" She served both of them steaming mugs of coffee.

"Perhaps. I am seeking a place, possibly to purchase. I have not been well."

The lady looked concerned at this.

"I fear that the city life we were used to did not agree with me. My friend, Carl, here, is from the country—well, a small town in Europe—and he has convinced me that a smaller town, with its clean air and quieter pace, would be healthier for me."

"Do you look to purchase a home or farm? We have many families who live in town, as the men practice their own crafts, but there are also farms surrounding us. And the Single Brothers' house is right here facing the square."

"All single men live together? What about the single women?" Johann had never heard such a thing.

"They have some rooms in the Congregational House, or Gemeinhaus. They do not have to live in these places, but many find it easier if they combine their skills and do so gladly. None of the single people are lonely in Salem. Most practice a trade or help in teaching our children."

"Thank you, kind lady. I think I can walk a bit now and explore this place more thoroughly." Leaving a few coins on the table, the pair headed out.

A large town square lay across from the tavern's front door. It had walkways around it and some also crossing it diagonally from both corners. Trees, which appeared to have been recently planted, dotted its fields. Several large buildings surrounded the square and streets led away from it, with single dwelling houses lining them. There was the

Single Brother's House on the northwest corner of the square, then an even larger building called the Gemeinhaus or Congregation House, as a gentleman walking by told them. Everything appeared neat and well-kept, again reminding Carl of the farming community of his childhood.

The larger buildings and the tavern were made of bricks, interlaced with heavy wooden beams. Smaller wooden houses were stuck here and there between them. A few even appeared to be made of rougher, whole logs. They must have been the older homes, Johann thought.

The air was clean and crisp, not too cold even on this November morning, and the sky shone a brilliant blue. A walk to the center of the square proved to be the most that Johann could manage. He leaned heavily on Carl's arm heading back and had to stop at the edge of Main Street.

A young, dark-haired man, sleeves rolled up, wearing a leather apron, appeared from nowhere carrying a small barrel.

"Please, sit, sir," he placed the barrel beside Johann, who sank onto it gratefully.

"Thank you," Carl began. "My master is not well, not yet."

"I was working at the Single Brothers' House and saw his difficulty," he pointed to one of the large brick buildings just north of the tavern. "I am Henry, Henry Salzwedel."

"Johann Pertl, and thank you," Johann inclined his head in a bow to the pleasant young man. "This is Carl Bauer."

"Very nice to meet you. May I be of any assistance?"

"Thank you. I believe I will be able to get back to the tavern after a short rest. I am afraid that I have been ill for some time and misjudged my strength."

"So, you are visiting Salem?"

"Visiting and perhaps seeking to stay, if it might be possible."

"We welcome men of good character to our settlement. Most of us are of the Brethren, but that is certainly not a requirement for living in this area. What is your profession?"

Carl stared at Johann, who stared back. Johann decided quickly that this remote frontier had to be safe for him. He could start to come out of hiding.

"I am a music teacher," he replied.

Henry broke into a huge grin, "That is fortunate, quite fortunate, sir! You will find Salem most welcoming, most welcoming indeed." He noticed that Johann looked down at his hands instead of acknowledging his words and tapped his fingers together restlessly. Carl said nothing. A strange lack of reaction, Henry thought. Most would have continued to explain what they played, where they studied. This pair sat in stony silence. But perhaps they didn't understand how important music was to this community.

"We are all most devoted to music, you see. In our church services, our love feasts—we even have Singstunde, singing hours. And most families can say that every member has had musical training. They play together in the evenings, even the smallest of children. You will be most welcome, sir, most welcome."

Johann nodded and looked at Carl, "Well, I think I may try to get back to the tavern. Carl, if you would be so good as to help." Carl nodded, stood, and grasped Johann's arm to pull him to his feet.

"Well met, Herr Pertl. I do hope to talk again," Henry continued to smile in the face of being blatantly, almost rudely, ignored. "Dear Lord, help me to love as you do," he whispered under his breath as the two newcomers made it slowly across the street.

Carl stopped at the bottom of the three stairs before the tavern's porch. Johann looked white and leaned heavily on his arm. Then suddenly he wasn't there. Carl was dismayed to see him unconscious on the street. As he bent over to help, two men ran noisily from the tavern's door to his aid.

"Is he in need of a doctor?" the older gentleman asked.

Carl didn't know what to answer. "I'm not sure," he admitted.

"Franz," the man said to his younger companion. "Get Dr. Lansbach, quickly." Franz nodded, turned, and ran north on Main Street. Turning to Carl he said, "Come, let me help you get him inside."

Carl picked up Johann easily by himself and followed the older man, who held the door open into the tavern. He accompanied Carl up the stairs and helped him into Johann's room. As Carl settled the limp figure onto the bed, a breathless, very tall young man carrying a small satchel entered the room. He addressed Carl with a voice full of concern.

"I'm Dr. Lansbach, at your service. I understand a gentleman fainted?"

Carl nodded and backed away from the bed. "He has not been well, but I have not seen him in this state for a long time."

The doctor sat on the side of the bed and picked up Johann's arm to feel the strength of his pulse. As he continued to poke, prod, and examine the small man, he kept up a steady stream of questions for Carl. His manner was gentle and sympathetic, and Carl found himself sharing everything, every symptom, setback, and worry of his own with the physician. He even told of their months of travel, the ordeal of crossing the sea.

"Well, I think that he is in much need of rest. It sounds as if you two have done nothing but travel, and very strenuous travel at that, for almost a year now. I also believe that perhaps his kidneys are weak. The color of the skin, the pains you have described. I think rest and some medicines to restore those, plenty of water, and he should recover."

They moved away from the bed and Dr. Lansbach pulled a bottle from his satchel to show to Carl. He began discussing the patient's care, so neither one of them were aware that Johann had opened his eyes.

"Carl?"

Carl and the doctor turned quickly to the bed. "Ja? You are better? Here is a doctor who has some medicines for you."

Dr. Lansbach sat down once more on the bed. "Herr Pertl? You have worn yourself down to nothing. This young man here has been telling me about your adventures in coming to Salem. I have to say, it is a wonder that you survived all of this."

Johann felt too weak to be angry at Carl for divulging secrets. He wasn't even able to lift his head as the doctor continued.

"I am prescribing rest, a few medicines, and much water and fresh air. I believe the Lord has health ahead for you, but you must rest."

"Thank you," Johann responded weakly. "Carl has helped me so much, but I have not been well for a very long time."

The doctor patted his hand as he stood. "Take these tinctures, rest, and I will come again soon. And I will pray for you. God be with you, Herr Pertl."

Carl watched him leave. These people certainly talked about God a lot. He was used to keeping a safe distance from the Almighty in everyday life. He did not know what to make of this easygoing familiarity with the Lord, but they all seemed welcoming enough. And everyone spoke German. He would have time to explore things for himself, with Johann ordered to rest, to see what he could make of the place.

CHAPTER 20
Salem
Spring 1793

Just as Dr. Lansbach predicted, Johann grew stronger day by day. Carl settled into a routine, helping around the tavern's kitchen while he made sure that Johann took every drop of medicine along with special tea prescribed by the doctor. Then, while his master slept, he wandered the town streets and even strolled by the many small farms surrounding Salem. By the time Johann began to sit up and take brief walks around the airy room and hall, Carl was quite familiar with the area.

Salem's winter weather could be cold and snowy, but periods of milder temperatures prevented the ground from being covered by snow for long. On warmer days, when the muddy roads dried, the pair ventured out on short walks. The town was too small for anyone to escape notice and friendly curiosity brought many new acquaintances their way. Carl noticed that there was not so much distinction here between master and servant. People greeted him as warmly as they did Johann and included him in conversations. He had become used to being invisible in the large cities of Europe with their centuries' old class system.

Johann's return to physical health caused his mood to lighten as well. The black hand holding his heart did not relax its grip, but he no longer fantasized about dying, seeing it as his only future path. Perhaps he could stay here, in obscurity, and even teach a few pupils to earn a small income. Their funds, seemingly infinite over a year ago, had dwindled noticeably. He remembered his pride in Vienna, how he only took pupils from the nobility, and then only those who had real talent or who could afford to pay extravagantly for lessons. Perhaps the humbler Johann Pertl could find, if not joy, at least some small purpose in teaching children.

During one of Dr. Lansbach's visits, Johann thought to ask him about his living situation. As the physician thumped his chest, bent over to place his ear to hear better, Johann broached the subject.

"Herr Doktor, I have been thinking that perhaps I might wish to stay in this area," he spoke into the top of the doctor's head.

The doctor smiled, straightened, and thanked God for another answered prayer, though he kept the thought to himself. He often stayed with this patient much longer than medical care necessitated. He enjoyed their conversation. This small man had earned a spot in his heart, and he believed strongly that he was meant to stay in Salem.

"Yes?" He didn't want to seem overly eager and scare him away. There was something different about him, something other than the pain he carried so obviously in his soul. God had purposes here for this man.

"Is it possible to purchase a home here? Or must one be a part of your church first?"

"Yes and no. Yes, there are homes available from time to time. And, no, you do not have to be a part of the Brethren, as long as you are of good character and deal honorably with those around you. I have come to know you over this month, Herr Pertl, and I would be more than happy to be a witness as to your suitability before our council of elders."

"Thank you, sir."

"In fact, I have heard just recently of the Widow Reuter's plans to give up her little house. She is in poor health and will be moving into the congregational house where our pastors stay. All of these decisions are under the oversight of our elders, but I know she would be most appreciative of the income from such a sale."

Johann grew more interested as Dr. Lansbach described the small, green house south of the town's center, with a garden surrounded by several acres of farmland and slightly removed from the center of things.

"Do you suppose you could show Carl where it is? I am not sure I trust these legs to take me so far yet, but I can rely on him in matters like this."

They set a time for the doctor to return and take Carl to see the widow's property. He left promising to bring the matter up with the council. Johann retrieved the leather pouch holding his remaining fortune. This would not purchase much in Austria, but perhaps prices in this New World were lower.

Carl returned flushed and winded from his tour of the property the next day. Usually very brief in his comments, excitement prompted him to release a torrent of words.

"Mein Herr, it is a very fine house and land. There is already a garden and a well so close. It is down the hill just there," he pointed to his left. "Do you think we really might stay? There is land, land for growing things, even animals. A small stable looks to be sturdy enough. I could find out about these plants they grow here. Pumpkins, I think, and other squash, cabbage..."

"But what about the house?" Johann had to interrupt the agricultural discussion he had no interest in. He appreciated the displaced farmer's enthusiasm for it, though.

"Oh, yes, forgive me. It is small, two bedrooms, a sitting room, and a kitchen. But it is sturdy, with a porch on the back, and not drafty."

"Would there be space for a fortepiano?" Johann put into words the desire that had been building in his heart. And he would need one, to earn more income.

"Yes," Carl thought a bit, "I'm sure one would fit in the sitting room." He imagined the keyboard instrument on the ship from Italy to London and could see such a thing easily against a sitting room wall.

"And what price? Did the doctor tell you?"

"No, all that is decided by their Board of Elders. He said he would tell you what they decide."

"Well, I would like to see the place. Maybe tomorrow."

It turned out that the price was just under the value of their remaining gold coins. The Widow Reuter was glad to leave the table, chairs, and beds that made up the meager furnishings of the place. Hating to spend even more, but seeing no other way, Johann placed an order for the best fortepiano to be found in Charleston. One of the furniture makers in Salem would be heading there in a week or so and could handle the details. He had discovered that it was the nearest city that afforded purchases of manufactured items. He hoped the instrument would open the door to more income. And now they owned a farm and Carl was a farmer, wasn't he? Perhaps he could sell vegetables or something and contribute to their needs.

Moving in involved no more than finding a spare cart to take their trunks the half mile or so to the small frame house. It had been built twenty years before by the first surveyor in the community. Johann looked up at the central chimney sitting atop a high gabled roof. The single front door placed on the left above a solitary stone stair invited him to enter. Warm sunlight filled the sitting room on the right, blessed with two large windows. A small room opened on the left and he could see the kitchen farther along on the same side. Walking into it, he spotted a larger room on the right. These must be the two bedrooms. Smaller, single windows provided light to see by, but they were more private.

A second door opened from the kitchen onto a small yard and large field beyond. A well sat by the back door. Carl was examining a small shed about twenty feet from the house. He emerged grinning, "A barn, ja?"

"If you say so. How much of this is ours?" Johann swept his hand toward the field.

"Quite a lot of it. There are stones marking the boundaries, but they are difficult to see from here. Would you like me to show you?"

"Perhaps later." Johann turned again to look over the house. "You know, Carl, I have lived many, many places but never owned any of them. Neither did my father."

"Yes, my family farmed always, but ever someone else's land," Carl nodded.

"This America is something, is it not?" Johann entered his house again, leaving Carl to his dreams about what to do with the land.

A few days later, they received word that the forte-piano had to be ordered and, barring rains or other mishaps, should be delivered within two months. This greatly pleased Johann, who had little to occupy his time. He could look forward to playing an instrument again before too long. Carl worked like a man possessed, making repairs on the small shed he called their "barn" and walking to town several times a day to return with various tools whose purpose Johann could only guess.

Carl also gained knowledge on these trips. While purchasing farm implements, he talked to the craftsmen and other customers to find out the best crops to plant, what the climate in spring and summer was like, and anything else he could learn to begin his life again as a farmer. He shared what he learned with Johann as they walked the boundaries of the fields behind the house. It had become their custom to do that at least once a day. Johann's health and strength increased daily, also. "Do what you need to do," Carl was instructed about the farm. He, grateful beyond words to be out of cities and back on the land, determined to make the most successful farm Salem had ever seen. He seemed like a different person, able at last to put his past behind him.

Johann realized within a few weeks that their money was almost gone. It was February and they had months before anything that Carl planted could supply their table. In fact, seed would have to be purchased, along with food and other necessities. It was time that he face teaching whomever he could, or they were in danger of losing this newfound status of his as landowner. The blackness always lurking around the edges of his thoughts threatened to invade once again. It was as if his capacity for pain or problems was already filled by the heaviness that lay over his soul, so any new issue rapidly exhausted him, leaving him in despair of a solution.

Carl recognized the signs of his master's heavy mood returning. Johann spent hours staring at a spot on the sitting room wall. On days when the North Carolina early spring felt like heaven itself, he managed to coax Johann onto the back porch, where he watched Carl hoeing, planting, and pulling weeds. Though Carl knew it was probably inappropriate, he tried to talk Johann into helping him, showing him the difference between young pumpkin vines and weeds. Within minutes, Johann was back on the porch, sitting in a broken chair, staring into the distance.

Carl grew angry. He had planted so much that he really did need some help. They were growing beans, cabbage, celery, cucumbers, field and garden peas, rhubarb, turnips, garlic, lettuce, watermelons, pumpkins, potatoes, leeks, sweet potatoes, spinach, asparagus, onions, salsify, and gourds. It would be a welcome change from their most recent diet of only pumpkins and corn meal mush. Johann's lack of interest spurred Carl on to even longer hours.

The fortepiano arrived like salvation itself. Carl still had no help with chores, but at least he did not have to worry over what Johann was about. He could hear the music pouring from open windows for hours every day. As for Johann, the music, as always, pushed back the edges of the blackness.

One day in May, Carl headed into town to purchase a few necessities. Soon they would have some of their own vegetables, but he still had to buy flour and salt. Coffee was a luxury they could ill afford, so did without. At the small store, he noticed the proprietor's son struggling to move heavy bags of meal. He offered his help, and the job was finished in no time. In gratitude, the owner offered to buy him a stein of ale at the tavern next door and Carl accepted.

He was astonished to see his friends, Peter with his sister, Greta, sitting at a table within. They both looked rested, healthy, and happy. Greta wore a blue dress that perfectly matched her eyes.

"Hello, dear friend," Peter rose to shake Carl's hand. A red flush of delight spread over Greta's cheeks. Carl thought her more beautiful than he had remembered. He stopped just short of enfolding her in his arms, shyness winning out over his natural desire.

"I am so glad to see you again," Carl said, eyes focused on Greta's bright blue ones as he waved his arms in the air. He did not know what to do in his excitement.

Peter laughed. "We have found work in Bethabara, just six miles from here. I am helping a miller and Greta has a place with a wealthy family. We are both able to stay with them, as long as I do a few things around the house every now and then." Peter stopped to take a long drink of the strong dark ale.

"And you, Carl? How are things with you?"

"Herr Pertl has purchased a small house with some land. It is just down this road from the tavern. I am farming again," Carl beamed at Greta.

"Good, good for you! It is a miracle that we are now so close to each other. And how is your master? In health?"

"Yes, better, but I still worry about his dark days. Things in his past sit like a heavy stone on him."

"We are doing very well," Peter changed the course of the conversation back to joyful things. "We have never made so much or lived so well." He elbowed Greta gently, causing her to smile and drop her eyes to her lap. "The miller came today to sell flour, so we tagged along to see Salem and help him with it. And you found us before we could even start looking for you!"

Carl grinned, "Truly things are well." His eyes met Greta's as the words left his lips.

"We have a plan," Peter dropped his voice to a whisper.

Carl raised his eyebrows as he drank.

"Greta and I, we have heard of a place west of here. Tennessee, they call it. There is land, rich land, and all you must do is find a piece and start to work. You do not even have to purchase it, as long as you make improvements on it."

Carl's heart sank. Had he found them again just to lose them so soon?

"But we must wait for a while, save more of our money. Carl, can you imagine? Owning your own farm?"

He could not. Johann's purchase of the small plot was the largest miracle he could grasp.

"It is possible, here," Peter pointed a large finger at the rough wooden tabletop.

"I would be sorry to lose you again. Bethabara isn't too far to see you every now and then. But how far is this other place? This Tennessee?"

"Come with us!" Peter was always full of ideas. "Two of us could manage a large farm, I know we could."

Greta's face turned beet red at the thought of Carl joining their family, living with them.

Carl, despite his attraction to Greta, instantly began to back away in the face of this new idea. "No, I could not... I could not leave Herr Pertl."

"Maybe not now," Peter agreed. He probably said too much too soon for his friend. "But what about in a year or so? He could hire someone else, I'm sure. We are not slaves, Carl. This is America."

After finishing their ale and telling tales of their lives in this new world, Peter and Greta left to find the miller. Carl promised to see them again, even if he had to walk the six miles to Bethabara himself. He described the little house at the bottom of the hill, so they could come find him when the miller returned to Salem. They in turn gave him detailed instructions about how to find them should he come to Bethabara.

Carl's heart was full as he returned home. Fear about leaving, even a few years away, battled with pictures of Greta that he could not get out of his head. He heard music as he neared the house. That meant that Johann would be in a better humor. He had best start thinking about cooking dinner and forget all these crazy, impossible things buzzing around in his head.

That evening, just before sunset, Johann and Carl walked the perimeter of their land. Johann had acquired the Viennese love of walking in nature whenever possible and was grateful that his health now allowed it. The air was humid, but a small breeze kept it comfortable. Rows and rows of young plants attested to Carl's labor. Insects buzzed loudly around them.

Johann was genuinely pleased when Carl told him about Peter and his sister visiting Salem. He noticed something in Carl's voice as he spoke of the girl, Greta.

"So, is she pretty, this Greta?" he enjoyed the chance to tease Carl a bit.

"Very pretty, yes, very pretty indeed." Carl's face turned bright red.

Johann laughed, "Watch out, Carl. I think she has captured you. Have you thought of marriage?"

Carl stood in shock as Johann entered the house. All these thoughts and feelings about Greta. But marriage? He and Greta?

Chapter 21
Salem
Summer 1793

Johann gazed over the neat rows of green vegetables, the proof that Carl indeed knew what he was doing on a farm. The garden provided enough for the two men and some to sell on Saturdays, when area farmers carried the fruits of their labors to the town square. That money enabled them to purchase what they could not grow themselves. There was no excess for luxuries or saving, but it suited their most pressing needs. And they could afford coffee again. He knew that he would have to start teaching to earn more soon, perhaps by fall. For now, though, they survived.

Carl was gone for the day. Since meeting Peter and Greta again, he saw them at least once a week, walking six miles to some town north of Salem and six miles back. Usually the visits happened on Sundays, leaving Johann alone for an entire day. Everyone else in the town was caught up in church services or time with family. These were his hardest days.

This evening he walked aimlessly up and down the rows of cabbages and potatoes, stopping when he noticed a weed or two, which he pulled and left to die on the bare dirt between rows. Here he was, the great composer, the toast of Vienna, weeding a garden! What in the world would become of him? At the bottom of the hill, he stopped at the large flat stone signaling the end of his property. Rows and rows of neatly tended plants stretched before him in every direction. A border of trees marked the horizon, darkened by the sun setting behind them. In the opposite direction he could see the back of another house, quite a distance from him. He didn't even know who might live there. He knew no one in the town other than Carl and Dr. Lansbach. Suddenly tired and confronted with the reality of his loneliness, he sat on the stone.

Johann was in the best physical condition of his life. A diet of mostly vegetables, much sunshine, and daily exercise had worked their wonders to produce a strength and health he had never known. But there was a wound in his soul that festered. Hatred and unforgiveness, the desire for revenge for his wife's betrayal, would drive him mad before long. He knew it, as well as he knew that he was incapable of doing anything to remove it. He longed to hurt her, but he had made that impossible by his insane escape. What was he doing? Here he was, living a futile existence in the wilds of America. He still had music, but without the twin gods of Fame and Fortune driving him in their pursuit, what was its point? A heavy sigh escaped as he lowered his head into his hands.

"God, I don't even want to live any longer," he looked up finally and spoke into the night sky. "Are you truly merciful? If you are, could you put an end to this?" It was the first prayer he had prayed in years. Perhaps his first honest one. He sat silently as darkness fell. His father's faithful Catholic teachings had removed from him the possibility of suicide. He was left with a vague fear of a God who surely was most definitely angry at his having escaped to a place where mass and confession were not an option. There was too much to confess at this point, anyway.

Not comforted, still heavily burdened, he returned to the house in full darkness. Carl came in directly after and headed straight to bed, tired after the long walk back. Johann stared at his ceiling through most of the night, caught in endless thoughts which all led to dead-end alleys.

Carl also lay sleepless in the next room, but it was a joyful hope that kept him awake rather than despair. He had spent the afternoon with Peter and Greta, but then had been left alone with her for an hour in a shady yard while Peter tended to some emergency. They speculated about the possibility of Tennessee, building a life of their own in freedom, and how this all might come about. He could still see her upturned face, eyes warm with affection, hanging on his every word. Unthinking, he had grasped her hand in a moment of excited dreaming, then continued to hold it because she did not pull away. When Peter arrived on the scene, Carl dropped her hand, suddenly self-conscious. But Greta's brother only smiled. Sleep finally caught up with him as he wondered where these feelings for her might lead.

Monday dawned hot and humid. Carl had onions and corn to harvest, along with the interminable weeding. Most days he didn't even notice what Johann got himself up to. Sometimes the music stopped, and its creator even came out to offer some help with the work of the place. Carl wished he would today. There was so much to do. He did not hear any music going on, so perhaps?

Close to mid-day, a visitor slowly approached the house from the south. Neither Carl nor Johann saw him coming. Carl was far out in the field and Johann sat staring at the keyboard before him, arms hanging by his side. The mood of the previous evening was still with him, only magnified by a night of lost sleep, making composition impossible. A voice at the door startled him.

"Hello? Is anyone there? Hello?" a strange voice called.

Johann opened the door to see an elderly gentleman in the plain brown clothing so prevalent in Salem. The man removed his tricorn hat to reveal a frizz of white hair surrounding a bald crown. He bowed, "Sir? May I introduce myself? I am Richard Gutman, your neighbor." He smiled broadly at the younger man.

Johann stood blinking, trying to adjust his sleep-deprived eyes to the bright sun. "Oh, yes, come in, please." He bowed slightly as he opened the door wider for this unwanted guest. Years of moving in circles with nobility had given him impeccable manners which never failed him. He stood aside to let the gentleman enter while thinking out loud, "Neighbor? I didn't know..."

"East of you, sir. Our back fields share a border, down at the dip in the valley." The man was tall and looked to be in his late sixties. His face and smile radiated kindness as he faced Johann.

"Of course," Johann still didn't know where the man's house could possibly be. "Forgive me, I am Johann Pertl. Welcome." He showed Richard into the sitting area.

"A fine fortepiano, Herr Pertl. Do you play?" he asked, settling onto a hard bench. The house's furnishings were more utilitarian than comfortable. No decorations of any kind graced walls or surfaces. There must be no female residents here, Richard decided, which would explain its bare simplicity.

"Yes, I do." Johann left it at that.

"And what about Frau Pertl? A young man such as your-self must have a wife?"

Johann did not feel especially young that day. "No, I am afraid not. My wife... passed away... in Austria. One of the reasons I was free to come here."

"I am sorry to hear that. You must be lonely, so far from town, and by yourself?" His tone was genuinely caring. The sparse furnishings and lack of warmth were explained.

Johann felt himself warming to this stranger. He had not put names to what exactly bothered him but supposed that loneliness must be a part of it. "I have a man who helps and runs the farm. He is out there now, working. The two of us manage."

Richard nodded. "Well, my own dear wife passed away ten years ago. I am fortunate to have a daughter, Luisa, who cares for me. She is growing older herself now, and I fear that my needs have stood in the way of her marrying. She says no, that she is doing what God wants of her, but still I worry what's to become of her when I go to eternal glory."

It took Johann a minute to realize that he was talking about death. "But surely that will not be soon! You appear to be in perfect health."

"I am nearly 70. One never knows at my age," Richard smiled, eyes twinkling as if it were a joke.

"But I have almost forgotten my errand," he continued. "I have been remiss in not inviting you sooner, but we would like to have you join us for an evening meal as soon as it might be convenient for you. Since our houses are the two farthest out here at the foot of the hill, we had probably best get to know one another."

The last thing that Johann wished to do today was to socialize. His eyes felt full of grit and his thoughts flitted around like scared birds, flying everywhere and nowhere. What should he say?

Richard sensed the hesitation, "Not tonight. Perhaps tomorrow?"

Johann nodded, "Thank you. That would be very kind." What harm could there be? And solitude was far from his natural state. He longed for conversation and friendship.

"It might be quickest for you to come while there is still light and use the path through our fields."

Johann wasn't aware of the path, so Richard took him into the back and showed him where a tall dead stump marked the start of it. The older man took that way back himself, greeting Carl and stopping to compliment him on his plants on the way. Johann watched the older gentleman and was struck once more by his kindness.

The next evening, Johann headed off to the Gutmans'. It took a tremendous effort of the will to step out of his own house, but an invitation accepted was binding. He had never spotted the other home before but found the path by the stump easily. Nothing about this invitation attracted him, but he supposed that he must be starved for conversation, for he was determined to go. At least it would be a change from Carl's endless vegetable stews. And he had slept the night before, so perhaps he could form a coherent sentence if needed.

The house before him appeared to be about twice the size of his own, but freshly painted with a light-yellow color. The yard and surrounding gardens were immaculate, not a weed in sight. There were even flowers planted in a border around the porch. The door opened as he climbed the steps to it and Richard welcomed him warmly, extending his arm for a hearty handshake.

"Come in, come in, neighbor Pertl! We are so glad that you have come. Luisa, our guest is here!"

A short young woman entered the room, wiping her hands on an apron. She had the white bonnet with pink ribbon that Johann had learned to be the uniform of a single woman. She smiled as her father introduced her, curtseying gracefully before him. Johann decided that, though not what most would call a beauty, she had a very pleasant appearance, especially set off by her large brown eyes. Her hair was dark, he judged by the few strands escaping the bonnet. She had her father's kind smile.

The men talked in the sitting room as Luisa finished cooking. Johann's mouth watered at the delicious smell of roasting meat and baking bread. Richard shared the story of his birth in Pennsylvania, growing up amidst Indian raids and wars, his move to Bethabara, then starting over in Salem right at the founding of the town. Richard had been a church leader through its early history. Johann spoke about growing up in Salzburg and living in Vienna. He stuck as closely to the truth as possible, leaving out the incessant traveling of his childhood, not wanting to divulge too much about his altogether far from ordinary early life.

Luisa had cooked a simple but delicious meal of pork roasted to perfection, green beans, corn, cabbage, and fragrant fresh bread with butter from their own cow. Johann had not had such a feast in years. He remarked over every dish, especially the final dessert which was a cake made with pumpkin and spices. Something about these people allowed him to relax and forget the crushing burden of his pain and the strange path it had carved out for him.

"Yes, my Luisa is a treasure. I feel so guilty at times, that her fixation on caring for her old father has caused her to turn away every suitor."

Luisa flushed at her father's words. How could he say such things in front of a single gentleman, as if begging their guest to notice her? And besides, she had not turned away every suitor. The familiar ache was duller now but could still make its painful jabs to her heart.

"There have not been so many suitors, Papa." She quickly turned to carry dishes to her work counter.

"She is such a treasure, a godly woman just as her mother was. It breaks my heart that she has no family of her own," Richard confided to their guest.

If he was attempting to interest Johann, he failed. So wounded by his wife, the younger man never made the connection. Content after his best meal in months, he made no comment.

Richard invited him to their sitting room, large and richly furnished. A small fortepiano sat under a painting of a woman in a white bonnet with blue ribbon. Johann assumed this was probably Richard's deceased wife. A wooden flute lay across the top of the fortepiano. But the most surprising thing was a large bookshelf, each shelf filled with bound volumes.

"You have quite a collection of books, sir," Johann stood before the shelves.

"Yes, theology mostly. They are responsible for my retirement from preaching."

Johann sat in a straight wooden chair by the fire and waited for an explanation.

"My health is not the best and the council thinks I have a gifting with words. So, they had me retire long before the time that most do. Many men gave me books and I ordered others. I have been charged with writing. I am working on some things to use in our schools right now, but perhaps I will attempt something of more import later," Richard explained.

Luisa came in, having cleared the table. She was too intrigued with their new neighbor to waste much time cleaning dishes in the kitchen. Sitting quietly in a rocker by the door, she listened to her father and their guest while working on some needlework. Without being too obvious, she took in his appearance through quick glances. His brown jacket and breeches were not overly fine, but clean. His dark blonde hair was tied neatly with a black ribbon. Though not handsome, his face was pleasing and had a healthy color, as if he had spent some time outdoors. She quickly looked down when his large blue eyes caught hers.

"And what about you?" Richard asked. "Do you read? How do you pass your days?"

How indeed, Johann thought. "I have been working about the farm somewhat. And I hope to obtain some music pupils this fall."

"Ah, a musician?" Richard leaned forward eagerly. "What do you play?"

"Keyboards. A little violin," Johann did not want to talk about this.

"Luisa here plays the fortepiano and the flute. You must come back! A musical evening. What a joy that would be," Richard was pleased to have thought of a reason to invite Johann for a second time. Luisa blushed furiously.

"Thank you, yes, that would be very enjoyable. I must be off now, though. I thank you both for your hospitality."

Johann stood to leave, as if the mention of music frightened him away.

"Here, let me see you to the path," Richard stood also, and Luisa handed him a small lantern, which he lit and gave to Johann. "You will need this to light the way."

The two men headed into the back yard and stopped where the path began. Crickets and other chirping insects filled the night with sound. A cool breeze provided relief from the heat of the day. Richard felt the nudging of the Holy Spirit.

"Herr Pertl, do you believe that God speaks to us?" Richard asked abruptly.

Johann stammered a reply, "Well, He has given us the heavens and His word. I believe that He has given us direction about how to live."

"No, no," Richard shook his head. "I mean to you..." Here he poked Johann's chest several times with a finger, "... to you, in here, words just for you."

"I am not sure, Herr Gutman," Johann admitted.

"Well, I am. And I believe He spoke to me about you, young man. You are unique."

Johann's eyes grew large in surprise.

"Yes, you are especially gifted in some area, beyond most men. But you do not know in your heart of hearts the peace that God gives. That is why He has brought us together. Next week?"

"What?" Johann was frightened by this man who said that the Lord Almighty spoke—and about him, no less.

"Dinner!" Richard laughed, "Next Tuesday. I will look forward to it." He left without giving Johann a chance to respond yes or no.

Upon returning to the house, Richard sought out Luisa in the kitchen.

"So, what do you think of our neighbor, Luisachen?" He found a mug and poured water from a clay pitcher.

Luisa had quite a few thoughts about him. "He is nice, Poppa, but something has happened to him."

Apparently, Luisa had noticed the same sadness that Richard had.

"He seems so troubled, as if a darkness has hold of him. I wish..."

"Wish, child?"

Luisa blushed for the third time that night. "Nothing, just that he might find peace. Do you think that he truly knows our Lord? Knows that he is loved?"

Richard shook his head. "We will have to see. I invited him back next week."

And, though she had years ago resigned herself to being her father's caretaker rather than someone's wife, Luisa's heart leapt at the knowledge that she would see Johann again. This frightened her. Long ago she had hoped for a husband, a family of her own, and had even felt strongly that God was leading her to a particular young man. He was not especially handsome or skilled in any specific way, but he loved the Lord so much that it spilled out of him onto everyone around. Especially to her. She pushed the thoughts, the old feelings, and the pain resolutely back into the corner of her heart long ago reserved for them. God had had other plans. Hanging her apron on a hook beside the door, she headed to her bed.

CHAPTER 22
Salem
August 1793

For several months, they kept up the same pattern. Carl visited Bethabara and his friends every Sunday. He thought about Greta more often on every day in between. His farm and house chores left his mind ample freedom for daydreams. Johann had dinner with Richard Gutman and his daughter every Tuesday. Their conversations grew deeper every week. Johann struggled with the things Brother Gutman was telling him about God. He heard him say over and over that "out of lost sinners He can make blest men," following that with a wink and nod in Johann's direction. Richard talked about a God who seemed so different from the one his own father and the Catholic Church had taught about. And, though he told himself he needed these evenings to learn about the faith of his Moravian neighbors, he sometimes found himself thinking of Luisa's brown eyes.

Carl found himself alone with Peter after a large Sunday lunch at their employer's Bethabara home.

"Next summer, Carl," Peter punched his friend's arm excitedly. "We are saving some money and earning extra besides. Next May we can go and find our fortunes in the west."

"How much will we need?" Carl felt dismayed more than excited.

"Just enough for the trip and a few months' food. We can work along the way if we need to. The North Carolina Road will take us to a place where we can find land and settle, I know it."

Peter asked every traveler coming from the west about conditions and opportunities there. All reports confirmed his thoughts about the fertility and promise of the wide-open land, despite the hard work necessary to build a life there.

"I'm not sure," Carl shook his head. The only income he and Johann had came from the produce he sold. It was barely enough to meet their needs.

"Well, tell Herr Pertl that he needs to start teaching music or whatever it is he can do to earn money. He doesn't pay you, does he?"

Another shake of Carl's head. No, Johann had provided all their travel expenses, purchased food and clothing, but had never mentioned pay. Carl managed to put aside a little from the things he sold, but that money belonged to them both. It was not his to take.

Greta was sitting beside him, listening. She placed a hand on Carl's arm. "Don't worry, Carl. God will provide. Frau Stettler always tells me that and it happens, just as she prays."

Peter and Greta heard many lessons from the Moravian brethren they lived among. Carl heard only music in his house. He was generally walking to Bethabara during the time Salem residents were hearing preaching in their church. He felt that he was falling behind in preparation for many kinds of things.

Peter made an excuse to finish some work in the stables. He always managed to give Carl and Greta an hour or so alone, with him just nearby enough to maintain propriety. He left them at the wooden table under the shade of a large oak.

"Greta, what am I to do? I am such a dunce. I have not been thinking about saving. There has not been much to save!"

"Let's pray," she stated firmly. "Frau Stettler prays with me, and it is such a blessing. I believe what she says about God. He cares for us. He wants more for us than we know."

She hesitated a moment and met his eyes directly.

"I prayed with her last Sunday after the service, Carl. I accepted our dear Savior as my Lord. Everything is different."

This also scared Carl, but he was intrigued. "And what does Peter say?"

She laughed, "Oh, he did the same months ago. We just didn't know what you would do if we suddenly told you we had become part of the Brethren. But nothing has changed in our love for you."

He looked startled at her use of the word.

"Peter still believes that God would have us go west, now more than ever. We can help spread His word, help to build a God-fearing community."

Now he felt more left out than before. But she had used the word "love."

"And I still wish to go with you," he stated.

Later, on the long walk back to Salem, Carl realized that not once had he thought about the effect his departure would have on Johann. Perhaps he should encourage him to take students, to earn an income. It would help when the time came for him to leave, though he could never tell him that he was thinking of doing that.

On the following Tuesday, Johann found himself enjoying warm bread, duck, green beans, turnips, corn, and something Luisa called "sugar cake." These meals made it possible for him to survive the rest of the week. He would not admit to himself how much the Gutmans meant to him and how these evenings shone in the darkness that swallowed the rest of his life. He thought Luisa grew more lovely every time he saw her, though he would have scoffed in Vienna at any woman wearing homespun linen dresses. Now he thought that she made them beautiful.

After dinner, as their custom had become, Johann and Luisa played music both together and separately while Richard rocked and smiled in extreme enjoyment. The Gutmans had been breathless with astonishment at the quality of Johann's playing when the musical evenings began. He explained that he had had the advantage of Vienna's finest teachers and never told them that almost everything he played was of his own composition. Richard suspected that this was the gift God had told him about in the younger man. Luisa decided that the Viennese teachers must be very fine indeed.

Johann accompanied Luisa's flute playing in some small pieces that she had in her possession. He thought that she played with great feeling but had probably never had the time required to become a technical master. In years before, he had satirically said that there was nothing worse than a flute except two flutes. But at the time he was straining under the yoke of having to produce works of quality under circumstances which allowed him no quiet to do so, and had heard a number of out of tune flute performances. How times had changed! When a flute was played in tune, as Luisa managed, it was not so bad. In fact, he started to have some ideas for new pieces, suited to her style and abilities. He wondered if he could find paper and write out the flute part of that flute and harp concerto he had composed for the French duke's daughter, Marie-Louise-Philippine. The names even matched—Louise, Luisa. He could manage playing both orchestra and harp parts on the keyboard, he was sure.

This evening there were books and papers strewn upon a table in a corner of the usually tidy sitting room. Johann was first in after the meal, so took the opportunity to read what was on the top page.

"Salvation and Grace," he read quietly. "A Study for the Young."

"Are you interested in it?" Richard's voice startled him.

"Oh, I am sorry. I did not mean to overstep, but I have not seen your work here before," Johann laid the page back down.

"But are you interested?" Richard asked again. His eyes locked on the younger man's.

"Yes, yes, of course," Johann took up his customary chair beside the fortepiano.

"So, what would you say that salvation is?" Richard's tone indicated that he was now the teacher and the pupil had better do his best.

"Well, it is what the cross is about. Our Lord died that we might attempt to emulate his good works and hope to enter heaven," Johann recited what his father and the Catholic Church had taught him.

"No!" Richard's fist banged down upon a small table near him, causing a pewter candle holder and several pages to fall to the floor. It startled Luisa into running in from her cleaning tasks.

"Forgive me, but we don't work and hope to enter heaven," Richard still sounded angry. "Our Lord Jesus was brought forth of a virgin, sinless, perfect, yet he gave his life willingly for us that we might be born again. We are new creations. And we are assured of heaven when we turn ourselves, totally and without reservation, over to him. More than that, we can live in the Kingdom of God now, while here. He has opened the door for us to receive grace. Abundant life! We do not have to work. We can't work at a thing. Our good works are as filthy rags. All we can hope to do is serve him out of a grateful heart. But to those who have received Him, He has given the right—the right, mind you—to be called children of God. And that is what we are!"

"But the Catholic Church insists upon many, many things. I fear that I have endangered my immortal soul by neglecting confession and not going to mass," the older man's passion drew the truth out of Johann.

"Johann, do you know that Jesus is your savior?"

"The church says that He is."

Richard rocked forward again, emphasizing each word by a finger poking Johann over his heart, "But what do you say, man? Who is He to you?"

"I suppose that I am not sure. I believe in God. I do know that." Johann felt as if he had failed some test and disappointed the older man.

"Well, do not fret," Richard leaned back in his chair. "It will come, it will come."

The words left Johann wondering what exactly he was talking about. Luisa joined them and Johann moved to the keyboard. He felt like a challenge, so plunged into his piano concerto in C major, playing both the orchestra and piano solo parts, leaving out only what was necessary because of the limitation of ten fingers. Luisa wept at the beauty of the slow movement, hiding her tears from her father and Johann by turning away from them in her chair. Who was this gifted man whom God had placed in their living room? How had he come to be here with them in the great expanse of North Carolina? She left the room quickly before either could notice her dabbing her eyes with her apron.

After, Richard walked with Johann to the path, as usual. The small lantern left them in a puddle of light surrounded by loudly singing crickets and frogs in the darkness.

"Johann, may I pray for you?"

This made the younger man instantly uneasy, but how could he refuse? He had only experienced prayer in the formality of a church setting. He tensed as Richard grasped his shoulder.

"Lord, I thank you for this man and his gift of music. Please, Lord, help him to see You, help him to come into the sure knowledge that he is Your child. May he repent of anything that stands between him and You, Lord."

Tears fell from his eyes as Johann felt the warmth from Richard's hand move into his chest. Something reminded him of being a child again and feeling secure and safe. Richard continued to say something, but it was so quiet that Johann couldn't hear. Finally, he spoke up again.

"Lord, we praise you. You alone, Lord Jesus, are our God. I ask you to extend the mercy of salvation and the gift of repentance to Johann. In the name of the one true God, Jesus Christ."

Johann mumbled his thanks and hurried toward his own dark home. The tears refused to stop and caused him to stumble on the path. The warm, safe feeling filled his chest, and his mind was at peace, but he did not know how to make either stay. By the time he lay in his bed they were nearly gone. The only after effect was an instantaneous deep sleep that lasted all night.

CHAPTER 23
Salem
September 1793

U pon awakening, Johann had a very clear impression that he should see about obtaining some pupils. He had put it off long enough. His months of solitude were at an end. Going outside, he found Carl near the shed, tending to their chickens and goats. He couldn't know that Carl was at that very moment trying to decide how to tell the "master" that he needed to get up off his backside and earn some income.

"Carl, I am going into town. I am going to see about perhaps finding some music students to teach. Earn a bit of money." He turned too quickly to note the astonishment on Carl's face and started the walk into town to find his friend, Dr. Lansbach.

"Herr Doktor," Johann inclined his head in a small bow as he removed his tricorn hat upon entering the doctor's home which served also as his office.

"Herr Pertl! Look at you! How well you seem," the doctor stood to welcome his guest.

"I am feeling much improved, thanks to you and my Carl," Johann took the seat Dr. Lansbach pointed to.

"Are you here for a checkup? Are you feeling ill?"

"No, not at all. I do seek some advice, though. When we were at the tavern, you mentioned that perhaps there might be a need for my services here in Salem, as a music teacher."

"Of course, yes. There is a great need indeed," Dr. Lansbach nodded. "We in the Brethren value education greatly. You have seen how we begin to educate our children, both boys and girls, at a young age. The Boys School was founded very early on and a school for young girls in 1772, so they are quite well established. Of course, the community's desire is to have music lessons at both. It is important that all children have proper musical training for church and home. Some adults also wish to improve their skills and study for the enjoyment of it at every age."

"I am settled now in a home and have a fortepiano, purchased from Charleston. Could you tell me how I might locate pupils? I do not know many of your kind townspeople."

The doctor thought for moment. "We have schools, actually, for both boys and girls, as I mentioned. There are also the Single Brothers' and Single Sisters' houses. But you may have interest from all age groups. Everyone here plays some instrument or sings. There are various types of musical offerings almost daily. I know, let me ask the Council. We have two councils, the Aeltester Conferenz, or Board of Elders, is responsible for the church and the Aufseher Collegium, or Supervising Board, watches over the financial and practical needs of Salem. I have friends on both."

Johann left, thanking the doctor for his help as Lansbach promised to let him know something soon. There did indeed seem to be the potential for a number of music lessons in his future. He met Carl who was carrying a box with some strange sounds coming from it. "More chickens," was his explanation. A few buildings down and Carl stopped briefly to speak to a man selling a few pigs and chickens. As Carl pulled a coin from his pocket, the man turned and appeared to stuff something into a burlap sack, something that protested loudly. "Rooster," Carl explained, handing the bag to Johann to carry. He held it at arm's length as they walked home together.

Early the next evening, a knock on the door heralded Dr. Lansbach's presence. He was at first alarmed by Johann's bloodshot eyes and lethargic manner. "Are you quite well, Herr Pertl?" he asked in concern.

Johann looked surprised, until he realized why the doctor had asked. "Yes, quite well, except for having been awakened hours before dawn by that cursed crowing. Excuse me, sir, the language. Carl purchased chickens and a rooster who sounds like a banshee."

Dr. Lansbach laughed, "Well, if you have hens, you must have one of those, too."

They settled into the two wooden chairs in the mostly empty sitting room.

"I have news and I hope it's acceptable to you."

Johann wondered what he meant.

"The Aufseher Collegium said that this matter of your teaching must be taken up with the Aeltester Conferenz also, since it would affect our youngsters. They are certainly very open to your working among us, even excited about it. But there are certain requirements."

"Go on?" Johann encouraged him.

The doctor looked down, "I hope you do not interpret this as an insult, but only as the desire of this group of men to protect the youngest among us. They would like to interview you about your religious beliefs."

Johann was taken aback.

"And they would like you to audition for them."

"Audition? Do you mean give them a free concert?" A trace of the great musician's pride flared up at what would previously have been a grievous insult.

"Oh, no, just perhaps one piece. I am sorry if I have given any offense, but as I said before, everyone here has some bit of musical training. They simply want to hear for themselves that you can do a better job than they themselves could," the doctor stumbled in his haste to get out the apologetic words.

"Please, friend, if I may call you so, do not worry. I understand. You have been nothing but helpful and I thank you." Johann recalled himself and his situation. The request was totally reasonable.

"They wish to hear you in the Congregational Hall. There is the Board of Elders, about twelve, and the Council, about fifteen, then there is also the Grosse Helfer Conferenz, the advisors of the other two groups."

This was sounding more and more like a free public concert. But what choice did he have?

"I will, of course, make myself available whenever they would like."

"Tomorrow?" The poor doctor winced in apology.

So, he would have to recite the catechism and perform something, though he had not seriously practiced in longer than he could remember. He flexed his fingers unconsciously.

"Yes, certainly," Johann responded. *Why not?*

The doctor took his leave, telling him to come to the Congregational Hall around 7 p.m. Johann headed into the kitchen to inform Carl about what he would face the next evening. The blonde giant shrugged as he continued to chop cabbage, "Good."

"Good?" Johann's eyebrows shot up at his lack of reaction. "A performance after all this time?"

"I know who you are," Carl stated as the cabbage hit the boiling water.

"And an inquisition about Lord knows what. I'm glad that one of us has no concern about it."

Carl grinned as Johann left to decide what to play for his audition.

Dr. Lansbach waited in the street before the Gemeinhaus the next evening, anxious that his friend arrive on time. At least fifty of the residents of Salem, all of them wielding some type of authority, waited inside. Many had invited their wives. He wouldn't be surprised if more than a hundred souls would hear Johann tonight and he dearly hoped the little Austrian would not miss many notes.

Johann arrived fifteen minutes early, to the doctor's relief. He wore a plain brown coat over a yellowish waistcoat. His clothing was clean and new but had given him a few moments of worry when he contrasted it with the fine coats and brilliant colors he had favored when performing for European royalty. That man was dead and this one needed students. He smiled in greeting at Dr. Lansbach's obvious excitement.

"Welcome, welcome. Many are here, but the Board of Elders would like to speak with you privately first." The doctor wondered that Johann had brought no musical scores with him.

"About my beliefs?"

"Yes, come with me." He led Johann into the large building, straight to the back into a warm room with a large table. Twelve men, both young and old, stopped their conversations as the pair entered.

"Gentlemen, may I present Herr Johann Pertl? He desires to teach music lessons here among us." And with that, Dr. Lansbach left Johann alone before them.

One of the older men stood, "Welcome, Herr Pertl. We are glad to see that you are in health. Please, sit here." He offered a chair in the middle of one of the long table's sides.

"I am Brother Kleinbeck, one of the pastors here," the older man continued, then gave the name of each man around the table in turn. "Please, tell us where you are from and what brings you here?"

His voice was warm and welcoming, hardly the inquisitor Johann had imagined beforehand.

"Thank you. I am Johann Pertl, Austrian by birth. I studied music in Salzburg and Vienna." He noticed several heads nod. Perhaps they were aware of the quality of the musical life in his home cities.

"I became ill several years ago and traveled, seeking cures." He had come up with this explanation earlier in the afternoon. "My servant, Carl Bauer, was with me. He learned about Salem from friends of his in Philadelphia. We thought that perhaps such a place and climate might help me. And, it has, though I credit good Dr. Lansbach more with my improved health than I do the pleasant climate."

Several smiles and nods.

"Good, good," Brother Kleinbeck responded, "We are always glad to hear good news such as that. And now you desire to stay?"

"Yes, if it pleases this group," Johann struck a humble note, one he was well familiar with in his dealings with the crowned heads of Europe.

"And are you a Christian, sir?" another of the men, whose name Johann had forgotten, asked quietly.

"I was baptized in the Holy Catholic Church," Johann continued. He was brought up to believe that baptism assured salvation, even if carried out on a newly born infant. "My parents raised me and my sister according to the strictest tenets of that faith. I have endeavored to continue in the teachings throughout my life, attending mass and confession." He thought of the Pope conferring upon him the Order of the Golden Spur and the numerous services in St. Stephens, Vienna's grandest cathedral, for which he had provided music.

"And do you believe that Jesus is the Son of God and Lord Incarnate?"

Johann wasn't sure who had asked that, and he blinked several times before responding, "I do." That was what he was supposed to say, wasn't it? He hoped that he would not be asked to recite the commandments, though he could easily do some of the prayers, if asked.

Brother Kleinbeck spoke again, "Herr Pertl, we are certainly welcoming of those who come from the various organizations of our Christian faith. We have Methodists and Quakers living in our town and, though no other Catholics that I am aware of, we certainly welcome you. We have the Ten Commandments and a Christian understanding of morality in common. Thank you for allowing us this time."

And, with that, the interview was over. Johann was escorted back to the large room by the door. The rows of seats facing a single pianoforte at the front of the hall comforted him. This he knew, this was home. Plain and unadorned, it still felt like a concert hall.

"May I?" he asked Brother Kleinbeck, pointing to the keyboard after being led to the front. Receiving a nod, he sat and ran through a few scales, both to warm up and check the tuning. It was satisfactory.

"Brothers and sisters," the good brother addressed the crowd, who stopped speaking. "It is my great honor to present to you Herr Johann Pertl. He comes to us all the way from Austria and wishes to teach music here among us. We of the Board see no moral failing in him and he has said that he believes that Jesus is his Lord. Please, allow him to show us what he knows of music."

Johann had decided beforehand to play his last published D major sonata. The young man so full of himself, so convinced of the superiority of his musical sensibilities in every way, was gone. In the past, he would have pridefully stopped playing and glared at the audience if anyone dared to speak or made a noise. But his time away from music had humbled him and he waited patiently while fixing his eyes on the keyboard for the room to quiet. He hoped only that he would meet whatever standards the assembly before him required. As soon as he had quiet, he began.

Nothing existed but him and the music. He appreciated their sensibility in not applauding between movements, taking only a short pause to breathe and allow a shift in mood and tempo. He finished the Allegretto, the third movement, and the notes died in the silent hall. He could not help himself from turning to them. No applause now? Had they disliked it?

He was very close to the first row. His friend Richard sat just in front of him, tears streaming down both cheeks. Brother Kleinbeck sat beside him and looked stunned. Then, blinking and clearing his throat, he stood to his feet and began to clap. That broke the strange silence, and all jumped up to join in. Johann stood and bowed, his left hand on the fortepiano.

Brother Kleinbeck turned and motioned for the others to sit. "Thank you, sir, thank you. I do not know when I have– Might you play another?"

There were enthusiastic shouts of "yes, yes" and applause. Smiling, Johann returned to the keyboard and entertained them with three more sonatas, one by his friend Haydn and two of his own. Perhaps he would not have to worry about enticing enough pupils to provide a livable income after all.

One of the councilmen who oversaw practical matters suggested that Herr Pertl entertain visitors tomorrow afternoon for the purpose of scheduling lessons. This served to relieve the crush of people who surrounded him, pressing in to get his attention and commitment to a lesson time.

When the crowd cleared away, Richard remained. "I thought I would walk back with you, since it is on my way."

"I would be glad of the company, sir," Johann spoke truthfully. He always wanted friends and family around after a performance, to ease the transition back into normal life.

"Would you be willing to give Luisa lessons?" Richard began the conversation.

"Of course, but I would not accept payment," Johann answered. "I think she plays well, though, I do not know..."

"She needs to work on something other than the house and me," Richard interrupted him. "I worry about her. She is very smart, and I think somewhat talented?"

Johann nodded in agreement.

"But she has buried herself in that house with me, an old man. Music gives her such joy. I would be grateful, sir."

"Then it is settled. Do you think that most of the people tonight were satisfied with the performance?" Johann was not fishing for a compliment. Like most musicians, he had a distorted view of his own performances, focusing inordinately on small mistakes or effects that perhaps did not come off as hoped.

"You will have more requests for lessons than you could ever teach," Richard predicted. He privately thought it would do the young man immense good to get to work within his calling. No one who recognized his prodigious musical talent could deny that God had gifted Johann in an extraordinary measure.

Johann did not know if that really pleased him or not. It seemed that he was entering life and work again, out of necessity. His mind raced back to the last year of his old life, in Vienna. He remembered his last concert, in early March, when he had premiered his Bb major piano concerto. Then the rest of that year was spent under a crushing load of composition, trying to earn enough to keep sending *her* to the spa in Baden. How he had missed her! He had been mortified, having to borrow money from friends to fund her apartment there and keep up the place in the city as well. A thick cloud of depression had settled over him six months before the illness struck in November. He remembered then believing it was because he missed his beloved so, but now he could recall signs that should have warned him of her infidelity, her blatant use of him, her deception. Anger threatened to overwhelm him, and the familiar black hand gripped his heart. He would give anything to exact some sort of revenge, hurt her for her humiliation of him.

"Johann," a quiet voice pulled him back to the peaceful Salem night.

"Yes?"

"You are the finest musician I have ever heard. So much spirit and grace in your playing! I bid you goodnight. Are you quite all right?" Richard couldn't help but worry about the younger man and these black moods that could overtake him from out of nowhere. He prayed for him daily. Sometimes it seemed that there was a storm before breakthrough, as if the devil himself tried to discourage those whom the Lord was wooing.

Johann was abrupt, "Yes, goodnight."

He was taken aback by the words "spirit and grace," the same that his rival Muzio Clementi had applied to his playing almost 15 years earlier when the Austrian Emperor Joseph II had forced them into an insane contest of musical abilities on Christmas Eve of 1781. The contest, which pitted him against the visiting Italian keyboard virtuoso, officially ended in a draw, but the Emperor was pleased to collect some private winnings from side bets as everyone agreed that Mozart had won. Remembering himself, Johann realized his rudeness to Richard, who had only been kind to him. He added "I think I am quite tired. Forgive me. The evening has required a lot."

"Indeed."

CHAPTER 24

Salem
December 1793

His favorite pupil came on Saturday evenings. Luisa, accompanied by her father for propriety's sake, brought joy with her. She practiced diligently for each lesson, but that was not the reason he enjoyed her so. Something else, her gentleness and exclamations over his musical ideas perhaps? Whatever the cause, she was his reward after each week of 50 or 60 lessons.

It really was not so terrible, teaching children. Luisa was his oldest pupil and the youngest were six or seven. These Moravian children were very well behaved and always respectful. He had taught primarily adults, even accomplished musicians, before. He supposed there was no harm in training the little ones in the right ways from an early age. And the income helped tremendously.

There were no music books to be had, at least, not for beginners. He wrote things out for his pupils, remembering the painstaking guidance his father had taken with him from his earliest memory. A great teacher, but unable to let his son grow into adulthood. Johann still carried the pain of that broken relationship. However, he had laid a solid musical foundation in his son, and it enabled him to write many valuable exercises for young students.

Early one Saturday evening, Johann concluded Luisa's lesson. They turned to see Richard soundly asleep in a chair in the next room and smiled at each other.

"He did not sleep well last night," Luisa explained.

"Well, let's not wake him yet then. Could I offer you some refreshment?" Johann was unused to playing the host.

"Water would be welcome, thank you."

He took a pitcher from the kitchen counter and headed out the back door to fill it from the pump. After locating a couple of mugs, he set them on the small kitchen table and motioned for her to take a seat. They could hear her father's snores from the sitting room beyond.

Uncomfortable silence settled over them. The time they had spent together had been in playing music, not talking. Neither knew what to say.

Johann began, "Did you like that new..."

At the same time, Luisa spoke, "I much like that new..."

Their eyes met as they laughed.

"My father enjoys your company very much," Luisa relaxed a little.

"And I his," Johann responded. "Have you been... has it just been you and your father for a very long time?" He was curious about her history.

"Yes, my mother passed away years ago. I was 15."

"I have also lost my parents," he said. "And I was closer to my mother than my father, though he taught me music. For that I will always be grateful."

Luisa sensed that there were things unsaid there. His next question startled her.

"And there were no suitors?"

At her surprised expression he continued, "Forgive me. I do not mean to be so forward or personal."

"No, that is fine," she lowered her eyes. "It's been a very long time." Her voice carried a sad note.

"I was to be promised," she continued.

His raised eyebrows betrayed his surprise in turn, as he had not thought her to have ever planned a life apart from that of her father.

"I was 16. It was just one year after my mother had gone to her eternal home. There was a young man who was preparing for the ministry. His parents and my father spoke, and an agreement was reached."

Johann waited and she gathered herself.

"We were well matched, or so I thought," she smiled at her 16-year-old dreams. "And he did profess his... well, he told me he cared for me a great deal." This was hard, but she wanted Johann to know the truth. She could see Paul's tall frame and earnest brown eyes as he had confessed his conviction to her that they should be together. He didn't use the word "love," but she had no doubt that the sentiment was there.

"Several months before we were to wed, some missionaries came to Salem. They were of the brethren and passed through on their way to Charleston. They planned to sell themselves into slavery in the islands to the south."

"What? Why in the world?" Johann had heard of the sugar plantations in these islands, Saint Thomas and others. Sugar plantations built by the forced labor of African people stolen from their homelands. He despised the practice, but knew it was spreading, even to the areas around Salem.

"You see, the slaves who work there, who have no freedom and no hope, are sore in need of the gospel. No one can take it to them. These missionaries decided that, if the only way to carry the good news of our Lord to these wretched souls was to become one with them, they would do it. The service would pale in the light of their future reward and the potential to reach so many of these poor people was worth the sacrifice. After all, was it not like the sacrifice of our Lord, leaving Heaven itself to live among us miserable creatures?"

"I had not thought of it this way," Johann was stunned that these men would willingly give up their entire lives for their faith.

"And Paul felt God wanted him to join them," she spoke this last quietly, folding her hands in her lap.

"I am so sorry..." his heart broke for what this must have meant for her at such a tender age.

"No," she raised a hand to stop him. "I believe he was right. Of course, it was difficult at the time. I was just a girl. But I fled to my Lord, who comforted me much. He assured me that he had a different purpose for me, and that I could show my love for Paul by praying for his success among the mistreated slaves of the islands. I do so still."

Johann wondered if her love for this Paul continued. She had to think of him much if she spent time in prayer for him as she said. And why should he be concerned about that, he asked himself sternly.

"And soon after he left, my father became somewhat ill. If I had married and started a new family, who would have cared for him? God knew. I had a different place, a different purpose for myself, here by my father." She looked toward Richard, who was beginning to stir.

"I believe your life, though undeniably one of sadness and loss, shows your character clearly. You are a loyal, faithful woman. I know you will be rewarded as such," Johann was uncharacteristically direct in his evaluation of her story.

"Where is everyone?" Richard's voice came from the sitting room.

"Father, you were asleep," Luisa stood and moved to his side.

"Lesson over?" Richard asked.

Johann nodded, "Yes, and a fine one it was, too."

He watched the two walk away arm in arm. So, he was not the only one suffering from pain and disappointment in his past. Luisa seemed to handle it with more grace and resignation than he had ever seen. Truly, her character was like gold refined in the fire, he thought as he headed to his bed.

Carl was not yet in that night. He had taken their horse to Bethabara. They had enough money now to support one, and Carl had found a mare in the town about to be put down because of a cough. Her owner gave her to the young man at no cost, shaking his head over the stranger's interest in a sick animal. Carl named her Magda, healed her within a week, and was rewarded with a fine, sturdy helper. She was his pet and followed him like a loyal dog. Johann didn't begrudge him the beast. After all, the man had saved his life many times over and supported both of them for most of a year on this farm.

Carl was deeply in love with Greta. He still spent hours with her and Peter on Saturdays, and their plans took concrete shape. Peter believed that next April would be the most fortuitous time for their journey. He had been working for extra money, which he saved, and had begun to stockpile tools and farm implements of his own as he was able to barter or purchase them. There was only one thing still undecided, in Carl's mind.

Would Greta marry him? The three would truly be a family then. A married couple, journeying to create a new home, would be welcomed anywhere. Single men on their own might be suspect, and he would never want to tarnish Greta's reputation, even among strangers. He couldn't bring himself to just come out and ask her, so the three went along as if nothing had changed.

And every time he returned to Salem for his week's work, he chided himself for not letting Herr Pertl in on his plans. Honestly, the town was growing and there were men to hire to help with the farm. His friend, his master, was teaching music now, not moping around in anger about his past wife. A paper mill had opened, and he was writing music again, too. He could think of many reasons that Johann would be fine without him, but never got up the courage to even hint that he might leave in four or five months.

Since there was money now for more than just the essentials, Johann purchased quite a bit of paper from Herr Shober's mill. The first thing he wrote out was not a new composition, but the flute part for his flute and harp concerto. He presented it to Luisa at a Saturday lesson.

"I hoped that perhaps we could try this on Tuesday?" he suggested. Their Tuesday evening meals followed by music had continued.

"Yes, of course," Luisa looked over the page eagerly. "Did you write this?"

He hated to lie but wasn't ready to disclose to anyone the extent of his musical abilities. "I heard it performed several years ago. I think I remember it well enough to put together an accompaniment."

"Good, Father will love it," and she gathered her music to leave.

"Luisa," Johann glanced over at Richard, dozing in a chair. Gazing directly into her large brown eyes he said, "I do look forward to it also."

She smiled and her eyes lingered on his. Reluctantly, she turned away and gently shook her father awake. As Johann saw them to the door, he began to berate himself. What was he doing? He was married. Was he now looking to become an adulterer? A bigamist? He disgusted himself. Best to put all thoughts along those lines out of his head. Besides, she was totally devoted to her father. Richard had said so, early on. And she had to be 15 years younger than him. No, he needed to concentrate on teaching. Forget the rest.

Next Tuesday's dinner was outstanding. More meat was available, now that it was fall, and Luisa had created a feast of pork with onions and apples, squash, and white cabbage. The men retired to the sitting room and their conversation turned to religion, as it usually did. Johann was curious about some more Moravian beliefs.

"So, what would you say are the basic tenets of the Brethren's faith?" Johann asked, once they were settled.

"That our Lord Jesus was born of a virgin, lived a sinless life, was crucified for our sins, and rose again for our salvation," Richard never tired of answering his questions.

"But all the traditions I see," Johann continued as Luisa entered. "The pink ribbon on her bonnet. Is that necessary for the Christian life?"

"Absolutely not. We have used our minds, in prayer to the Almighty, to seek wisdom in how to live, and we believe Christian community is His will for us. These small things only serve to organize and help us but are not essentials."

"Well, I think that your daughter is intent upon playing something new for you," Johann rose to go to the keyboard as Luisa blew air into the cold wooden flute. She placed the page of music he had given her last week on top of the fortepiano. Johann had none, but they were used to him playing without it.

At the concerto's end, Richard could not say enough. "My dear man, that slow movement is enough to make the angels weep. This is truly a masterpiece. Who wrote it?"

"I heard it a few years ago," Johann told him, "By some German composer, I suppose."

"Well, it is truly remarkable. Could I possibly hear it again?"

Luisa laughed and countered, "Perhaps just the slow movement? I am a little tired, Poppa."

Johann obliged by performing it with her once more. She formed the musical phrases expertly, playing even more poignantly than the first time. He smiled to think that perhaps his teaching was affecting her musicianship after all.

Later, on the way home, Richard broached a different subject.

"As you are aware, Christmas is next Wednesday, and we have some very lovely celebrations around it. I know you are not keen on the idea of coming with us to our church, but what about for this special occasion? We have a Love Feast on Tuesday, Christmas Eve, with coffee and buns, lots of singing. Why don't you come with us? It is your regular night to visit anyway."

Christmas. He had dearly loved celebrating it with his family and the thought of spending it alone stirred up some familiar self-pity.

"I would be honored," he replied.

"Thank you. It will make Luisa happy. She worries about all the time you spend by yourself."

So, Johann spent the walk home pleasantly contemplating the thought of Luisa worrying about him.

Carl spent the Sunday before Christmas in Bethabara. Since acquiring Magda, his sweet-natured brown mare, he had been able to arrive in time to attend services with Peter and Greta. He wasn't sure that he understood all the pastor spoke of there, but it made his friends happy and gave him more time with them.

After the noon meal, Peter had to see to some emergency at the mill. Greta and Carl sat in a small room in the house where she worked. The lady of the house liked Carl, who was always willing to jump up and take heavy loads from her or help her husband with the animals. She suspected that he was more to Greta than just her brother's friend. Since the weather had turned cold, she gave them permission to use a small study beside their large living area. A fire kept the place cozily warm and inviting.

"How did you find the service this morning?" Greta asked.

"Good, very good. I like the music and all the German singing. Sometimes my mouth gets tired of trying to speak English."

Greta laughed. "I know what you mean! What did you think of Pastor Jarvis's message?"

Truthfully, he could not remember. "Good, also good."

Greta was frustrated at Carl's refusal to speak about faith. He seemed so shallow about it at times. And she was frustrated with herself for loving him anyway.

Peter returned and the three spent a few hours talking about pleasant dreams for their future. After Carl retrieved

Magda from the barn and headed back to Salem, Greta went into the kitchen to see if Frau Jarvis needed help.

"So, how was the time with your young man?" the older woman asked, eyes twinkling.

"It was all right," Greta answered, grabbing a bowl that needed washing.

"All right? That sounds like not such a good time at all."

"I guess not. I mean, I very much enjoy seeing him. But he never talks seriously."

"Hmm—seriously?"

"Well, I asked him about Brother Jarvis's message this morning and it is as if the words just slid off him like water off a duck's back." Greta's tone betrayed her irritation.

"Greta," Frau Jarvis faced her and took the bowl from her, set it on the counter, then grabbed her soapy hands in both of hers. "I know that you care for this Carl. No, look at me. But I think that he has not yet given himself to the Lord Jesus. If he does not, you cannot be unequally yoked with him."

Greta looked at her questioningly.

"You cannot marry a man who does not believe as you. It is strictly forbidden and would bring you much misery besides," the older woman's words were full of authority.

"Yes, you are right," Greta agreed, though the pain felt like a knife in her heart.

"Now go on to bed. We have a lot to do in the morning. Christmas is coming!"

That night Greta prayed and cried herself to sleep, telling God that she would do what He wanted and asking Him to help her forget Carl, if he was not for her.

The Gutmans came by Johann's house on Tuesday evening in a carriage. They used it so rarely that Johann didn't realize they owned one. It was a blessing, though, in the late December cold. He wore his best coat, a golden-brown linsey-woolsey that his newfound teacher's income had allowed him to purchase. None of the Moravian men wore anything like the bright colors fashionable in Viennese society, which he used to prefer. That kind of posturing seemed so vain and useless to him now.

Richard saw Carl in the sitting room window. "Isn't your friend coming?" he asked Johann. Having not even considered it, he replied that he guessed not.

"Well, ask him. We have another seat here. No one should be alone on Christmas Eve."

Carl was stunned at the invitation, but quickly made himself presentable. Richard, always radiating interest in others, kept a lively conversation going on the short trip into town. He explained how a Lovefeast was kept in the spirit of the Agape feasts and meals of the early church described in Acts. The point was fellowship, harmony, and the strengthening of communal bonds. The two men sitting across from him forgot their own worries and began to look forward to the event to come.

The four entered the congregation hall, where Johann had performed his audition. Many chairs were set up and a brass ensemble regaled those entering with hymns Johann had never heard. He found himself sitting between Richard and Carl while Luisa left to join the single women's area across the aisle. He could still see her, though, and his eyes kept wandering to her in her seat with the older single women.

The service began officially with a choir's rendition of *Rejoice, Rejoice, Believers.* Johann was entranced with the new hymns. He was glad to hear at last the small instrumental group that Richard had spoken of—violins, a viola, clarinets, bassoons, and horn. Though not up to the standard of the professional orchestras of his past life, they certainly acquitted themselves well. They accompanied the singers and performed some instrumental selections on their own.

Several young women began to serve buns to the seated congregation, followed by others passing out steaming mugs of milky coffee. The instruments continued to play as people enjoyed the refreshments and spoke quietly with one another. Then the young women circulated again, this time passing out beeswax candles with red ribbons tied to them. Other lights were darkened as these candles were lit, producing a beautiful effect. A young child stood alone at the front and sang about the "morning star." The congregation sang the lines back to the child, then all ended in unison.

The service was over, but no one was anxious to leave the hall. Musicians were providing background music as quiet voices and laughter filled the room. Richard was telling Johann and Carl how the red ribbon on the candles symbolized Christ's sacrificial love when a hand grasped Johann's arm.

"Herr Pertl?" It was Pastor Kleinbeck, whom he had not seen since his audition in September. "I do hate to impose, but several of us here were wondering if you might also help us to celebrate this most holy evening?"

For a moment, Johann was confused. Then he understood. "By playing something?"

Bro. Kleinbeck nodded enthusiastically.

"Of course."

Walking to the fortepiano, he wondered what would be appropriate and thought of the Christmas Cantata by the elder Bach, the composer he respected above all others. But he had no orchestra, no singers. He settled upon playing a theme from the work followed by variations that he made up on the spot. Bach's music was intellectually challenging and the task to which he had set himself required his utmost concentration. He was unaware that the voices in the room had stopped, and most had returned to their seats to listen. Finishing with quiet reverence, he realized that all eyes were upon him. He stood, gave a brief nod, and returned to his place by Richard, among a sea of heartfelt thank you's. He was gratified that he was able to be a part of things.

On the ride home, Richard invited them both to the Christmas service in the morning, promising them a more traditional format, complete with sermon. Luisa told her father that she would have more than enough prepared for Christmas dinner. Carl begged to be excused, as he was expected in Bethabara, but Johann again felt grateful not to be alone on such a day. The simplicity of the evening's service had touched him more deeply than some of the grandest masses in Vienna or Rome. He wondered at the changes in himself.

Early on Christmas morning, Carl headed to Bethabara to attend the service there. Magda felt frisky in the cold, and he made it in record time. The music and singing stirred him deeply, and he could watch Greta sitting with the single women without even turning his head. The sermon was about God's love and being willing to step out into it, just as Mary and Joseph had done. He felt courage rising within him to finally ask Greta what he needed to ask her.

Stepping outside with Peter afterward, he drew his friend apart. "May I have some time alone with Greta? On the walk home?"

Peter agreed easily and wondered what Carl was up to. As his sister joined them, he made his excuses and told the pair to go on ahead.

Now was the time, Carl knew it. As soon as they had distanced themselves from the crowd lingering in front of the church, Carl stopped.

"Greta, I need to speak with you."

Rather than the excitement she had imagined at these words, Greta felt deep sorrow as he led her to large log that served as a bench under a maple tree beside the church.

"I would like to marry you, Greta. I truly would." He seemed like a little boy in his shyness. It must have taken all his courage to ask her.

Feeling as if she were pronouncing a death sentence, she spoke the words that she knew she must.

"No, Carl, I cannot. I am sorry. I am very, very sorry," she held her hand to her mouth as tears started to fall. She couldn't gain control of herself to add anything more. Leaving him stunned, she jumped up and practically ran to the Jarvis's home. How could she ever forget the stricken look on his face?

Peter caught up to Carl. Surprised to find him alone and obviously upset, he asked "Where is Greta?"

"She left. I offended her."

"I don't believe that!" Peter exclaimed. Though she had never spoken of it, he knew the depth of his sister's feelings for Carl. "What happened?"

Anger took over. He practically shouted, "I asked her to marry me, understand? And she refused. I am going back to Salem." Peter watched Carl march away to the stable in disbelief. This could not be right. He needed to talk to her. Quickly.

CHAPTER 25
Salem
January 1794

O n the second Sunday after Christmas, Carl headed
into the cold morning air to see to the animals. He
had worked at great length to fill all the holes he could find
in the stable walls and spread extra straw last night, but he
had no doubt that he would have to break the ice in the
water troughs this morning. Since Greta's rejection, he had
been working like a man possessed, trying to keep his hope-
less thoughts at bay. He was not entirely successful, but he
did not know what else to do. He felt like his life and happiness had ended once more.

Johann woke up and was surprised when Carl came in
the back door. This was the second Sunday that he had not
set out right at dawn to visit his friends. The two men had a
comfortable camaraderie but rarely spoke of more than the
day-to-day running of the house and farm. Deciding that
something was going on, Johann asked him about it while
Carl was heating some cornmeal mush for their breakfast.

"So, you are not going to Bethabara today?" Johann
poured himself coffee. He would teach an infinite number
of toddlers their notes if it would assure him of always being
able to purchase coffee.

"No." Carl threw a spoon forcefully into a bucket of water.

"Are your friends quite well?" He refused to let the younger man off so easily.

"I don't know. I suppose so." Carl practically threw the bowls onto the table.

Johann sat, holding a coffee mug with both hands, soaking in the warmth and studied his friend. Quietly he asked, "Carl, what is the matter? Something here is not right."

Before the blonde giant could answer, there was a knock at their front door. Wondering who could possibly be here this early, on a Sunday when the entire town spent the whole day in church, Johann went to answer it. The young man standing there looked vaguely familiar, but he could not place him.

"Herr Pertl? I am Peter Antes. Is Carl here?"

There was a loud crash from the kitchen. The two looked at each other.

"Yes, he is. I am glad to meet you, Mr. Antes, please come in."

He offered Peter a seat by the fortepiano and returned to the kitchen to find Carl bent over, bracing himself with his hands against a wooden table. A broken bowl and mush lay on the floor.

"Carl, you must go to your guest. I will take care of this."

Reluctantly, Carl straightened up, gave him a cold stare, and headed to the sitting room. Just seconds later, Johann heard the front door close. Sighing, he looked for a rag to clean up the mess.

The two began walking into town, but before Peter and Carl got to the tavern, the fireworks began.

"Why are you here?" Carl spat out the words.

"Why do you think? We haven't seen you in two weeks."

"And that should please Greta very well."

Peter was ready to face this, the crux of the matter.

"Carl, do you know why she refused you?"

Carl stopped and stared at him, his face a picture of pain.

Peter exhaled and put a hand on his shoulder. "Come, let's find somewhere warm to talk."

The tavern was not open to serve them, because it was the sabbath, but the owner welcomed them to seats at a corner table in bright sun while he went back to preparations for church.

"Carl, please listen. Greta is as upset as you are."

Carl looked at him and snorted, "I cannot believe that."

"Just listen. The reason that she refused you is that she is not sure of where you stand with God. She loves you, believe me."

"What?" Carl sat upright in his chair and stared in disbelief at Peter. This was the last thing he had expected to hear. During his sleepless nights, he had rehearsed his faults, his awkwardness with people, his nose that was too big, his general stupidity all around. Greta had probably been wise in rejecting him, though that thought pierced his heart with a crippling pain. He never imagined God entered into this.

"Remember when we told you months ago that both of us—at different times, but both of us—had turned our lives over to our living Savior?"

Carl nodded. Could this have ruined his chances for marriage? Perhaps she believed she was to be a nun?

"We study God's word now. We try to live according to it as best we can." Peter stopped, praying silently for the right words. "Greta is not free to marry as she pleases."

"What do you mean?" Was she now somehow in bondage to these people, this church? He feared the worst.

"In the Bible, it says clearly that we are not to be 'unequally yoked.' A Christian cannot marry someone who is not."

"But I am a Christian," Carl protested.

Peter spoke gently, "Carl, do you know what salvation is?"

"Not really, no."

"Do you know Jesus, in here?" He placed a flat hand on his chest.

"I don't understand these things." The blonde giant shook his head, then hid his face in his hands in defeat. He had attended mass in Dürnstadt, but only remembered the proper times for standing and kneeling, the way to accept the wafer, and being bored as the priest droned on in Latin. Some of the paintings in the church were interesting to look at, but he never really understood what was going on.

Peter sat back, hands on the table, and smiled. "Let me explain it."

He launched into God's plan at the beginning, how Adam and Eve sinned and threw away fellowship with the Almighty by their disobedience, how God provided the only way back to himself by sending his Son. Jesus lived perfectly sinlessly, then gave himself up for us who could not. Each person had to accept that, accept him, by faith. Then would begin a relationship with a loving God which would last for eternity.

The tavern owner and his family walked by on their way out the door. He approached to ask the two men to leave but heard what Peter as saying. The owner nodded when his eyes met Peter's, giving silent permission to stay, and they slipped quietly by. Carl was entranced by Peter's words and never saw them exit.

"So, what should I do?" He unwittingly asked the question the people asked the Apostle Peter in Acts 2. His heart has been pierced, Peter thought to himself.

"Let's return to your farm. You can get some warmer clothes and saddle Magda. Then come with me to Bethabara. We can talk to our pastor there." Peter had only been in the faith for a short time and wasn't totally assured of his abilities in evangelism.

Johann was surprised to see the two men again, quieter and on much better terms with each other. Carl told him he would return that evening and two set out. He had traveled this road many times, always with Greta first in his thoughts. This time was different. He was uncomfortable, longing for something, yet was strangely at peace at the same time. He couldn't get there fast enough.

Carl and Peter arrived as the church service was still underway. They stabled their horses and found some bread and butter inside. Before long, the family and Greta returned. She nodded to Carl, then quickly ran upstairs. Last to enter was Pastor Jarvis. Peter rose and spoke privately to him at the door.

"Carl?" Brother Jarvis approached, and Carl stood. They shook hands. "Come into my study. The ladies will fix us a meal and we can talk in the meantime."

Greta braced herself to go downstairs. She knew that Sister Jarvis needed her help, but she didn't want to walk by Carl again, didn't want to see his blue eyes with their sadness and accusation. What could be happening? Peter had said nothing, leaving before their meeting, which was very unusual. When she arrived downstairs, she saw that the men were elsewhere, which was a great relief. Her mistress told her they were talking in the study. She had a terrible time focusing on even the simplest tasks as they put pots of vegetables on to boil and bread by the fire to heat.

An hour later the meal was ready, and the three men entered the kitchen. Peter's face bore the widest grin she had ever seen. He looked directly at her and winked. *How strange!* Brother Jarvis had a hand on Carl's shoulder as they entered. *Also strange!* The tall blonde man gave her a long look with his blue eyes, but she did not see the angry furrowed brow she expected. Instead, his eyes locked on hers with no shadow of anger or hurt. Sister Jarvis called their six children and they all settled themselves at the table.

Brother Jarvis said grace and food was passed around. "Well, we have much to be grateful for today," he announced before taking a bite of potatoes.

What was going on? Greta felt near exploding. She kept her face turned away from Carl but felt his eyes on her.

"Our friend Carl here has just prayed to enter into a saving relationship with our Lord." He and Peter beamed at the table. Greta burst into tears and ran out of the room. Carl, swimming in a sea of peace such as he had never known, wondered now what he had done wrong, stood and went after her.

"He was very open. He just had never been told the truth," Brother Jarvis explained to a table now quietly chewing.

Greta was in the front room, sitting in one of the wooden side chairs, trying to regain her composure. Her heart stopped as Carl came in.

"I understand now," he bent one knee to the ground beside her chair. Taking her hand in his large ones, he continued. "Please forgive me for my stupidity. I did not know."

She silenced him with a quick kiss, their first. "I do love you, Carl, I do."

They returned to the table together. That afternoon, the couple spoke with Brother Jarvis, who counseled them to think of themselves as betrothed, but to wait for several months before marrying. He would take it up with the council of elders, whose responsibility it was to approve marriages in the community. Truthfully, he believed that Carl was sincere, but there might be those who would think that the young man's confession of faith was merely words to manipulate Greta into marrying him. In the pastor's estimation, those had been real tears of repentance, but it wouldn't hurt Carl to have some time to grow a bit.

It was a totally different man who rode back to Salem that evening.

CHAPTER 26
Salem
May 1794

M onths passed with the same Sunday visits to
Bethabara, but by May everything had changed.
All was finally in place. Carl returned to Salem late on the
first Sunday in May. Peter had purchased a wagon and a
horse; they had counted their savings and, if they were
careful, had enough money to last a year between them;
Brother Jarvis and the council agreed to marrying Greta and
Carl before they planned to leave; and just today God had
providentially given them a group to travel with. Some of
the Brethren from Pennsylvania were due to travel through
the area in a few weeks, headed west, and would be glad of
a few more men added to their number. Only one thing
remained: telling Johann.

Summer was a busy time on the farm. Carl had worked
as hard as possible, knowing that he might be leaving the
place without adequate care for some time. He planned to
advise Johann to hire a farmhand or two quickly, so the
crops and animals would not suffer. Catching him during
the rare times that he had no students, Carl had managed
to show him the basics about taking care of their chickens,

cow, mule, and Magda. There was no shortage of people to advise and assist the musician, Carl kept telling himself.

He saw a solitary candle's light coming from the sitting room as he entered the back door after bedding down Magda for the night. Why not tell him now? Everything was in place. They could not be surer of God's leading. Carl decided to act, while he was still full of the peace and joy his fellowship with Greta always gave him.

Johann sat at a desk, writing by the candle's light, deeply engrossed.

"You are still up, I see," Carl spoke quietly.

Johann sat back quickly, startled, then lay his quill down on a pewter plate. "Yes, just trying to finish this piece. I had no idea it was so late."

"May I speak with you?"

Johann tensed. This was very unlike his servant and companion, who could go a whole day speaking fewer than a handful of words. He wondered if something was amiss.

"Of course," he turned the desk chair completely around to face Carl, who sat on a wooden chair across the small room.

"I have some plans."

This must be about something to do with the fields or the animals, Johann decided.

"I am going to marry Greta in two weeks."

"Congratulations! That is excellent news." Johann was not surprised. He had surmised that something about the girl had been luring his servant-friend away on Sundays. His mind instantly jumped to some assumptions.

"Her talents in the kitchen will be welcome here. I'm sure we can find adequate furniture for the room you are in now," Johann continued.

"No, she will not come here."

Johann froze in his hasty plans for the couple's future.

"We have decided to move west, with Peter, her brother. He has things planned and we have some people to travel with. In a few weeks."

"What? What are you saying?" Johann's voice grew louder as anger took over. "This is not something I will allow! You cannot leave."

Carl stared at him.

"I won't hear of it. I'm going to bed. Just... think of another plan," and the small man stalked to his room.

After several hours of lying awake, the realization dawned that there was nothing he could do to stop Carl. This betrayal felt much like the one he had experienced two and a half years ago. He suspected he might be overreacting. Anger was easier to admit to than fear. Was this his destiny, to be totally alone?

After a week of tense silence, despite Carl trying to give Johann as much helpful instruction as possible, the young man resorted to the only help he could think of... Brother Gutman. Carl found a warm welcome at the Gutman house on a Saturday afternoon. He surprised them, as he had never come to their home without Johann before.

Sitting on the porch, sipping cool light ale provided by Luisa, Carl told the story of his friendship with Peter and Greta. Richard excitedly congratulated him when he heard of his conversion and baptism, then became ecstatic at the news of the impending wedding. He agreed totally that the hand of God was in this adventure. He also understood the pain that Johann must be suffering. Luisa's heart also ached for the musician.

"I do not know all that you and Herr Pertl suffered in your travels before landing here among us. He is not forthcoming about his life before," Richard began.

Carl nodded. He had vowed to never tell anyone his friend and master's secrets. He was a man of his word, though the opportunity had never been more tempting.

"But he has to understand that you are your own man. That is what this country is about, each man having the freedom to choose his own way. I will pray for him, Carl, and for you, and if I am given the opportunity, I will try to talk to him about it. I think that I can easily find a couple of young men from the Single Brothers' house who need to earn an income. Don't fear. I will keep an eye on Herr Pertl and the farm. You and your bride go forth and multiply!"

This last caused Carl to blush furiously. He finished the ale and left, thanking Richard, much relieved that someone would be checking on Johann.

The next day brought his final visit to Bethabara as Greta's suitor. In less than a week, they would marry and head out to a new home, new hopes. Carl and Peter discussed packing plans. Carl had been bringing his part of the supplies for the past several months. The group that they would join was expected by mid-week, so there would be no delay. Greta had news of a wedding gift from the Jarvis's. A cousin of Frau Jarvis owned a small home on the outskirts of town. She had to leave to help care for her ailing mother in Bethania for several weeks. Sister Jarvis had had no trouble in getting her to agree to let the newlywed couple stay there for a night or so, to have some privacy. The long trip ahead in a group of ten or twelve men certainly would not be conducive to marital intimacy. Greta giggled as she shared the news and watched Carl's face turn bright red. But he was thankful.

Carl left, agreeing to return on the following weekend. It was all planned: Friday for the wedding and a dinner, then a packing day on Saturday, a rest and church on Sunday, and the journey's start on Monday. Johann's bad moods faded into insignificance beside the joy and adventure ahead. Carl had done all that he could to prepare his master and the farm for getting on without him. He believed that God had brought them into each other's lives and now had different purposes for the two men. They would have to part ways. He was having a hard time letting go of a sense of responsibility for Johann, but it was time.

The first days of the week were no different. Despite a lengthy teaching from Richard about forgiveness on Tuesday evening at the Gutman's, Johann barely spoke. Carl approached him Thursday evening and spoke to his back.

"I will be leaving in the morning."

He saw Johann's shoulders sag. The little man turned and spoke quietly, "Then I suppose I must let you go."

Silence accompanied Carl to bed and excitement kept him awake. He arose before dawn, since he would have to walk this last trip to Bethabara while carrying a large load. Quickly, he gathered his things, stuffing them into a cloth bag that would be easy to swing over his shoulder. He thought of food, only because it was such a long way, so went into the kitchen to grab some bread. He did not see Johann anywhere. Picking up his load, he went out the front door into the street.

There stood Johann, holding a fully saddled Magda by her bridle. "Take her," he said.

Carl couldn't believe it. He took the offered reins.

"I don't know how to take care of her anyway," Johann added.

"Thank you, thank you." Carl was as touched by the kindness of his manner as by the gift of the horse. Maybe Johann had found it in himself to forgive.

"Thank you, Carl. You saved my life many times over. Go with God." Johann went into the house without looking back and Carl rode north to his new life.

Later that day, to escape the silence and melancholy of his home, Johann walked into the town. He stopped by Dr. Lansbach's office to tell him the news of Carl's leaving, which saddened the doctor. He thought highly of the young man who had saved his patient's life with his knowledge of the healing properties of plants. The two talked for a while before a patient arrived and Johann had to leave. As an afterthought, the doctor handed him a newspaper.

"It's from New York," he told him. "I'm finished with it. Enjoy!"

Glad of a distraction for the evening, Johann headed home to grab some food before a couple of students arrived for their lessons. There was some bread and cheese. The thought of having to struggle with meals on his own suddenly overwhelmed him. He fell heavily onto a kitchen bench. He had no idea how to run a household, much less a farm. What was he going to do?

Later that evening he had more bread and cheese along with a couple of red tomatoes he spotted in the garden. The house was too quiet. He was totally alone. It would never change. Despair and loneliness threatened to overwhelm him. He would be dead if Carl had not appeared in his life that night, the night that Wolfgang Mozart had died.

He grabbed the paper and headed into the sitting room to read it.

New York was quite a large place and the paper included news from the continent that many of its citizens had recently left. He read about a war between France and Austria with interest. Tucked at the bottom of the page, he was startled to see a small headline, "Composer Mozart's Wife Dies." In horror and shock, he read the few lines describing how Constanze Mozart Nissen, nee Weber, passed away giving birth to her second husband's son.

Blinded by rage and sorrow, he turned over the chair as he sprang from it. No rational thoughts formed in his mind. He had to get out. Tears alternated with shouts of anger as he wandered in the night. Without knowing how, he found himself at the flat stone by the path he used so often. Collapsing on it, he dropped his head into his hands.

She was dead. She was dead and he still hated her. And now Carl, too. No, he didn't hate Carl. It was painful, this desertion. It was abandonment. His chest felt crushed to the point that he struggled to breathe. His fears had come true—he was alone. Tears began to flow again. God, he wished, please let me die. The absurdity of trying to escape his past life, the futility of continuing this existence here, made him wrap his arms around himself and moan. He slipped from the stone to the ground and lay face down on the dirt of the path.

"God, please let me die. Please take me. I cannot..."

Why am I calling out to him? The thoughts came so fast as to overwhelm him. *God doesn't exist. If He does, He doesn't concern himself with you.*

Then, from the very core of his being, he called out again, "God, if you are there, take me."

Suddenly the turmoil stopped. Peace began as a pin-prick of light in the middle of his being. It shot out tendrils as it grew and each one caused a new area of his being to relax. Thought had nothing to do with it. He turned over and fixed his eyes on the stars blazing above. That God, the Creator, the Master of those stars, was filling his creation with Himself. Johann could only receive. He knew that God was real and that He loved him. Not because of his miraculous musical abilities. In spite of the pride, fear, hate, and utter selfishness that had motivated his entire life, God loved him.

More tears, this time gentle, repentant ones, fell. "Jesus, forgive me." In the presence of God, he could say nothing else. Then the peace returned, the sense of floating, of something outside himself holding him.

He had no idea how long he lay on the ground under the hand of God. When he caught himself falling asleep, he pushed himself to his feet and made his way back to his house. This time he felt grateful for it, for the intricate web of circumstances which had brought him here, for the life he had in this place. He fell into bed and slept for ten hours.

The peace was still there when he woke. He lay in bed wondering what he should do. Everything was different now. With a start he realized that his wife was dead, and he was free. All he had been able to comprehend last night was that he hated her and because she was gone, he would never be able to tell her that, never be able to exact revenge. Had he had plans of finding her and berating her for her sins against him? Not consciously, but he supposed that he had held onto a wish for retribution or justice. He was at a total, calm loss as to what he should do. Then one name popped into his mind, "Richard."

Johann got up quickly and marveled that it was mid-morning. He had struggled with insomnia for so long that he couldn't remember when he had slept as late. He dressed, managed to remember Carl's instructions about making coffee and made it much too strong. Fueled by it, he quickly fed the animals who made irritated noises at him in their hunger and headed to the Gutmans'.

Luisa answered his knock, pleasantly surprised to see him this early in the day.

"Welcome, Johann," her smile warmed his heart, especially this morning.

"Is your father home, Luisa?"

"Yes, come in. He is in his study in the back, writing, I think." There was something different about his countenance. Something important was going on. She guided him to her father, carefully closed the study door, then returned to the kitchen, praying.

"Well, well, Johann," Richard rose to greet him with a handshake.

"Good morning. I am very sorry if this is an inconvenience. I must speak to someone. I..."

Choking back tears, he was unable to speak and too overwhelmed to be ashamed of them.

"Here, sit, sit." Richard had been a pastor for many years and recognized what was happening.

Still standing, hands clenched at his sides, Johann began, "I am not who you think I am. My whole life here is a lie."

Richard's eyebrows went up, but he didn't speak.

"In Austria, I was a composer. My name was Wolfgang Mozart."

So, I was right, Richard thought, he does have talent.

"I was married, and I know now that my wife was having an affair for several years. I loved her deeply after... Well, her older sister rejected me. I was ready to resign myself to being single after that. But then, there was Constanze. We married in 1782."

Johann sat as Richard motioned to a wooden chair beside him.

"All went well for a good number of years. But then she kept going to Baden for months on end, she said for her health. I was working and working. I could never earn enough to make her happy. Those last few years in Vienna... I exhausted myself. Then my health failed." Johann paused, hands gripping his knees in tension.

"I became ill to the point of death, and I remember I fell into a deep sleep, for days perhaps. Then, I woke up. It was the middle of a winter night. I tried to call to Constanze, tried to let her know that I wasn't dead. I managed to get out of bed and then I saw her in another room."

Johann's eyes dropped to the floor.

"She was with a man, in bed with him. I was her husband, and she was doing this with my dead body in the next room!" Johann's voice got louder with anger and Richard shook his head in sympathy.

"I left. I went out into the cold. I suppose I thought I'd let Vienna's winter finish me off. I never wanted to see her again. And there was Carl, right before my house when I fell in front of him."

"So, you didn't know him before?" Richard asked.

"No, no. He just appeared when I needed him."

"Ah, the hand of God," Richard observed.

"Precisely. He helped me. I was an insane man, still very ill and bent on getting as far away from Vienna and her as possible. I thought that Mozart may as well have died, so I took my mother's family's name. Johann is actually one of my own, though not what my father chose to call me."

"So, we traveled, Carl and I. He was running from something, too, though he never gave me the details. I believe he was falsely accused of some crime. He has quite a gift with healing and faithfully found the herbs and things that he thought I needed. I guess he was right because he brought me alive to this place. I will miss him." Johann reveled in the freedom of honesty. His load was lightening with every truthful word.

Richard added, "He worried very much about leaving you. He even stopped by here, to make sure that we would check on you. I believe that God has a new life for him, a wife, and a purpose. Otherwise, he never would have left."

That felt oddly comforting, though Johann had much more to tell.

"He left yesterday morning and I, I am ashamed to say, I felt only anger. I did give him that horse he loved. Then I went into town and Dr. Lansbach gave me a newspaper from New York, a few months old, but I was glad to get it."

Johann took some seconds to breathe deeply. "When I took time to read it last night, I found an article about my wife. She had married another man after my disappearance, and she died bearing his child."

Richard sat very still, unable to imagine the pain, and wondering what would come next.

"I think I went insane. I threw things and ran out of the house. I could barely breathe. I was so full of rage and hatred..."

"And the pain of betrayal." Richard offered.

Johann nodded, then continued. "I found myself on that boundary stone between our properties. I don't know how many hours I sat there, even lying in the dirt."

He looked Richard in the eye, "I begged God to kill me."

"But He didn't."

"No," Johann looked down. "I screamed and raged at Him, at Constanze, at Carl. I decided that I would refuse to believe in Him and find some way to end my life."

"But you didn't."

"I was... I am... sick of the lies, the hatred, my pride. I am sick to death of me. I finally called out to Him to save me. I'm not sure why or how," Johann again looked at him. "But an incredible peace came in, here," he pointed to his chest. "I don't know what to do now, but I think God told me to come to you."

Richard spoke quietly, "Johann, you have had an encounter with our living Savior, the Lord Jesus Christ. We can't help but see ourselves in filthy rags when we first see him for who He is. Do you want to give your life to him, to call him your Lord?"

"I do." Johann wanted to do anything to make this peace last.

"And do you acknowledge that you are a sinner, that there is nothing in you that is good, that you have rebelled against God's truth?"

"Yes, that is true."

"And do you believe that Jesus died for those sins, that he went to the cross for you?"

"Yes," Johann brushed at the tears that fell again. Would they never stop?

"And do you believe that he rose again, to sit at the right hand of the Father? To give you new life and to intercede for you, to prepare a place for you in heaven, where He will welcome you in His own time, not yours?"

"Yes, yes."

"Let me pray for you. Father, I give you thanks for Johann, for revealing your truth to him. Lord, he has stated that he believes that he is a sinner, that Jesus died for his sins, and rose for his salvation. Please make these truths ever more important to him and cause him to follow You for the rest of his days. In Jesus' name, amen."

"There is one more thing, Johann."

How could there be anything more? Johann thought every part of him had been pressed clean.

"I believe that you need to forgive. Our Lord says that we must forgive others as He has forgiven us. There is your wife. Anyone else?"

Johann became very still. Finally, he answered, "I was able to set words to music in my operas, words about reconciliation, forgiveness. But I never..."

"Whom do you need to forgive, Johann?"

"Of course, you are right. Constanze, Carl, then I also think my father, and Archbishop Colloredo."

It was a start, Richard thought, "Now you pray. I'd like you to say out loud that you forgive them."

Johann had never prayed before anyone, but began, "Father in Heaven, I do want to follow You. I forgive Carl. I forgive Constanze." Here he stopped, overcome by emotion. "Also, my father and the archbishop. For everything."

"In Jesus' name," Richard added, smiling.

That peace was still there along with a feeling of lightness, of cleanness, that Johann had never known before.

Richard felt that he should add, "You are a new creation now. The old has gone, the new has come. I don't believe that continuing to live here as Johann Pertl is a lie. God brought you here. Taking a new name is appropriate because you are a new man. And don't worry, I will tell no one your previous name. You came to me as a pastor, in confession, and as such, I will hold your words in confidence."

"Thank you. I felt this morning so confused about what to do now. Not fearful, but without direction."

"You have spent several years living totally in hiding, but the reasons for that are gone. Just continue here, with your teaching. God will show you the way."

Richard got up and pulled a book from one of his shelves. "Here, I would like you to have this."

Johann accepted the book.

"It's a Bible, God's Holy Word. Have you ever read it before?"

"No." Of course, he had been taught that the Bible was the inerrant Word of God, but it was best left up to the priest to study and explain it to his flock. He had only ever seen it in Latin.

"This one is in German. Read something in it every day. Start with the gospel according to Mark."

Seeing his confusion, Richard took a small scrap of paper, found the spot, and marked it for him. Johann read the first verse, "The beginning of the gospel of Jesus Christ, the Son of God," and smiled at his friend. "This *is* a beginning, isn't it?"

Luisa had a light lunch prepared as the two entered the kitchen. She had been praying nonstop since Johann came and couldn't sit idly waiting. She was eager to know what had happened.

"Rejoice!" Richard proclaimed, "Our brother who was lost is found!"

"What?" she exclaimed with joy. Could it possibly be? Her prayers of a year answered at last?

"Johann here has given his heart to our Lord. He is truly one of us!"

"That is wonderful!" Luisa clapped her hands in delight. Johann smiled at her, looking directly into her eyes with no hesitation.

"Let us celebrate!" Richard sat at the head of the table, "Look, Luisa has prepared the fatted calf!"

"Poppa, you are silly. It is rabbit."

Johann laughed, basking in the altogether new experience of God's love and peace.

CHAPTER 27
Salem
July–December 1794

At first, Johann struggled to do anything other than read the Bible that Richard had given him. He did manage to feed and water the animals left in his charge and teach the pupils who showed up at his door with annoying regularity. But every other moment found him poring over pages in the thick book, exclaiming with excitement when words that he had heard all his life took on an entirely new meaning. He forgot to eat, until sounds from his belly interfered so with his concentration that he had to rummage for something edible in his kitchen.

Questions proliferated as well. Most of them were about the Old Testament versus the New. Did Jesus mean for them to throw out the law? Surely not. What did it mean that He was the fulfillment of the law? Johann brought his questions to Richard during Tuesday dinners.

After only two weeks, he realized that he was not going to be able to take care of the farm. He repented of his pride and wished he could apologize to Carl for being such a stubborn, unwilling student. He approached his friend Richard for help once again.

"I know of a situation which might yield you some workers while helping to correct an injustice," the older man responded. "Some weeks ago, two freed slaves appeared here. They have been staying with one of the African families just outside of town." Salem had Black people in its population since it was founded, both free and enslaved. Richard was a staunch abolitionist and sought to help restore dignity to these people whenever he could. "Let me check to see if they might be interested in earning some wages."

The two young men agreed and began by working under the supervision of the man who also managed the Gutmans' own land. They soon proved themselves capable and managed Johann's farm on their own. When they were near the house, they greatly enjoyed the music pouring from it most days. He in turn was fascinated by their occasional singing and sometimes followed them around the field to hear it clearly. Richard also found an older widow in need of additional income who could cook one meal a day and do other household tasks in the afternoons. Johann did not like spending his funds like this, but it did not surprise him that it took two men and a woman to do the work that Carl alone had handled.

Johann's desire to be with the brethren became second only to his passion for the Bible. His nature was social, and the past few years of isolation were foreign to his character and had contributed to his depression. He was pleasantly surprised that something was happening at the Congregation House almost every evening: vespers, love feasts, prayer meetings, celebrations of music called Singstunde, and other evenings of music just for entertainment. Rather than refuse invitations from the Gutmans, he eagerly accepted them and finally just learned the schedules and went on his own, though he always sat with Richard. The Brethren's worship held a great deal of joy. Johann relied on it for his spiritual food just as much as the teaching.

A major event was his baptism in September. He had heard a sermon about it and asked Richard whether it was a lack of faith to think that he should be baptized now. He had been baptized as an infant by his parents. Richard explained that the Brethren believed that a person should be baptized when he was conscious of good and evil and had chosen the Savior for himself. Well, he had certainly done that now. A deep sense of peaceful well-being followed the ceremony.

Johann slowly entered the musical life of the congregation. Though the musicians who served were amateurs, many had had the advantage of excellent training and were familiar with the musical life of Europe. He heard Hummel, Salieri, Haydn, and even, from time to time, Mozart, played by the ensembles of Salem. He was asked to participate and did so gladly, even taking up a violin to substitute for an ill performer, much to the surprise of Luisa and her father. The musicians were delighted with the polished, graceful stranger who seemed humbly unaware of his miraculous talent.

This slow entrance into the musical life of the town was the subject of much prayer. The now-deceased Wolfgang Mozart had viewed himself as the foremost composer and performer of his time. His father, recognizing his prodigious talent, taught him music and, even more, that he was worth so much because he could perform so well. One of the reasons that Johann had had to forgive his father was that he had dragged him all over Europe to make the Mozart name famous and every other composer and performer jealous.

Johann recognized that another part of his years of depression came from his withdrawal from a life of performing and having his compositions performed. He mused for days upon what the effect of not being able to play or compose might be... if he were to lose a hand, for example. He finally concluded that, whatever else he might do, God had created him a musician. He firmly believed now in the Brethren's goal of living an honest, industrious, and useful life to the praise of God. There was no pride in that. How could there be when he was a creature and not the Creator? He decided to attempt to walk in thankfulness always and pray that God guide him in how to use these gifts.

Johann developed the habit of reading a psalm and a chapter in Proverbs daily. One day almost a year after Carl had left and his life had begun, he read Psalm 68 and verses 24 and 25 jumped out at him:

Your procession is seen, O God, the procession of my God, my King, into the sanctuary—the singers in front, the musicians last, between them virgins playing tambourines.

The phrase "the musicians last" stayed on his mind all day. He knew that he had read other things about being last, but where was it? He returned to the book of Matthew, which had been his study over the last month and finally found it. Matthew 20:16

So the last will be first, and the first last.

Johann felt strongly that God was speaking to him, correcting the lies that he and his father had believed and based their lives upon. Most musicians competed incessantly against each other for notice, financial reward, and ultimately the gratification of self. They, and he, were always seeking to be first. Was it possible to use one's gifts out of a pure heart and not seek one's own glory? To please God by thanking him for musical ability and using it to serve others?

He remembered some stories he had heard about J. S. Bach. One of Johann's great friends had been the Baron van Swieten, the Viennese ambassador to Berlin. On Sunday afternoons in Vienna, he and the Baron passed pleasant hours discovering the music of Bach and Handel which the baron brought home with him. He learned counterpoint by playing the music of the elder Bach, marveling at the weaving of lines together in a supreme intellectual exercise, pleasing to both the ears and the heart.

The Baron told him that Bach wrote "J.J." for "Jesu juva" or "Jesus help me" or "N.J." for "In nomine Jesu" on his blank composition pages. Then he inscribed "SDG" on all his works. "Soli Deo Gloria" or "To God be the Glory." What would that mean for him, for Johann Pertl? J.S. Bach wrote, as he said, for the glory of God and the refreshment of men's souls. In the past, the Protestant composer's faith lay remote, far outside Johann's own experience. Now he began to understand. He was here in Salem, where his gifts were greatly appreciated, but he himself was not worshipped or held up as being more important than the butcher, for example. That seemed right, somehow. These Moravians did love music, though, and studied and listened to the best they could acquire. Perhaps God put him here to both preserve his life and serve them.

It was easy and less expensive to purchase paper now. Brother Christian Stauber had learned papermaking in Pennsylvania and another mill had been built on the Petersbach, west of Salem. He still had countless unborn pieces within himself, he knew.

A plan came to him. Perhaps he could continue to compose? He had heard enough of their anthems and arias that several of his own making were knocking around in his head. And sometimes they did not have music for their pleasant entertainments and fellowships, because a particular instrument was lacking, or a strange combination was all that was available. Two clarinets, two bassoons, and two horns for example. Perfect for a partita! What if he wrote music for them, but did not publish it? They could use it for God's glory, but he would keep it. If it was not published, he could avoid all the stress of his prior life while putting himself last. This place was perfect for him–his gifts were needed, would be much appreciated–but he himself would not be elevated. It was death to his flesh, but real life for his soul.

Richard confirmed what Johann had decided. "You, sir, are a peacock among plain brown chickens. We don't know what to make of you! If you think this is what the Lord wants of you, I will pray that you are able to do it. And I am grateful!"

Self-sacrifice was not uncommon among the Brethren. Many lived while subordinating personal desires for the good of the community and out of worship for God. Richard saw the rewards of such a life and was impressed that Johann had reached that level of maturity so quickly.

In spite of his time being full and the enjoyment of returning to composition and participating in the worship of the community, Johann was still uneasy about being alone. He had never done well outside of the closeness of his family. Then he had had Carl, who was a constant presence despite all his taciturn silence. And he realized that he couldn't take his eyes off Luisa whenever they were at church at the same time, or he was in the Gutmans' home.

Could the joy of marriage be his? He scarcely allowed himself to think of it. He did not believe that she would give up her calling to take care of her father. And he was older! Now 38 and she was possibly 23. It would be best not to think of it.

Luisa, on the other hand, found herself consumed with thoughts of the musician who was so often in their home. His music played itself in her head all day and most of the night. She couldn't stop daydreaming about him. She prayed for long periods about it, pleading with God to take this desire away if it was not of Him. She was past the age that most women married, and her father needed her.

Richard, meanwhile, could practically feel the waves of attraction passing between these two young people he loved so dearly. He caught Johann tracking Luisa's every move and watched the way Luisa almost swooned as Johann played the fortepiano for them. He also began to pray, felt sure of God's will in the matter, and decided to kick Johann in the rear to wake him up.

But, as it so often turned out, God was working in Johann also. He finally decided to hint at his thoughts to Richard, test out the waters, to see what the older man thought about the possibility of gaining a son-in-law. He resolutely determined to accept a negative response as the will of God and tried to convince himself that might well happen. He worked himself into an unusual state of nervousness before their next dinner.

"Sir, may I speak with you in private?" Johann asked after the meal one Tuesday evening in June. He had been obviously on edge, but Richard did not think the request unusual. The younger man often had questions of theology or about his own walk with God that required them to speak alone. Luisa watched them leave as she carried dishes into the kitchen, praying herself about what was going on. It was growing harder and harder to stem the feelings she had for Johann.

"Yes?" Richard asked as they took their customary places in his study.

"I have been praying much about a matter," Johann began, and Richard noticed an uncharacteristic flush creep onto his face.

"I have been here for several years, and I believe that God would have me stay."

"Good," Richard encouraged him.

"I have also known you and your daughter for several years now. I greatly respect Luisa." He looked at Richard, who now suspected that he might know what was going on.

"I have established myself as a teacher and my income, while not overly much, is enough to keep a family."

"You want to marry my Luisa!" Richard broke into a wide grin.

Johann was astonished, both as his quick grasp of the matter and his extremely positive reaction.

"Yes, but I believe that she perhaps does not want to marry? She sees her duty to remain as your helper here?"

"Poppycock. Let me talk to her." Richard pushed himself out of his chair and Johann realized that he meant right then and there.

"Perhaps I should leave?" Johann tried to make his escape.

Richard waved him back down. "You sit right there and don't move."

A few minutes later Richard came in, dragging Luisa by the hand. "Here she is," he stated proudly, placing her hand into the younger man's. He then turned and left the room.

Johann jumped to his feet, "Luisa! I... what did he...?" Then, realizing he was holding her hand, he pressed it between both of his.

"Luisa, I know that I am much older and that I do not have a position worthy of you."

She stared in shock. Could this be happening?

"I have my small property and a goodly number of music students. I also know that you have pledged yourself to your father's care. These things have chased each other around in my head until I would be totally rid of them. There is no resolution save one. So, I would like to offer myself as your husband. If you will have me, that is," his eyes locked on hers.

She nodded, unable for a second to form words. Finally, she said, "Yes," and broke into a huge, beautiful smile.

He wrapped his arms around her and held her for quite a long time. Resting her head against his chest, she whispered, "Father is probably near bursting."

Richard saw them come from the room holding hands and knew that all was right with God's world.

They were married in a small ceremony on December 5, 1794. Johann liked the irony of it, the third anniversary of the "death" of Mozart, though he kept it to himself. Luisa exchanged the pink ribbon of a single sister for the light blue of a married woman at last.

CHAPTER 28
Salem
October 2019

A nna thanked God that her last class on Friday was cancelled, allowing her to leave for Winston-Salem a couple of hours early. The trunk of her car was loaded with several lamps stolen from her apartment, old clothes for working in a dusty attic, two folding tables borrowed from Steve, a cooler with sandwich fixings, and her MacBook Pro. Everything needed for a dreamy weekend with piles of old music. She was in heaven.

Arriving before dark, it took her an hour to haul everything all the way into the attic. She quickly downed a turkey sandwich and headed upstairs to start. Opening all three trunks, she thought over her plan of attack. It still seemed best to her to sort the music by genre first, sacred and secular, then categorize the instrumental pieces by size of ensemble, solos, duets, trios, quartets, then larger ensembles. The religious music was not her specialty, but surely she could figure it out as she went. Donning a pair of nitrile gloves, she began taking music carefully out of the first trunk, keeping her eyes open for written words.

By midnight fatigue caught up to her and she decided she could not go on. Her heart burst with excitement, but her eyes refused to focus. So far it was mostly instrumental works—lots of keyboard pieces, string trios, quartets, and serenades for octets and nonets with all kinds of different instrumentation. There were some tempo indications and a few dynamic markings. She put those bearing written words on the top of their respective piles. Taking off the gloves, she headed down into the house for a quick shower before falling into bed. Despite racing thoughts darting around her head about the mystery of the music and worries about changes in her life, she nodded off immediately.

Anna was up at dawn on Saturday, too excited to waste more time sleeping. Two more trunks to go. The second one yielded a pile of anthems, based on psalm passages as far as she could tell. Lots of written text there, a few in English, but the bottom three-fourths of the pile was all in German. Then she pulled out a thicker score, tied together with old string. At first glance, it looked like an opera piano-vocal score. The title said "für Kinder" and she also spotted the word "Weihnachten." A children's musical for Christmas? She knew the early Moravians were very focused on education and their children. Did they also have children's musical programs as some churches did today?

At the very bottom of the second trunk, she discovered another, thicker set of pages, also tied together. It bore the title "Fortepiano-Schule," which meant to her mind a set of exercises for teaching piano. Browsing through its pages, she saw exercise after exercise with lots of instructions written beneath each one. This could be a gold mine for research into performance practices of the early 19th century if she could prove its age.

It was afternoon and she was starving. Time for another turkey sandwich before the third trunk. Her phone lay on the ancient kitchen table, and she noticed with guilt that Steve had been trying to call. She let him know that she was fine, the work was going well, and that she missed him, too. She was relieved to see that even during this growing romance, she was still herself. Still obsessed with music history. That made her wonder about exactly what was going on in her mind and heart. Why was she worried about change? Finally, after finishing lunch, she admitted the truth to herself. She was in love with Steve, and it was the first time this had ever happened to her.

Smiling, she climbed back into the attic. Romance break over. She had already filled the two 8-foot tables she brought with piles of music, so she found a set of four small folding wooden ones and carried them up the stairs one by one.

The last trunk held larger works: the score and parts for two symphonies; several wind concertos, including two for trombone–she couldn't wait to show Steve–one for flute and two for clarinet; along with five piano concertos. Solo piano works were tucked in everywhere, as in the other two trunks. She sat on the floor, leaned against the large beam in the center of the attic, and removed her gloves. The only thing conspicuously missing from every piece, as far as she could tell, was a composer's name.

It was 6 p.m. Sorting the contents of the trunks had taken all day. She decided that she needed something more substantial than another turkey sandwich, but she'd better clean up first. No, first she would call Steve and let him know about her progress. This romance thing needed attention, too.

"You're kidding! Trombone concertos? There aren't many of those," his reaction was just as she'd hoped. "Especially not from that time period."

"Yup. The Moravians dearly loved their trombones."

He laughed. "So, what is your next step?"

"I'm going to create a database, a catalog of all of it."

"Do you think you can do that by tomorrow night?"

"I doubt it," she laughed. "I think it's more like months of work. I'll get started in the morning. I've got a friend who lives here and I'm going to see if she's up for dinner. I need a break!"

Anna's friend Madeline York was indeed up for dinner and thrilled to be able to catch up with Anna. Madeline taught technology at the Salem Academy for Girls. She was a foot taller than Anna, with reddish-gold long hair. They had been inseparable since second grade at Brunson Elementary, when Madeline's family moved to Winston-Salem for her father to become the composer-in-residence at the U. N.C. School of the Arts. The two had grown up together, sharing their passion for music starting in their pre-teen years. Madeline played the violin through school but majored in education. She still held a chair in the second violins in the Winston-Salem Symphony. Though it had been six months since visiting face-to-face, they picked up as if no time had intervened at all.

Over chicken pot pies at the Salem Tavern, Anna told her about her great aunt's death and how she was sorting through things at the house. Madeline commiserated with her on losing Aunt Alzbeta. The grand old lady had always made Madeline feel as if she were a family member. Anna kept the music a secret, not really knowing why, but uneasy about sharing anything having to do with it yet. Madeline had news; she had just become engaged to a Wake Forest math instructor. That prompted Anna to share a little about Steve, and Madeline's comments had them giggling helplessly as if they were still in 7th grade. They would have to have a double date soon.

The two young women walked back to the old yellow house and talked a while. By 10 p.m., Anna could not stop the yawns and apologized for being exhausted as Madeline left. She slept soundly until dawn again when she headed back upstairs to begin cataloging.

This was going to take a while. She created a database to include title, instrumentation, key, and notes about interesting features for each piece. Some had no title, so she made up the most descriptive one she could, putting it in brackets to indicate that it was not actually on the music. By 3 p.m., she estimated that she had made it through about a twentieth of one trunk's worth. But it was time to head back for another week at school.

Before she left, she picked up one piano piece that had some words written on it: "For Luisa's birthday" and "Allegro" along with some single-letter dynamic markings. Realizing that she did not want to hand over another original to Dr. Miller, she made a quick trip to a business supply store and copied it.

Steve met her for a late dinner when she returned to Chapel Hill.

"You look exhausted," he greeted her with a quick kiss.

"Thanks a lot!" she responded, sinking into a booth at Jason's Deli.

"I didn't mean..."

"It's ok. I *am* exhausted. This is going to take me a lot longer than I thought." Anna took a drink of her iced tea before sharing details of what she had found and how far she had progressed.

"This is such a huge amount of work, and right in line with your studies. Do you think you could work it into your program? Get credit for it somehow?"

"I've had the thought," Anna admitted. "If I could just get some confirmation that the music is worth something, original maybe. I don't know for sure that somebody didn't just copy a lot of stuff and store it away. And for what reason?"

"A true musical mystery. What's the next step?"

"I brought a copy of a page with more words written on it. Dr. Miller said he had a friend who could do handwriting analysis. But I'm not sure what the purpose of that is."

"What do you mean?"

Their food arrived. Once plates were passed out, Anna responded.

"Well, I assume that a handwriting analyst matches some writing to a sample of someone else's writing. A known quantity. So, what if this was just some obscure person obsessed with copying music?"

"Then it won't match anyone else, and you'll have your answer, right?"

"Or I'll never know. Except maybe I could check some of those genealogy notes that my aunt had. One of the pieces mentioned a 'Luisa.' The house was built in 1803. Maybe I could find out about her, see if she lived in the house."

Steve watched her come back to life with the thought of another possibility to research. "So, music history is sort of like being Sherlock Holmes. Hunting down clues?"

"You've got it!" she laughed.

On Monday morning, she contacted Dr. Miller and made an appointment for that afternoon. Steve was teaching and could not accompany her, which had upset him. She argued that it would be fine, in the music building in the center of a school day. But she was not looking forward to it.

Dreading the encounter, she hesitated at Miller's office door and prayed. The resulting peace made her wonder why she didn't remember to do that more often. She had barely entered his office when he accosted her, "So, do you have more of that music for me?"

His tone and manner raised red flags for Anna. I'd better be careful, she thought.

"I brought a copy of a page that has some text on it, as you asked," she responded. He did not offer her a seat.

"Let me see." He grabbed it quickly from her hand and stared at it for a long time, saying nothing. Anna became a little uncomfortable.

"It seems as if someone copied some late Mozart. I'll have to check the NMA when I get time."

Anna felt a twinge of disappointment. It sounded like he believed the music was from a copyist, which was what she feared.

"I'll have my friend look at this text for us. Now, what was the name of the librarian who gave you this music?"

Anna's heart skipped a beat before she remembered the lie she had told about the music coming from the public library.

"I'm not sure. She oversaw their archives."

"Well, I hope they have the originals in appropriate containers and haven't handled them without gloves."

Anna did not want to dig herself in deeper, so she didn't respond at all.

"All right, Miss Stohr, thank you, and I'll let you know when I learn something."

Anna left, not feeling good at all about that conversation. He didn't believe her about the library, she could tell. But if the music was just copies of known works... Maybe she could check out the *Neue Mozart-Ausgabe,* that huge collection of all the composer's works, herself. The university music library had it, along with the collected works of all the other important composers. It was even available to scholars online. If she could find one of these piano sonatas in there, that would be her answer. But where would she find the time?

It turned out that Anna did not have time to try to play match the sonatas before the weekend came around again. She headed back to Salem for another bout of cataloging. This time Steve promised to come on Saturday and, if he couldn't help in any other way, at least treat her to a decent dinner.

She made it through more of the music in the first trunk by the time Steve arrived on Saturday. It was too early for dinner, so he wanted to know what he could do to help. Anna found a history of her family that her aunt had tried to interest her in years ago. She couldn't be bothered with it when she was in high school; now it might provide some important material. She brought Steve some tea and settled him on a beanbag chair under a bright light in the attic. Then she handed him the *History of the Stohr and Pertl Families, 1756-the present.*

"Just look for anyone named Luisa," she told him.

A few hours later, she finished the trunk.

"How is it going?" she asked her assistant.

"I found a couple," he lifted the book with two papers marking the relevant spots. Anna moved her chair over to look at what he had found. She leaned against his arm as he found the page.

"Here is the first one: 'Luisa Stohr nee Smithers, married Peter Stohr in 1890.'"

"No," Anna shook her head. "That is too late to be our Luisa. The paper wouldn't have been right."

"OK, well there is another one." He turned to the next marker.

"Luisa Gutman married Johann Pertl in 1794. Then they had a bunch of children. Oh, here it says that her husband Johann was quite a musician. He taught piano and violin and—look at this—he wrote numerous compositions that were used in both services and secular entertainments."

Anna leaned in closer, "That's him! Must be! When did he live? What are his dates?"

"It says he arrived in Salem from Europe in 1793 and bought a house here, but he died in 1840. I'm not sure how old he was exactly."

"Wow. That really could be him. I found a piano method in one of the trunks, just the thing he would have used in teaching. I wish I could find out more about where he came from."

"It says he was baptized just before their marriage. Maybe he came to the Moravian faith late in life?"

"That wasn't uncommon, from what I've read. Great job! You may have found our mysterious composer!"

They went to Ryan's Steakhouse to celebrate and forget about the piles of music for a few hours.

CHAPTER 29
Salem
1795–1810

L ife after their marriage worked out well for Johann and Luisa. They decided that Johann would move into the larger house Luisa shared with her father. That would allow Richard to continue as part of their family, which pleased all three of them. Johann offered residence at his farm to the men whom he had hired to tend it after Carl's departure. They accepted gratefully and settled on the percentage of its proceeds to pay him. He was able to hire men to add an extra room onto the Gutmans' home. This was at the northern end, opposite Richard's study on the south. Johann moved his fortepiano and desk there, so both men could be engaged in their individual pursuits without music lessons disturbing Richard's writing.

Within six months, Luisa was expecting their first child. Johann found himself suffering much anxiety when he learned of their blessing. He and Constanze had had six children, four of whom died as infants. Johann hardly knew the two boys who survived. She took them to Baden or her mother's home frequently. He had also been working incessantly during those days to support the family. But the pain of losing four children still haunted him.

He did not want to frighten Luisa in any way, so he was unwilling to talk to her about it and fought unsuccessfully against anxious thoughts for weeks. One afternoon, several of his pupils had to cancel their lessons to hear a visiting Bible scholar. He left, but instead of heading to the Boys' School, he continued to God's Acre. Finding a spot under a large oak, he sat to seek the Lord. With tears, he confessed his shortcomings as a father to the children of his first marriage. He forgave Constanze again and prayed blessings over his two sons if they were still alive as he hoped. He gave the children that he and Luisa would have over to God, asking that they would know their Savior and be obedient to him their whole lives. And he asked for wisdom to be a good father. That led to more prayers of forgiveness for his own father. He could see things differently now and be grateful that God had placed him with a man who could so thoroughly sharpen his musical gifts, even if mainly in the service of his own ambitions. Peace and gratitude began to fill his thoughts. He also heard the words, "the helmet of salvation." Yes, he had let anxious thoughts take over his mind, rather than holding onto the fact that he was reborn, a new creation in Christ, and could trust God. He headed home rejoicing over the blessing of a child for him and Luisa.

Johann's work became the foundation of the town's musical life. He taught scores of children and adults and played at both sacred and secular musical events whenever asked. Writing music was his anchor and his escape. Luisa loved the renewed joy with which he showed her every new work.

Johann tried his hand at setting some of the psalms he had grown to love as anthems. They were received enthusiastically by the musicians and congregation at the church.

The brethren were sorely disappointed, however, when Johann refused to give them copies of the pieces to add to their church library. The Collegium Musicum der Gemeine in Salem, or Musical Society of the Congregational Community in Salem, was founded around 1780, and its members prided themselves on having accumulated a massive library of sacred and secular music along with instruments of all types. They adored Johann's works and eagerly anticipated every new one, then argued with him bitterly over his refusal to release them to the Collegium's library. He placated them somewhat by promising to provide the scores whenever needed and to write more besides. When he brought the music home that evening, he was at first at a loss as to a safe place to deposit it. Then he remembered the trunks that he and Carl had used in their long journey from Austria to Salem. They lay in a storeroom attached to the back of the house. He dragged one into his music room, where it made a perfect cabinet for the scores he placed within.

In May of 1802, in the second year of Thomas Jefferson's presidency, Richard took to his bed with severe chest pains. By that time, Luisa and Johann had three children, Richard, Thomas, and Sarah. Johann kept the three amused and quiet while Luisa conferred with the new doctor in Salem, Dr. Vierling, who had taken over Johann's dear friend Dr. Lansbach's practice.

"He should not be in too much pain," Johann heard the doctor say just before the front door closed. He left the children playing quietly with blocks to find Luisa in the hallway. Her face was pale, her eyes welling with tears as she shook her head before he wrapped her in his arms.

Richard was awake later in the afternoon. He smiled at each grandchild as Johann lifted them up one by one. The old man placed his right hand on each child's head and closed his eyes. Johann knew he was praying blessings over them, though he could not speak the words out loud. The children were too young to realize what was happening but looked up at their parents' solemn faces and knew it was a time to be quiet.

Richard died peacefully in his sleep that evening. Johann lost his spiritual father and Luisa was inconsolable, though both believed firmly that they would certainly see him again in eternity. The children cried with their mother, and she tried to explain why they could no longer see their beloved Opa.

While the family was still grieving, Johann learned a plot of land close to the southwest corner of the town square was for sale. It was large enough for a substantial house, across the street and a little past the tavern. After speaking to the town council, he approached Luisa with his idea.

"I would like to consider perhaps moving."

She looked surprised.

"What would you think of moving closer into town? It would be easier for the children. The boys' classes have been large and there is talk of establishing a larger girls' academy soon. I have been asked to consider teaching the younger students there, also, rather than having them all come to my studio. We could sell both of our properties, separately or together, and build in town."

"I think your idea is good. I have lived here my whole life, so it will be a change. But perhaps starting over is a good thing." Luisa kept expecting to see her father in his chair or at the table. This house held beloved memories, but perhaps it was time for a new chapter.

Johann was glad that she agreed. Part of his plan was to help her in her sadness over Richard's passing. He caught her from time to time just sitting in the old study, staring at the empty chair surrounded by books where her father had spent so many happy hours.

It took four months to build the two-and-a-half story frame house. Once the family had relocated, buyers were quickly found for their old homes. Johann's tenants were thrilled to purchase the farm they had been working for years and another family from Pennsylvania bought the Gutman property. Soon after their move to the yellow house in town, one more child followed, completing the Pertl's brood of four, including two boys and two girls. Johann thoroughly enjoyed simply playing with them and Luisa was never surprised to find the whole crew climbing trees or building forts, Johann included.

One winter afternoon in 1810, as Johann worked with a piano student in the music room, a large wagon pulled to a stop in front of their house. Luisa spotted it instantly and left her kitchen, drying her hands on her white apron. There seemed to be a lot of children in the back of the wagon. Her heart began to beat quickly as she saw a giant of a man help a woman down from the high seat.

"Johann, come quickly," she called as she opened the front door.

Johann frowned. Luisa never interrupted his lessons. Something must be wrong.

He hurried to the porch only to see Carl and Greta approaching, followed by what looked like a crowd of children. "Thank you, blessed Lord," he whispered to himself.

Carl hesitated as he saw the familiar figure of his small master from so many years ago. The man looked totally different–healthy, not at all showing his more than fifty years. And, Carl realized, he seemed happy. Johann rushed to him, shaking his hand and patting his shoulder. "I am so glad to see you, Carl, so glad." Relieved, Carl patted his former master on the back while the two women smiled broadly.

"I told you," Greta touched her husband's arm.

"And, you see, I am married also. Do you remember Luisa?" Johann introduced her proudly.

Carl nodded and bowed. So much had changed since he had left.

Luisa quickly settled the adults in the kitchen with coffee and cake and sent the children to the back yard with cookies. Johann dismissed his student who was staring at the scene and promised a longer lesson next time.

"So how has your life gone, Carl? Where do you live?" Johann began.

"We are here from Tennessee. We have a farm there, a large one. Since Tennessee is a state now, it is peaceful there. It goes well," Carl, never much for words, took a long drink of the rich coffee.

Greta continued, "Yes, the Lord has blessed us over much. Land and children. We settled with a group of Quakers who moved from Virginia, so we have had the protection of a community."

Luisa couldn't resist asking, "How many children?" She had not been able to get a count for all their moving around.

"Eight," Greta said proudly. "Five boys and three girls. Two of the boys are twins!"

Carl grinned at her. No one was a better wife and mother than his Greta.

She continued, "We are back to claim an inheritance. Do you remember when my brother Peter and I lived in Bethabara? The Jarvises were so kind. They took us in as family. Brother Jarvis has just passed on to his reward; his wife has been gone for a long while. We received word that he made mention of us in his will. Carl agreed to leave our land in Peter's care so we could return to see about it."

She didn't mention that Carl also wanted to find news of Johann. All these years later, he still felt somehow responsible for the small man. It bothered him that he never knew how he fared after Carl had left. He was afraid that perhaps he had died.

"And Peter is well, also?" Luisa asked.

Carl nodded, "Yes, very well. He married soon after we arrived, a Cherokee girl who had accepted our Lord."

Johann's eyes widened at this. "He married one of the savages?" What a place, this New World.

"Yes, but he would have our heads if we called her that," Greta grinned. "She is the kindest, gentlest, best of women."

"They have six children of their own," Carl added, "on the land right beside ours."

"Well, we have not been so busy as you," Johann put his hand over Luisa's. "Only four, I'm afraid. Perhaps we should...?"

Luisa withdrew her hand and slapped his lightly. Carl and Greta laughed, and things became more comfortable.

Luisa tried to persuade the Bauers to spend the night, though she had no idea where she would put them all. They refused and insisted on returning to Bethabara, as they had to pick up things and get on the road back to Tennessee the next day. Even though winter was just ending, a farm that large always had work. They hated to leave Peter and his brood with extra chores longer than needed.

Greta and Luisa went to gather the children spread out over their yard and through the neighborhood, giving Carl and Johann a moment of solitude.

"Carl, I need to apologize."

Carl's eyebrows went up.

"I never thanked you for all you did, back then. I know that I was... difficult." Johann searched for words to convey that he understood the sacrifices Carl had made. His illness, the lengthy path to their new lives, seemed ages ago now.

He looked up at his dear friend, so much more than a servant. "I dragged you across two continents, across the ocean...with your sea-sickness!"

Carl was able to smile at the memory now. He had never again taken a voyage by ship.

"You saved my life, over and over," Johann choked at the words, "though I didn't want saving. I was dead inside, dead to God, dead to everyone."

Shows of emotion always made Carl uncomfortable, but this time with Johann felt sacred.

"When you left, you did me the greatest favor of all."

Carl couldn't understand. "What do you mean?"

"I couldn't care for myself. I know, you showed me all about the blasted chickens and the cow, but I really could not. I was totally alone. Then I received word that Mozart's wife had died, over there, in Germany." The name "Mozart" felt uncomfortable on his lips, as if he were talking about a stranger.

"I finally called out to God. After all those years of hating and hopelessness. And he heard me!"

Carl's eyes misted over. He never imagined Johann without the hatred and anger. Only God...

"Everything that has happened since has been his doing," Johann clasped Carl's arm. "You were his agent, his messenger sent to bring me to him. Can you forgive me for thinking only of myself?"

Carl nodded, grabbed him in a bear hug, managing to get out the words, "There is nothing to forgive. God meant it all for good."

"And now we are content, yes?" Johann continued, pulling back to look up at his old friend. "As it says in the Word, 'Godliness with contentment is great gain.'"

Carl nodded.

"All those years ago, I sought only my own fame and wealth. Then I hated, almost to the point of my own death. How blind I was! And how gracious our Lord. See all he has given us?" Johann motioned to the house behind him.

Suddenly a large crowd of children poured from the yellow house's front door to the strange sight of their stalwart fathers, looking at them with tears in their eyes.

After the Bauers drove away, Johann thanked God for the opportunity to reconcile with Carl at last. It seemed his past was finally put to rest.

CHAPTER 30
Salem
1810–1840

Johann served his Lord and his community with great passion, even into his fifties and sixties. The health problems of his youth plagued him no longer. The love of his family and the gratitude of the community for his talents brought joy to him daily. His abilities were the backbone of the town's musical life. As the years went by, he taught fewer students and generally only the older youth and adults. He marveled that he did not find teaching tedious or boring, but genuinely cared for the students who came to him. Yet another proof that God makes new creations of his followers.

He was always willing to compose anthems for services or instrumental pieces for any odd group that happened to be available for an evening's entertainment. String quartets and trios, clarinet duets, serenades for strings and winds, and even a symphony or two lay in the trunks which held his works. He wrote a string quintet complete with two violas, just as he had years ago. The memory of Haydn and he himself playing the viola parts in his Vienna apartment brought a smile of remembrance. He could look back without pain now. Another miracle.

There were some decent wind players in the small town, so he produced several serenades, like the one for clarinets, horns, and bassoons he had composed in Austria so long ago. Emperor Joseph had dearly loved a band. On occasion he expanded the works to include basset horns, trombones, or a bass to suit the musicians available to him. He also decided to collect and organize the materials that he used most often in teaching, so a method for instruction in playing the fortepiano joined the works in the trunks. He added notes, maxims he had learned from his father and tips picked up from Johann Christian Bach and his friend Franz Joseph Haydn. He made several copies with Luisa's help and loaned the method to students, but always insisted upon its return.

The Moravians were in the custom of having the children perform a Christmas play each season. One year, the young man who wrote the plays for the school had the brilliant idea of asking Johann to set the words to music. Over the years, ten operettas for children joined the pieces in the trunks.

Salem was far removed from the large cities of the new United States of America, but most of its citizens, along with those of the Moravian centers in Pennsylvania, had been trained in music in the European classical tradition. The Musical Society of the Congregational Community in Salem had accumulated a huge library of sacred and secular music. Whenever possible, they obtained new works and eagerly performed them for each other. Though it was only a trickle and certainly not current, Johann was able to hear these new pieces from time to time. There was a common library of music, containing works by Haydn, J. C. Bach, Stamitz and Abel, along with older works by Handel,

J.S. Bach, and, of course, Mozart. Later, the more modern Beethoven, Cherubini, and Weber were added. However, their most beloved musician, Herr Pertl, kept his compositions to himself, away from the library.

From time to time, Johann conducted a small children's orchestra, made up primarily of his pupils. The older boys loved him and often gathered around him afterwards. Johann had some favorite pupils. One gifted young man, Samuel Richter reminded him of his best pupil in Vienna, Johann Hummel. He had even had the young Hummel live with him and Constanze to study both keyboard and composition back then. He could think of Constanze's name now without any ache, like a scar over an old wound that served as a mere faint reminder of past pain.

One day Samuel asked his teacher, "Herr Pertl? Why don't you like Mozart?"

Johann froze. What a question! He asked, "What makes you think that, Samuel?"

A younger boy, also a violinist, piped up, "You never talk about him. You tell us stories about the others, like Haydn and Bach. But you act mad when we practice Mozart."

"And we like his music! Very much!" Another of the youngsters joined in.

"Well," Johann folded his arms across his chest and took a step back, thinking quickly about what to say. "He was an arrogant, prideful man. I never liked him. But his music is all right, I suppose."

That seemed to satisfy the students and he congratulated himself because every word was true.

"Did you really know him, Herr Pertl?" Samuel felt awe at the thought of his own teacher interacting with such a musical luminary.

"Too well," Johann replied, "too well. Let's be off now." He shooed the boys out of the rehearsal room, putting a quick stop to that conversation.

Johann was also quite interested in the new works which arrived from time to time. Beethoven's First Symphony was performed by the Collegium Musicum of Salem in 1808. It was a revelation to Johann, with its dramatic *sforzandi*, enhanced use of wind instruments, and frequent modulations. It prompted him to write a couple of his own, incorporating some of the new ideas he had heard in the Beethoven. He remembered listening to the younger man play a work of his own when Beethoven was just 17 and heard the promise in the composition. However, some family tragedy had prevented the young German from studying with him in Vienna. It was good to hear proof that he had been right. Beethoven was brilliant.

The few recent works that made their way to Salem intrigued Johann with the different directions that composers appeared to take. He liked the chromaticism and bolder modulations of the new music. It seemed bent upon eliciting strong emotions from those who heard it, overly dramatic in some ways. Even more interesting were the songs of the black inhabitants of Salem which he heard from time to time. These new influences crept into his own work, where he made them his own.

In his early years, Johann had delighted in grand, expansive pieces. "Lots of trumpets and drums," as he called it. But his last works in Vienna, written in that horrible final year there of failing health and marriage, were less bombastic, more intimate, and introspective. The smaller groups of musicians available to him in Salem only encouraged him in this way. He had to compress the expansive ideas in his mind into miniature masterpieces, no less innovative as he grew older for all their small scale. He crafted perfect gems of pieces, exquisitely beautiful, which reached right into his listeners' souls.

Their oldest son, Richard Leopold, did not follow in his father's musical footsteps, but begged to be apprenticed to a furniture maker in the town. Johann had tried to teach the boy keyboard, but that ended in fights which only Luisa's intervention could stop. However, in the Moravian community, a person lacking musical training was a social anomaly. Johann, not wanting to control his children's lives as much as his father had done, insisted only that Richard study one instrument of his own choosing. Much to his father's consternation, Richard chose the trombone. Johann made him practice outside in the garden.

As Richard learned the furniture trade, he accompanied his teacher on an annual trip to Charleston, South Carolina. It was the closest major seaport to Salem and the nearest place to purchase the hardware and other supplies needed for the finer items of furniture they were starting to make. In Charleston, Richard sometimes had a few hours to himself. He wandered the streets and discovered the Seigling Music House on King Street. Perhaps he could find a gift for his father there.

The proprietor was eager to assist him and showed him some items recently arrived from Europe. A stack of piano works caught his eye, each one with the title "Sonate pour le piano-forte," by L. van Beethoven and published by F. W. Arnold. He took five of them, all in different keys. Mr. Seigling assured him that they were the latest works of a great German master and that, if his father was a music teacher, he would be very glad to have them.

Richard had no idea how much his gift, more proof of Beethoven's genius, would mean. Johann spent hours playing over the sonatas and studying them. The one in Bb major, entitled "Grosse Sonate für das Hammerklavier," was next to impossible for him to play. Never had he seen such challenging music and for the first time in his life he wished for larger hands. Well, there was no help for it. He would have to resort to something he hadn't done in years. Practice. After weeks he finally agreed to performances of them, but only for a hand-selected audience of family and friends, forewarned that it would require at least three separate concerts and rapt attention on their part to get through these sonatas. They were very different from his own clear, precise works in their dramatic effects, surprising sudden dynamic changes, and expanded harmonies and range. The concert series introduced the serious musicians of Salem to the most profound examples of recent European music. Johann managed to break their hearts with the beauty of his playing.

Afterward, he told Luisa, "This Beethoven has changed music forever. Good for him!" Those who attended that performance talked about it for years after, and the sonatas had a major effect on his own composition, though he vowed to never write anything that he himself couldn't play.

As Johann neared the age of 70, he decided to retire from teaching. He and Luisa had been frugal with their income, allowing him to enter a period of rest that he accepted gratefully. Her inheritance, the sale of their farms years earlier, and a small excess from his musical income had provided enough funds for their old age. He read, especially the Bible, napped, and escorted Luisa on walks around Salem during good weather. Her favorite afternoons with him were spent listening as he improvised for sometimes hours at a time at his beloved American fortepiano. Richard, with his business connections, had ordered one with a full six-octave keyboard from the Boston manufacturer Timothy Gilbert. His children presented it to him on his sixtieth birthday. They were all happily married and growing their own families, so the house was always full of grandchildren who were the joy of his heart. He felt blessed above all men.

The only shadow over this period in Johann's life was the person who was hired to replace him as teacher, Luther Hauser. Mr. Hauser also composed and played several wind instruments. Johann had reservations about the man's character, though he was a thoroughly trained and accomplished musician. He seemed self-focused and arrogant to the older man. His compositions were distinctly uninspired.

When preparing for an evening's performance, the members of a wind sextet angered Hauser by asking him to please see if Mr. Pertl would loan them one of his serenades. Since this was after trudging through one of Hauser's own, he interpreted it as an insult. Then, when the clarinet player returned with the parts, and they ran through it, Hauser realized that his own work was much inferior. Jealousy and anger took over.

After the performance, Johann left the audience to find the players and asked for his music. They told him that Mr. Hauser had taken the parts. Annoyed, Johann searched for the composer until finding him in the back of the hall.

"Sir," Johann asked, "may I please have the return of my score and parts?"

Hauser turned, "I'm sorry, but these are the property of the Collegium." Having them in his possession he intended to pass them off as his own work back in Pennsylvania.

"I am Johann Pertl, and I wrote the piece you played this evening. The musicians here know that I give them music whenever asked, but I always want it returned."

The clarinet player who had borrowed the parts saw them and sensed something uncomfortable going on. He approached the two men.

"Mr. Pertl, thank you so much for loaning us that partita. It's always been my favorite."

"You are welcome, William."

The younger man continued, "Mr. Hauser, can I help gather them to return to Mr. Pertl?"

Outnumbered, Hauser handed over the music. "I believe it is all there."

Johann nodded and returned to Luisa, who was waiting for him. Her eyesight was failing, even though she was much younger than her husband, and he took her arm to escort her back home in the evening shadows.

"I do not trust Mr. Hauser," he confided in her as they walked.

"Things are changing in Salem," Luisa replied. "It seems that Christian character is no longer the first thing considered when people are sought to fill positions here. But I heard that he was successful in the churches in Pennsylvania."

"Ah, well, Pennsylvania. That's the problem then."

She hit his arm lightly at the joke.

Johann and Luther Hauser reached an uneasy understanding over the next decade. Johann loaned him music but was especially careful to see it returned. He realized that the chances of his music being recognized as that of a composer dead for decades were almost nonexistent. However, he simply did not want to deal with any changes to his life as it was. People clamoring for his music might do that. At this point, he could not tolerate change. Hauser resorted to copying what he could of Johann's compositions and tried to alter them just enough to escape being accused of stealing. The results were far inferior to the originals, and he remained a second-rate composer in the community's eyes. His long simmering resentment threatened to boil over at times.

CHAPTER 31
North Carolina
November 2019

"You know you have not given me much to work with."

"I know, I know," Frank Miller sounded exasperated, clenching the phone in a tight fist. "Just tell me what you've been able to find."

Sam Popkin, expert forensic handwriting analyst, continued. "I looked at letters and word spacing, letter and word slant, size and proportionality of letters, unusual formations of letters, flourishes, and other individual attributes. Then I compared the small samples you gave me to the known composers of the period you told me to check."

"Go on," the edge in Frank's voice betrayed his impatience. His fingers twitched in anger. He hated the way Sam had to draw these things out.

"But there was no way to consider spelling, grammar, or punctuation in what you gave me. The samples were just too small."

Frank gritted his teeth but waited.

"So, I went through and evaluated the similarities to samples from ten known composers. I also looked at the music itself, since sometimes composers' hands are pretty distinctive. And I found one that I believe is probably a match..."

"Good grief, just tell me who you think it is!" Franks' impatience boiled over.

"I can't be 100% sure, but it looks like everything I see is a match to Mozart."

"Mozart." It was a statement. The blood drained from Dr. Miller's face. This was unbelievable. Too good to be true. "How sure are you?"

"I'd have to get a much larger sample, but I matched every attribute on what you gave me to photos of known samples from Mozart. I'd say I'm probably 98% certain."

Frank looked at the copy of the work he had provided Sam. It made sense. The style, the precision, the unearthly beauty and simplicity of the melody. Mozart.

"Sam, look, do me a favor, don't tell anyone about this. I'll cut you in when I find out more."

"Ok, but where did you get it? Is it a new piece?"

"I don't know, ok, I have to check some things. Just stay quiet about it. I'll see if I can get you some more samples."

"All right. It's big, isn't it?"

"The biggest," Frank replied before hanging up.

He had to get more if there was more. Frank jumped up from his leather desk chair, his pulse pounding. Mozart. This one page was enough to cause a world sensation and could net him thousands if he played his cards right. Pacing back and forth on his expensive Oriental rug, he formulated a plan of action. He decided to go to Winston-Salem and find out more for himself. Grabbing his coat, he left his office quickly. As he breezed by the department's administrative assistant, he commanded her to cancel his afternoon classes. She sighed and glared at his departing figure. Dr.

Miller had not even waited for an acknowledgement. No other faculty member ever treated her like that.

He broke the speed limit heading to Winston-Salem. His GPS directed him to West Fifth Street, on the outskirts of downtown. There was plenty of parking available mid-day and his tires screeched as he slid into the space closest to the library's entrance. Taking the few steps to the glass front door quickly, he located an information desk.

"Can I help you?" the woman staffing the desk looked bored.

"Where are your archives?" Frank asked, a little winded.

"Archives? What do you mean?"

"Your historical collection?"

"I'm sorry, but I don't know what you are asking about. What are you looking for exactly?"

"Old music. I'm Dr. Frank Miller from UNC. A student showed up in my office with some old music and said she had gotten it here."

The woman shook her head, "I don't know about anything like that. I've been here a long time and never heard..."

"May I speak to your supervisor?" His tone was totally flat and cold.

She glared at him over her reading glasses but punched a button on the phone in front of her. "Mr. Webster? There's a patron here who wants to speak to you."

A gentleman who looked to be in his sixties soon arrived and asked Frank in a friendly manner, "Can I help you?"

Frank repeated who he was and what he was looking for.

"I'm sorry, but there must be some misunderstanding. We don't have anything like that in our collection. Now the Moravian Archives or the Moravian Music Foundation in Salem certainly do. Perhaps your student was mistaken?"

"Or perhaps she lied to me." Frank concluded the conversation angrily and left, fuming. He decided to return to Chapel Hill and see if Ken Fussell might know what was going on. If this piece really was by Mozart, he had to assure that he was the one who announced it to the world. It would be the crowning achievement of his career.

Dr. Fussell was surprised to see Frank Miller at his door this late in the day. He knew that Miller didn't like him much and the feeling was mutual; Miller had pulled some strings to knock him out of the running for department chair a few years back. The lies planted refused to die. However, he decided to stick to his resolution to forgive him and invited him in.

"Ken, you've got a student who brought me a piano piece a few weeks ago."

"Oh, yes, Anna Stohr. I dated the paper, but we thought we'd get confirmation from you that it looked to be about 1800-1830."

Frank nodded, "Do you know where she got it?"

Ken furrowed his brow. "I don't remember what she... Oh, yes, she had a relative die in Old Salem and was spending some time up there. That seems a likely place, I suppose."

"Do you know an address or anything?"

"No, I'm sorry, but I don't."

"OK, thank you." Frank left and Ken felt slightly uneasy at how wound up the other man seemed. He hoped he had not said anything that he shouldn't. He had probably better warn Anna that Miller was on the warpath, he thought as he picked up his phone.

Searching the Winston-Salem city directory, Frank found one Stohr with an address in Old Salem. Inwardly cursing the number of meetings and obligations facing him over the next few days, he realized further action would have to wait until the weekend. But he resolved to head back to Winston-Salem as soon as he could.

Anna left Chapel Hill again on Friday afternoon. This time Steve didn't think he would be able to go with her but promised to come later if he could. The weather was clear, cold, and beautiful. She had put Dr. Fussell off about her decision on a dissertation topic until she could figure out if these trunks of music were originals or not. If they were, this would be fantastic research for the next couple of years. She had also called her mother and asked them to hold off on selling the house. Her parents understood when she told them about finding some music there and needing time to sort through it. Truthfully, the place was growing on her, and she wondered if her parents would consider keeping it if she agreed to be the caretaker. With only the dissertation lying ahead, she would not have as many obligations on campus. She could make it work until she finished school, she was sure.

Arriving after dark, she hauled her one small bag and laptop into the house. It was cold, but she loved the peace and stability the place always brought to her. She turned up the heat and turned on a few lights. Her stomach growled, but she wanted to see the music again before doing anything else. She headed up to the attic.

It was still there. The number of pieces spread in neat piles took her breath away. This had to be a real find, she just knew it, but she had better grab some food before diving in. Reluctantly, she went back down to the kitchen to see if anything edible remained in the old fridge. After devouring some reheated restaurant leftovers from the freezer, she climbed back up to the attic and spent several hours adding information to her database.

She woke early on Saturday after a full evening with the music the day before. This work was fascinating. Though focusing on just the basic details of the pieces, she couldn't help reading some of the notes from time to time. Humming one of the clarinet concerto's melodies, she realized that it was quality stuff, hauntingly beautiful. Who was this mysterious Johann Pertl anyway?

With only a few breaks, she decided to keep working into Saturday evening. Since Steve couldn't come and Madeline was booked, she might as well just stay at it. She was typing away, examining the score in front of her intently, and never heard the front door open downstairs. Her aunt had rarely locked it, so Anna usually forgot to do so except when she headed to bed.

Frank had seen a light from upstairs in the old yellow house. That had to be Anna's car on the street, because of its UNC student parking sticker. If she was going to lie to him, he was going to take matters into his own hands and see what she was up to before he confronted her. He had done what he needed to advance his career his whole life and wasn't about to stop now, especially if this girl had stumbled on some unknown Mozart piece. Trying the door, he sighed quietly in relief when it opened easily. There was one light on in the kitchen. Moving soundlessly, he found the stairs ahead. He crept up them, excited at the prospect of scaring her in the process of getting some answers.

Anna was "hearing" the piano piece in front of her, so didn't notice the man entering the attic behind her.

"So, Miss Stohr, holding out on me, are you?"

Her blood froze as she turned to see Dr. Miller of all people in the attic in front of her. His eyes swept eagerly over the stacks and stacks of music piled on the tables and floor.

"Dr. Miller! What in the world?" She stood to face him quickly. She couldn't imagine what he was doing here. All the mistrust and suspicion she held toward him instantly came to the surface. Anna didn't like the look on his face. Naked greed and anger.

He bent over and picked up a piece from the top of the pile nearest to him. He moved slowly, reminding her of a predator, never taking his eyes from her. He glanced at the music in his hand—a score for a piano concerto. It suddenly struck him. *What if all of this was Mozart?*

"Do you know what you have here?" he asked in a menacing tone.

"Music," she hesitated, sensing that she needed to downplay the find. "Someone, an ancestor of mine, copied some pieces for the Collegium and the church."

"Really? You don't know?" He smirked at her in disbelief.

She stared back in fear. "Know what?" The intensity of his focus on her had her totally unnerved. She felt like a dove in the presence of a hawk.

Would it be worth it? His mind raced. If this was Mozart, it would make him a millionaire, more famous than he ever imagined. Sam said he was 98% sure. He spotted an ax on the floor against the wall. If he could just get this girl out of the picture...

Anna realized in horror that he was moving, slithering, toward her ax. "What are you doing?" Her legs refused to obey her instinct to run, and she felt glued in place.

"Come over here, please. Away from the music." His voice was full of menace as he picked up and held the tool in his hand. Even on the verge of murder, he knew he couldn't have her bleeding all over these pages.

Anna refused. He would have to come after her. She spotted a wooden chair not far to her right and determined to swing it with all her might if he approached. Would she reach it in time?

Suddenly Frank fell forward with a cry onto the floor and Anna saw Steve standing just behind him, arms out like the wings of an avenging angel, a mad one. He must have pushed the man down. As Miller turned over, ax still in hand, Steve bent down and punched him in the face several times, hard. Miller's head hit the floor with a crack as he lost consciousness.

Anna couldn't speak as Steve stepped over the professor quickly to wrap his arms around her. Tears began to flow.

"Are you ok?" he asked.

"I can't believe he snuck in," she could barely speak as the reality of what had happened sank in. "Oh, Steve, I am so, so glad you came."

"Something told me to get myself up here tonight," he bent over and kissed the top of her head.

Anna looked down in revulsion at the man on the floor. His face turned her stomach, bloodied and swollen.

"Let me call the police. He looked like he was going to murder you!"

"I think he was," Anna shook her head in disbelief. "Why in the world? He's the one who was going to find out who may have written this music."

"I wonder if he did. And why would he be willing to kill you over it?"

The police arrived soon and found Frank sitting on the floor while Steve loomed over him, glaring, ax in hand.

They arrested the professor and he left, handcuffed between two officers. His parting words to Anna were, "You have no idea what you've got. Or what you've done. I will ruin you."

Anna and Steve returned to Chapel Hill early on Sunday. She was too shaken up to stay at the house any longer to work on her cataloging. She called Dr. Fussell at his home, something she had never done before. After hearing her quick summary of the attack Saturday night, he insisted that she come over to see him and his wife to tell them the whole story. Steve went with her, reluctant to let her leave his sight after the previous evening.

"I have to apologize," Dr. Fussell began. They sat in the Fussell's comfortable living room with cups of coffee. "I'm afraid he found out where you were thanks to me. He came in the other day, tense and frantic to know where you'd found that music. I told him I didn't know, but that your aunt had died recently. I guess he put the pieces together."

"I should apologize to you," Anna began. "I haven't been totally honest about it with you. I found three large trunks of music in my aunt's attic. I've been working on cataloging it on the weekends."

"You didn't owe me that information, my dear," he told her. "That's your inheritance."

She hadn't thought of it that way before. Relieved at finally being able to talk about it, she told him all she had found and the questions she that filled her mind. She was able to remember fairly accurately the number and types of pieces. He was amazed at the amount of music involved.

"And, finally, what had Miller's handwriting expert friend discovered? It made him willing to kill me over it!" Anna raised her hands to punctuate her disbelief.

Dr. Fussell sat back, "I tell you what. I think I know whom he called. Probably Sam Popkin. I've met him a time or two. I'll talk to him. Meanwhile, you take that piano sonata you found and see if you can locate it in the NMA for a start. We can work together on this."

"Thank you so much!"

"It may very well be possible that you've found your dissertation topic," he told her as she and Steve left. "At last."

CHAPTER 32

Salem
1840

Johann was feeling his age. He never performed for any outside of his own family these days and taught only a few of his own grandchildren. All of them seemed to have at least a bit of talent, and he held great hopes for the youngest boy, John, who showed an uncanny ability to play back whatever he heard. His son-in-law assured him that the lad was named after him, just with the Americanized version of "Johann." That was fine with him. This new country had proved as wonderful as Captain Handford told him it would all those years ago.

He had filled the three trunks that he and Carl had brought from Europe with his compositions. One day, as an afterthought, he removed a cloth sack from a bottom drawer in an old chest. Inside were six snuffboxes, several of gold. Carl had carried the things all the way from that cursed apartment in Vienna to Salem. He placed them in the top of the oldest trunk and locked it, unwanted mementos of the world's recognition of his early life. Perhaps some descendant of his could sell them.

Johann had turned 84 in January of 1840. He knew that he walked more slowly, but his eyes and ears still worked. He was concerned about Luisa, though. She was totally blind, but he imagined her outliving him by decades, since she was so much younger. He decided to confide in his oldest son, Richard. Someone needed to know about the music and be prepared to take care of his dear wife.

All the children dropped by frequently, so it was no surprise for Richard to come by on a Saturday morning in May. He worked as a partner with the furniture maker who trained him and always had plenty of news to share with his parents. This morning was different, though, as Johann asked him to come with him to his study alone. He told Luisa that he needed his son's advice on repairing a cabinet. Richard had not been there in quite some time. The piano still stood in the center of the room, bringing back some distant memories of a few painful music lessons. There was a desk against the wall, under a window onto the back yard. Lined up on the south wall were three old trunks, battered and worn.

"Richard, you know that I have never given any of my music to be published while I have been here in Salem." He looked up at his son, who stood at least a full foot taller than his father.

Richard nodded solemnly. It had been the subject of many an argument with others in the town, who thought his father's works to be of the highest quality, even innovative and more than worthy of dissemination. But Johann steadfastly refused.

Johann went to the closest trunk and turned the key in the lock. "Here it is." He opened each trunk in turn and his son saw that all three were absolutely filled to the top with music.

"I have begun to think that perhaps there might be a use for it after all."

Was he serious? Richard thought. Everyone loved his father's music, begged him to give or sell them copies. There was talk that his music alone could bring fame to Salem as a center of the art. As it was, the town had a good reputation musically, but not what many believed it could be, if the secret of Johann Pertl got out.

"There is a very good chance that your mother will out-live me. We have our savings, but I would hate to think that she might lack anything when I could provide it for her. And the grandchildren might need funds for education later." Johann closed the lid of the trunk he stood by.

"When I go on to the greater life, I would like you to sell this for me. Use the funds for your mother first, then as any of the children have need of it. I trust your judgment."

"Father, I..."

"I know you will know where to take it, in Charleston or Philadelphia, I suppose. But just not until I am gone. Promise it."

Richard was humbled by his father's words. "I swear it."

"Good. Now let's see if there is any coffee left in there." Johann placed a hand on his son's shoulder and the two headed into the kitchen.

May was a wonderful time of year in Salem. The dog-woods were in bloom and the weather warm without the oppressive heat and humidity of summer. Sitting in the shade of an oak tree in their backyard, Johann thought about the story his son Richard had brought back from Charleston. It was about Beethoven, that composer he so admired. The poor man was dead now, for quite some time apparently. Who knew he himself would have outlived him? From what Richard said, Beethoven had lost his hearing during the latter part of his life. The thought brought a cold horror that any musician would understand. But here he was, an old man, still hearing and playing music to his heart's content. He had noticed a certain shortness of breath from time to time, not related to any activities as far as he could tell. But that was to be expected, wasn't it?

The back door slammed open, and four children raced to his chair.

"Grandpa! Grandpa!" a chorus of voices surrounded him.

"My goodness! I thought the natives had returned! Or some strange wild flock of birds!" He helped the two smallest climb onto his lap and the others grabbed the arms of his rocking chair. Johann's grandchildren loved him wildly. His lifelong sense of humor had returned to its full force after marrying Luisa, and he was often the mastermind behind outrageous pranks with the youngsters.

"We are going on a picnic!"

"We are? Who said?" He made them laugh by wiggling his eyebrows up and down.

His youngest daughter, Rebekah, appeared at the door. "Don't hurt your grandfather, children! He is fragile, you know."

Johann stuck his tongue out at her, which caused peals of laughter among the children.

"We just spoke with mother and we're going to take a wagon to the creek at the bottom of the hill," she informed him.

He wondered how many of them would be included in the "we." He and Luisa had had two sons and two daughters, Richard Leopold the oldest, then Thomas Peter, then Sarah, and finally Rebekah. All were married and all had several children. The whole family might mean twenty people.

It turned out that it was the whole family. The women had decided that, on this beautiful day, their men could be persuaded to take off early in the afternoon and spend time together. They tried to gather once a month as a family. Johann, Luisa, and the youngest grandchildren had seats in the wagon, surrounded by baskets of food; their parents and older siblings walked. Johann felt like a king surrounded by his court. God had truly blessed him beyond all he could ever have imagined.

The women had prepared a feast and worked at setting food out on a white tablecloth covering some boards. The children screamed and chased each other through the field on the opposite side of the small creek. The men talked seriously for only a few minutes. Soon, they were busy chasing the children and the screams increased. Johann, as the patriarch of the clan, was settled under a large tree. His son Thomas spread a worn quilt and helped him position himself sitting with his back against its trunk so he could observe his large clan.

Luisa, almost totally blind, came over to him on the arm of their oldest granddaughter, Maria. At 17 she was a beauty and Johann believed her to be one of the most talented of all their large brood. She could have given his sister, Nannerl, a run for her money at the keyboard. He hoped she would marry a man who would encourage her musical pursuits. She lived with them at present to help Luisa and study with her grandfather.

"So, husband dearest, are you ready for lunch?"

"What? I can't hear you above these screaming heathens we have produced."

Luisa smiled. She and Johann had been blessed. He stood with only a little help from Maria to take Luisa's other arm and the three headed to a spot where a feast had been spread across a makeshift table. Maria saw them seated on a small bench at one end of it. Everyone else sat on the ground or old quilts to eat the fried chicken, biscuits, cold salads, and pies offered.

After lunch, the men found spots to doze off while the children played more quietly, floating sticks and leaves down the creek. Johann felt short of breath again and also drowsy. "Luisa, dear, I believe I'll return to that tree and stretch out on the blanket for a short while."

"Good. I think I'll ask Catharina if she wants to put the baby to sleep beside you. He is sounding a bit fussy." Thomas's wife walked and rocked a one-year-old, the youngest of the clan. She was relieved to put the nearly asleep infant beside his grandfather.

Johann propped himself up against the large tree trunk and put a hand gently on the baby, who fell asleep instantly. Catharina rejoined her sisters-in-law by the table. Strange, Johann thought, my arm doesn't feel quite right. He closed his eyes and quietly lost consciousness. The family at the table looked over from time to time at the tableaux of their beloved father sleeping peacefully beside his grandchild.

After a bit, the baby woke and cried loudly. Johann did not stir. Catharina went quickly to retrieve her child and thought it odd that her father-in-law could still sleep. Looking more closely, she noticed that his lips appeared blue.

"Thomas!" she cried in a tone that caught everyone's attention. Thomas and Richard ran to where their father lay. He was gone.

Later, Luisa talked about the blessing of simply falling asleep beside his much-loved grandchild. She was truly thankful, but the open wound of missing him refused to heal. With a heavy heart, she exchanged the blue ribbon in the bonnet she still wore for the white ribbon of widowhood. She turned to prayer and found comfort in hours spent with her Lord. Truthfully, she longed to join her father and Johann. Maria stayed with her, and her other children and grandchildren saw that her every need was met. Her daughters talked about how they saw their mother praying her way into the next life.

Richard got into the habit of stopping by his mother's house every day on his way to his own. He felt the responsibility of overseeing the family and knew that he would probably have to investigate selling the music in the trunks within the next year. Right now, though, his mother needed companionship and the love of her children more than any tangible assets.

He entered the front door of the yellow house and was surprised that his mother was not seated in her favorite chair by the fireplace. He could hear something going on in the back of the house, though.

"Mother?" he called as he went through the kitchen.

Luisa was standing in the door by Johann's studio, holding onto the door frame, looking into the room with sightless eyes. She had not let anyone disturb it since his death a few months ago. In the room, Richard saw a man's back by one of the trunks on the wall. He had the lid open and a piece of music in his hand.

"Sir?" he shouted in indignation.

"Richard?" Luisa turned. "Richard, Mr. Hauser said that your father had borrowed some music from him and had not returned it. I told him that he was welcome to look for it."

Hauser closed the lid of the trunk quickly and turned to face Richard, now striding into the room.

"Hello, Mr. Pertl. Yes, your mother spoke the truth. I came to see if I could find a violin sonata of mine that your father borrowed."

"Sir, I sincerely doubt that my father ever desired to borrow or play anything of yours," Richard ungraciously alluded to the fact that there was no comparison between the compositions of the two men.

"Well, I am sorry you are upset. I will leave now," he nodded to Richard and stopped in front of Luisa. Richard saw a single sheet of music in his hand.

"May I have that back, please?"

"Yes, of course, you startled me. Here." Luisa backed into the kitchen and Hauser moved quickly through the rooms to the front door, Richard following him closely.

After firmly shutting the door behind the unwelcome visitor, Richard returned to his mother, still standing by the study.

"Mother, I believe he was trying to steal some of father's things."

"Oh, surely not," Luisa sat at the kitchen table. She knew Johann never trusted the man, but no one would take her beloved husband's possessions as she stood looking on. But that was the problem, wasn't it? She couldn't look on. He could have been doing anything in there and she would not know it.

"Where is Maria?"

"She goes on errands and visits her family most days now. I told her to. I'm fine. I just sit in my chair and nap until she returns."

Richard had to do something. He was due to leave town on a business trip in just a few days and would be gone for several weeks. Mr. Hauser knew his mother would be alone periodically and that she couldn't see what the thief was up to. Hauser could even sneak into the house if he moved quietly enough. What could he do?

He saw Luisa settled into her chair with a cup of tea, then began to look around the house for a place to hide the trunks, at least until he could return and deal with the music properly, as his father wished. No place would work. The things were impossibly big, and there were three of them no less. Nothing upstairs looked promising, either, until he saw the ladder leading to the attic. What about there?

He climbed up the ladder-like stairs, telling his mother not to worry about the noise he made. "Just checking on something in the attic!"

There wasn't much stored there. What if he could manage the trunks up here and hide them against a wall? He had been working on his own house and had quite a bit of wood at hand. Suddenly a foolproof solution presented itself. He would haul the trunks up here and put up a wall with no door. That should keep them hidden until he could find a buyer for the contents.

Returning to his mother in the sitting room, he told her, "I believe the roof is in need of some repair, but I can take care of it in the attic. I will be over tomorrow and get it all fixed before I have to go to Charleston on Thursday."

Maria opened the front door, "Hello, Uncle Richard!" She set down a basket to take off her shawl.

"Maria! I am so glad that you are home. I have to leave but walk with me for a minute." He turned to his mother and kissed her on the cheek, "I will be back tomorrow, Mother, and I'll just tell Maria what I need to do."

When they were outside, Richard instructed his niece not to leave Luisa unattended and told her about Mr. Hauser's deception. He knew that she was not aware of the trunks of music, but it was enc gh that the man had tried to steal something of theirs. Maria agreed to see that she or someone from the family was with Luisa at all times.

The next day, Richard drove up in a wagon loaded with a pile of boards. He spent several hours carrying them into the attic one at a time. Maria fixed him and her grandmother lunch, then told him that she was going to ask her mother to come over for the afternoon. She had agreed to help with some things at the church. This was the perfect opportunity, Richard thought.

"No need! I will be here, and I can keep an eye on things. Mother usually naps in the afternoon anyway, correct?"

"Yes, indeed," Luisa interrupted. She didn't like the way her children and grandchildren sometimes spoke about her as if she could not hear them. She was blind, not deaf. "And I plan to take a long one today!"

"Good, Mother. I will be working with some materials upstairs, so don't be concerned about anything that you might hear."

After Maria left and Luisa retired to her room with the door closed, Richard started to move the trunks upstairs. They were much heavier than he thought. He succeeded in dragging them up to the second floor without making too much of a commotion. But there was no way he could get them up to the attic by himself. Then he remembered the rope in his wagon.

Retrieving it, he carried it up the attic stairs. There were some sturdy cross beams overhead. Throwing an end of the rope over the middle one, he tied the other end to one of his planks on the floor. Descending again, he was ecstatic to see that the rope was long enough to tie securely around the first trunk, through both side handles. Doing so, he moved it into position at the base of the ladder, clambered over it, then used the leverage of the rope over the beam as a pulley to slowly inch the trunk into the attic. Just as he finished with the last one, he heard the front door open. He hurried down to see who had arrived.

It was Maria returning. "You must be working very hard, uncle, to get your clothes so dirty."

"It's a dusty place up there. I'll be finished for the day soon."

He returned to the attic and placed the trunks along the south wall. Then he nailed some small boards into place across the ceiling, being careful not to put holes into the roof. Below it, he did the same along the floor. By that time, he was exhausted and losing daylight. He closed the attic and bid his mother and niece good evening.

It took another full day to nail boards in place to create a wall concealing the trunks. The last step was to paint it, so that its appearance matched the north wall. Finally finished, he felt confident that no one would find the trunks until he was ready to arrange the sale of their contents. This time he bade his mother farewell for several weeks, as he had one day to get his own things ready for his trip to Charleston. He told her he expected to see her in a few weeks.

A few days later, after word spread in the close-knit community that Richard Pertl was on a trip, Luther Hauser showed up at the old Pertl residence again. And again, Luisa let Mr. Hauser in to look through Johann's studio for that sonata he was missing. This time, she heard him moving around quite a bit in there.

"Mrs. Pertl, do you happen to know where your husband's trunks went?"

"Trunks? Why, no, I remember them, but I haven't seen them in years."

He didn't know if she was being serious or taunting him in some way. "They were here last week, against that wall over there. Now they are gone."

"I'm sorry, but I am sure that I don't know anything about them."

Frustrated, he left, but only after snooping around the shed in the back, checking the root cellar, and peering into every room that he could see.

A week later, Richard concluded a profitable time of selling and buying and left Charleston to return to Salem. One of the rivers that he had to cross was swollen with rain water from somewhere west of there and a bridge was washed out. Deciding to try to ford it anyway, he stopped his horses to check that his load was secure. He estimated the waters to be lower than the bed of the wagon and guided his team slowly into the river. The force of the current made his horses nervous, but he soothed them as best he could with his voice. In the middle of the stream, he felt a sudden lurch to the right. Fast moving waters carried half of one of his wheels downstream along with some fine wood he had purchased. Cursing, he entered the water himself to cut his horses free. They could easily save themselves if unencumbered by the wagon. He had to dodge their flailing hooves as the waters streamed around them. Just as his second horse headed for the bank, a broken branch carried swiftly by the current hit him in the side of his head. Unconscious, he slipped beneath the waters. His body was found on the river bank several miles from the crossing a day later.

Luisa took to her bed after the death of her oldest son. She was glad Johann had not lived to see Richard's passing and was sure that he and Richard worshipped the Lord together in heaven even now. Her will to live faded with sorrow and she passed into her reward just a few months after her beloved husband. It was strange, but none of her children were able to find their father's music. They knew that he had kept many pieces in his private library but looked in vain. They searched his music room thoroughly but could find it nowhere. Some even checked the attic, but to no avail.

CHAPTER 33
Salem
November 2019

A nna cancelled her commitments on Monday and headed to Winston-Salem with Steve, who had found a substitute band director after monumental effort. She felt an urgency about all of this, and nothing seemed more important than discovering who Johann Pertl was. Steve was equally intrigued. They walked hand in hand the five blocks to the new Moravian Archives building, beside God's Acre. Anna's student ID gave them access to all the church records they needed.

She had spent Sunday evening in the music reference section of the Wilson Library in Chapel Hill, going through the solo piano works in the *Neue Mozart-Ausgabe* to try to locate the piece they had given to Frank Miller. Even with Steve's help, it took hours of poring over the large books. They worked far past the time all other students had left. She determined to her complete satisfaction that the piece was not there. Its distinctive theme was now stuck in both of their heads.

Since everything had escalated, she had no qualms about calling her advisor on nights or weekends, whenever needed. He was as eager to get to the bottom of things as they were. She called late Sunday evening and told Dr. Fussell that they were going to go to Old Salem and check church records for anything that they could find on Pertl. He reported that he had a call in to the handwriting analyst and wished them luck.

On Monday morning, Fussell tried to grade a stack of papers. His thoughts kept turning to the mystery of this old music and what would drive Miller to attack Anna for it. About 10 a.m. the phone rang.

"Hello, this is Sam Popkin. I understand you wanted to talk to me?"

"Yes, Sam, thank you for calling. I know that Frank Miller asked you to look at a piece of piano music and do some handwriting analysis on it," Fussell responded.

"Um, yes, but it's a private matter."

"Well, Frank Miller is in jail. He tried to murder a student of mine over this music."

"Oh my God."

"So, you see, it's rather important that she and I know what this is about."

There was a moment of silence.

"Mozart." Popkin sounded defeated.

"Mozart?"

"I am reasonably sure that the handwriting is Mozart's. If I could have a larger sample, I could be certain."

"We'll get you that larger sample." Dr. Fussell had to sit down after hanging up. Mozart.

At almost the same time, Anna and Steve were going through church records from the 1790s. They finally found something in the record of baptisms from 1794.

"Look," she cried excitedly, standing up from the old wooden chair. "Here it is."

She had to interpret the German script for him, "Pertl, Johann, baptized September 20, 1794. Born January 27, 1756, Salzburg, Austria."

Anna's face went white. "Oh my gosh, oh my gosh." She put the paper down quickly, as if it burned her hand. "I should have known."

"What?" Steve insisted. What was so dramatic about that date and place?

"Wait, let me..." She grabbed her phone and opened Safari. "Let me just check..."

In a second, she handed him the phone. She seemed ready to hyperventilate, with her hand on her chest as she gasped for air.

There in Wikipedia it stated, "Johannes Wolfgang Chrysostom Theophilus Mozart, born Jan. 27, 1756, Salzburg, Austria." The words were under a portrait of the composer by Joseph Lange, which had Mozart's image on an unfinished background.

"And look. His mother's name was Anna Maria Walburga *Pertl*." Anna couldn't speak. She could barely breathe and sat back down quickly.

At that moment, her phone rang. It was Dr. Fussell.

"Yes, we have found something, too. It confirms..." She had to stop. "It says that Johann Pertl was born on Jan. 27, 1756, in Salzburg, Austria."

Dr. Fussell said, or screamed, something unintelligible.

"Yes, Mozart." She ended the call.

Hopelessly overwhelmed, she looked at Steve who had pulled out his own phone. He grinned widely as he held up another portrait of the composer.

"I think you have your great-great-great-great-great-great grandfather's eyes."

Winston-Salem
May 2020

Anna was hard at work in her new office in the Moravian Archives Archie K. Davis Center. She stood up to take a break from her laptop and moved to look out the window at God's Acre and the tall buildings of Winston-Salem beyond. The graveyard's stone squares gleamed white under a Tarheel blue sky. Aunt Alzbeta was there, along with her grandparents, and many other family members. And Mozart. It was still hard to believe. They would probably never know how the composer had escaped death and made it to North Carolina, then lived undetected for almost another fifty years. But the handwriting, style, and sheer genius of the music confirmed it. Mozart. It defied all reason, but once you heard some of the music, you knew. And, when all the initial excitement was over, she remembered the old cloth sack with the little boxes that she had stuck away in a corner of the attic. Working with the Department of Research of the Old Salem Museums, they were able to determine that they were snuff boxes from the late 1700s. Several matched descriptions of those known to have been presented as gifts to the genius child prodigy, Wolfgang Mozart. The evidence was indisputable.

She had indeed found her dissertation topic. More than that, her life's work. She had to hire an assistant to help with all the calls from news agencies, publishers, and musical organizations who wanted to publish and perform from the "greatest musical find of all time," as the *Journal of Musicology* called it. Her father connected her to a friend of his who was an expert in copyright law, to help protect the scores more than to ensure any great profits from them. This case defied all previous guidelines and court determinations. She determined to work slowly and carefully after moving the collection to the Moravian Archives and consulting with the Moravian Music Foundation. The staff there hired a second security guard, started a capital campaign to double the size of their facility, and took in almost 20 million dollars in two days. They were happy to provide her with an office on the second floor. She was happy, in turn, that it was ready for her just as the coronavirus pandemic hit the area without mercy. She counted it a blessing to have such a beautiful, if isolated, work setting.

Frank Miller lost his job at the university after being charged with attempted murder. He was still awaiting trial and could possibly be sentenced to ten years or more. At least there was one thing that could cause a professor to lose tenure, Anna thought. Miller's friend's conclusion about the handwriting match was confirmed by three other analysts. Dr. Fussell, in his happy position as Anna's advisor, gained as much of a career boost from the discovery as she did. His encouragement and guidance helped Anna stay sane. Soon his colleagues spoke openly about him being a shoo-in for department chair.

Steve proposed on Valentine's Day, less than a month after confirmation of their astounding discovery. He applied for all the band director positions in the Winston-Salem area and hoped to find employment there by the next school year. A wedding was in the works for just a few weeks away, outside and with few guests because of the virus, but she preferred it that way anyway. They hardly had to discuss where they would live. The historical yellow house in Old Salem was theirs, a wedding gift from Anna's parents.

They decided to keep the old place as Aunt Alzbeta had left it, except for the addition of a king-sized bed upstairs. It looked ridiculous in the small, 19th-century room, but Steve was not exactly 19th-century size. Anna was living there now while Steve dealt with finishing the school year and moving and storing his things in time for the wedding. They were putting a lot of their own belongings into storage to keep the house and its furnishings intact for the time being.

Anna knew that someday they would have to leave. Inevitably, the place would become a stop on the Old Salem tours. The Museum had already approached them about inventorying the house's contents, seeking to verify any furnishings that had been in the home during the early 1800s. The home of Wolfgang Amadeus Mozart, aka Johann Pertl, for the last forty years of his life. What would Aunt Alzbeta think? Anna smiled as she returned to the score spread before her. Sometimes joy could be too much for words.

Acknowledgements

This book grew out of several years of wishful thinking related to Mozart surviving his last illness, my love of Old Salem, and my deep respect for the history of the Moravian Church. I should probably apologize to Constanze Mozart for using the possibility of her affair with a lieutenant whom she met at the spa in Baden as a pivotal event in this novel. Most music historians believe she was a faithful wife, though the Mozarts, like all couples, had their ups and downs.

I would like to thank The Smiths (our small writing group, "The Wordsmiths") for their encouragement at the very start of this project. I never imagined myself writing fiction until Elise Kail, Laurie Sherrod, and Sherry Thomas read a chapter I had written with this book in mind and urged me on. I can't thank you enough!

Thanks also to my husband, George, ever patient and willing to draw the house that inspired the whole thing, and my daughter Beth, constantly in my corner. Thank you to BettyAnn Whitten, photographer extraordinaire, also a great encourager. Many thanks to Richard and Phyllis Davis, who kindly hosted us in North Carolina and enabled me to finish some research there. Thanks also to John and Ann Lane, the first to read the whole thing, for your advice, support, and ridiculously over-the-top praise, which I deeply appreciated.

Bibliography

Bidwell, John, and American Antiquarian Society. *American Paper Mills, 1690-1832 a Directory of the Paper Trade with Notes on Products, Watermarks, Distribution Methods, and Manufacturing Techniques.* Hanover, NH: Worcester, MA: Dartmouth College Press; In Association with the American Antiquarian Society, 2013.

Bourdon, Austin. "Johann Christian Bach's influence on Mozart." Honors Thesis, University of Richmond, 2010. https://scholarship.richmond.edu/cgi/viewcontent.cgi?article=1166&context=honors-theses.

Bower, Jennifer Bean. *Moravians in North Carolina.* Charleston, SC: Arcadia Pub., 2006.

Brion, Marcel. *Daily Life in the Vienna of Mozart and Schubert.* New York: Macmillan, 1962.

Clutton, Cecil, Edwin M. Ripin, and Laurence Elliot Lipin. "keyboard instrument." Encyclopedia Britannica, November 2, 2021. https://www.britannica.com/art/keyboard-instrument.

Fries, Adelaide L. *The Road to Salem.* Winston-Salem, NC: John F. Blair, 1993.

Greenberg, Robert. "Music History Monday: How Did He Do It?" RG Music. June 26, 2017. https://robertgreenbergmusic.com/music-history-monday-how-did-mozart-do-it/.

—. "The Mozart/Clementi Duel." RG Music. January 23, 2017. https://robertgreenbergmusic.com/mozart-clementi-duel/.

Gutman, Robert W. *Mozart: A Cultural Biography*. New York: Harcourt Brace, 1999.

Hahn [Webster], Katherine Ann. "The Wind Ensemble Music of David Moritz Michael." MA thesis, University of Missouri–Columbia, 1979.

"Mozart.com" Mozart Media GmbH & Co KG. Accessed July 15, 2020. http://www.mozart.com/en/home.

Norwich, John Julian. *Paradise of Cities: Venice in the 19th Century*. New York: Doubleday, 2003.

Old Salem Museums & Gardens. Old Salem Museums & Gardens. Accessed November 2, 2021. https://www.oldsalem.org/.

Owen, Mary Barrow. *Old Salem: North Carolina*. 2nd ed. Winston-Salem, NC: Garden Club of North Carolina, 1946.

Songer, Mark. "Forensic Handwriting Analysis – Expert Introduction to Handwriting Analysis." Robson Forensic. January 1, 2014. https://www.robsonforensic.com/articles/forensic-handwriting-analysis-expert.

Stead, Geoffrey. "Crossing The Atlantic: The Eighteenth-Century Moravian Experience." *Transactions of the Moravian Historical Society* 30 (1998): 23–36. http://www.jstor.org/stable/41179469.

CPSIA information can be obtained
at www.ICGtesting.com
Printed in the USA
BVHW081742150222
629079BV00002B/87

9 781662 840487